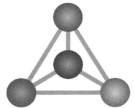  

ENTERPRISE
CONNECTI

www.Pra_____.com

Enterprise Architecture

A **Pragmatic** Approach Using PEAF

v2021

Kevin Lee Smith

First published: August 2014
Last updated: January 2021

ISBN 978-1-908424-09-9 (hardback)
ISBN 978-1-908424-10-5 (paperback)
ISBN 978-1-908424-11-2 (ebook)

Published by:
Pragmatic365 Ltd
25 Buttermere
Great Notley,
Essex CM77 7UY
England

Currently Available Reference Books	ISBN	Pre-requisites
The Pragmatic Family of Frameworks A Pragmatic Introduction	978-1-908424-42-6	
Enterprise Fundamentals A Pragmatic Approach Using PEFF	978-1-908424-42-6	
Enterprise Transformation A Pragmatic Approach using POET	978-1-908424-07-5	PEFF
Enterprise Architecture A Pragmatic Approach using PEAF	978-1-908424-10-5	POET

Currently Available Focus Books	ISBN	Pre-requisites
PEAF 4 TOGAF Kick-start Your TOGAF Adoption. Pragmatically	978-1-908424-25-9	
Transformation Governance A Pragmatic Approach using Transformation Debt™	978-1-908424-48-8	
Enterprise Architecture Tools A Pragmatic Approach to EA Tool Selection and Adoption	978-1-908424-54-9	
What is EA A Pragmatic Explanation	978-1-908424-57-0	
Transformation Culture The Inconvenient Pragmatic Truth	978-1-908424-59-4	
Transformation Maturity Assessment A Pragmatic Approach using the PTMC	978-1-908424-63-1	
Connecting the DOTS™ The Death of "The Business" & "IT"	978-1-908424-68-6	

Coming Soon	ISBN	Pre-requisites
Enterprise Direction A Pragmatic Approach using POED	978-1-908424-16-7	PEFF
Enterprise Operation A Pragmatic Approach using POEO	978-1-908424-19-8	PEFF
Enterprise Support A Pragmatic Approach using POES	978-1-908424-22-8	PEFF
Enterprise Engineering A Pragmatic Approach using PEEF	978-1-908424-13-6	POET

This work was inspired by all those who seek to make the world a better place, rather than those who seek to own it.

"We cannot solve our problems, with the same thinking we used when we created them."

Albert Einstein

"Sometimes it is the people who no one imagines anything of, who do the things that no one can imagine."

Alan Turing

"Computers are useless. They can only give you answers"

Pablo Picasso.

"You cannot 'cost justify' Architecture"

J. A. Zachman

"We have seen the enemy, and the enemy is us (management)."

W. E. Deming

"If I have seen further, it is by standing on the shoulders of giants."

Isaac Newton

Acknowledgements

The author would like to acknowledge the extensive help and advice provided by Murphy to get this book to market, particularly for the constant companionship and irritating interruptions (which provided much needed relief although I didn't know it at the time) and a chance for mutual tummy tickles.

I would also like to thank my wife, Virginia, for her moral support and the constant supply of Marmite on toast.

Please note that, to preserve commercial and personal confidentiality, any stories and examples in this book will usually have been adapted, combined and in part fictionalised from experiences in a variety of contexts, and do not and are not intended to represent any specific individual or Enterprise.

Registered trademarks such as PEAF, Zachman, TOGAF, ITIL, COBIT etc are acknowledged as the intellectual property of the respective owners.

Pragmatic thanks the following people who have contributed their ideas.
(In country alphabetical order)

If you would like to contribute ideas or have any comments or suggestions for improvements or corrections, please **contact us** .

| Australia | Hungary | New Zealand | United Kingdom | United Kingdom | United Kingdom | United States | United States | Zimbabwe |

Contributor	Area of Contributions
Taiss Quartapa Interim Executive Enlightened Interest Group **Australia**	Exploring the impossible is my calling. Whether that means working on the Enterprise Architecture, reinventing the internal processes of a global company or creating a new, innovative approach for the retail experience, solving the impossible is what I seek to do. I'm driven to deliver impactful results which enhance aspects of people's lives. POET > Culture > Slaves-to-Psychology > The-Dunning-Kruger-Effect
Tamás Nacsák Senior Enterprise Architect Telcotrend **Hungary**	Tamás Nacsák, is a Senior Enterprise Architect, worked twenty plus years in IT mostly in the telecommunication industry; the last twelve dedicated to Enterprise Architecture. He is currently working as Enterprise Architect on several Telco companies and at Hungarian State Tresury. POET > Culture > The-Architect > The-Pragmatic-Architect-Creed
Brendan S. McEnroe Chief Technology Officer // Enterprise Architect Trade Window Limited **New Zealand**	Brendan is a Certified Enterprise Architect, technology thought leader and start-up founder with 30 years' experience. He has a demonstrated history of digital strategy, innovation and leading high performing teams on large scale technology projects, across UK and NZ organisations. PEFF > Adoption > Measures > PTMC > Tools
Gareth Llewellyn Enterprise and Solution Architect Freelance **United Kingdom**	Over 28 years, Gareth has been a trusted advisor to executives and key decision makers. He has architected strategic transformations for medium to large commercial organisations, and to federal, state and local government across the UK and Australia. Gareth uses design thinking to transition businesses to their target operating model, delivering profound outcomes while reducing cost & risk. POET > Culture > The-Architect > What-Does-An-Architect-Do
Amber Smith Trainee Cabinetmaker Humphrey Munson **United Kingdom**	As someone who likes to learn, and loves a challenge, I have tried working in many different industries, some of which I loved, some I absolutely hated. I have come to know myself through trying new things. Recently, I have attained a job which I absolutely love, and aspire to turn into my career. Cabinetmaking allows me to be practical, creative, and keeps me on my toes! POET > Culture > Slaves-to-Psychology > The-Dunning-Kruger-Effect
Abdul Aziz Business Architect and Cybernetician Vanga Limited **United Kingdom**	A passionate strategist, enterprise architect and business change leader endeavouring to help executives, managers and operatives navigate complexity with principles and values that enable their organisational purpose. Abdul has over 20 years' experience in all aspects of "changing the business" across multiple industries holds an MBA with distinction from the Alliance Manchester Business School. POET > Culture > Architecture-and-Engineering > Fundamentals

James McGovern
Research Director
Gartner
United States

Over twenty years of experience applying technical, process, and people skills to improve individual, team, and organizational performance and overall efficacy. Advanced knowledge of enterprise architecture and enterprise security with a focus on high-profile customer-facing applications. An impassioned leader who mentors with purpose and understands that strong working relationships create great

PEAF > Culture > Roles > EASG-Enterprise-Architecture-Steering-Group

Pedro M. Correa
Harbinger of things to come
Papyrus Software
United States

Regional IT industry leader with SMET background and 25+ years of international experience in the Americas. Award winner for: leading regional sales and service delivery CoE while working as CTO (EDS), for Regional LATAM Sales/Marketing Director (Texas Instruments) and for Business Analyst/PMP (IBM)

PEAF > Methods > Phases > Roadmapping > Intermediate-Journey

Murambwa Clever Haparari
Technology Lead and Design Authority
FBC Holdings
Zimbabwe

Technology Innovation and Enterprise Architecture Leader with a vision to become an Enterprise Transformation leader driving Enterprises for the consistent achievement of their Strategic goals of Effectiveness, Efficiency, Agility and Sustainability of both the Operations and Transformation capabilities through appropriate adoption of the Enterprise Architecture Paradigm.

PEAF > Artefacts > Meta-models > Structural

Contents

Methods.. 135

Artefacts... 197

Guidance 227

Items 271

Culture 309

Appendix 357

FOREWORD

Enterprises have been and will continue to live in a state of flux. A never ending sea of change that buffets them and blows them around, seemingly at random, in an unending churning ocean. Even when it is calm, a storm can blow up "out of the blue" and literally sink the ship at a moment's notice. Most Enterprises invest huge amounts of time and effort in battling the storms. Very few spend any resources on preparing the ship. Instead the call is "all hands on deck" to land the next catch and set the next net. Without proper preparation, every Enterprise is sailing full speed into their own perfect storm.

If we are to sail safely in these unpredictable waters we must make preparations and plans to allow us to respond when treacherous conditions face us. For if we wait until that time before we act, it is unlikely that we will survive.

> "When you are drowning, it's too late to learn to swim."

While the seas are calm, an unprepared ship and crew is generally indistinguishable from a well prepared ship and crew. In fact the unprepared ship will often seem preferable to many, setting sail before other more well prepared ships - not having to waste time gathering and studying the correct charts, loading extra emergency rations, checking the presence and quality of the life-rafts nor performing preventative maintenance on the engine. Often the unprepared ship will set sail and return with a hold full of fish while the prepared ship is still making good their preparations.

The unprepared ship will often catch more fish than other more well prepared ships - not having to comply with safety regulations they are able to cast and wind in the nets much faster and therefore fill their holds faster. Holds also have more space due to the absence of emergency equipment which means more fish can be stored before having to return to port to offload them.

It is not a case of "if" the ship will meet the storm. It is a case of "when".

What preparations has your Enterprise made for its own "Perfect Storm"?

Kevin Lee Smith
*The **Pragmatic** Mariner*

Who Should Read This Book?

Anyone and everyone that is involved (in whole or in part) in the Strategising and Roadmapping phases of Enterprise Transformation (e.g. CxO's, Executive Management, Enterprise Architects, Strategic Transformation Planners, members of the PMO, etc.) and with the Governance and Lobbying of project execution (e.g. Project Managers, Business Analysts, Enterprise IT Architects, Solution Architects, Technical Architects, etc).

The book is intended for Enterprise Architects, Business Architects, IT Architects, process-designers and others who deal with the practical implications of whole-of-enterprise issues.

It should also be useful for Strategists and Service-managers, and for anyone else who works with other enterprise-wide themes such as supply-chains, value-webs, quality, security, knowledge-sharing, sustainability, business ethics and social responsibility, or health, safety and environment.

What Does This Book Tell Me?

PEAF does not tell you how to be a CxO, Executive, Strategic Planner, Enterprise Architect, Business Architect, Solution Architect, Portfolio Planner, Portfolio Manager, etc, etc, etc.

What PEAF does do is expose a holistic environment and context of Methods, Artefacts, Culture and Environment that all of those people exist within. The glue that brings all the parts together into a choreographed whole which makes the whole so much more than just the summation of its parts.

PEAF asserts that people working within the Strategising and Roadmapping phases of Transformation already know how to do what they do. The problem is not them. The problem is the context (Methods, Artefacts, Cultural and Environmental things) that they are forced to work within. PEAF aims to increase the maturity (effectiveness and efficiency) of that context, enabling people to achieve their full potential. Increasing the maturity of the context they work within, to one that supports, enables and makes their work easier rather than one which hinders, impedes and makes their work more difficult.

PEAF places its emphasis on the one practical issue that causes the most problems for EA efforts: how to get started and keep going, delivering real and verifiable results within the constraints and complex, challenging realities of any large Enterprise. In a sense, PEAF was born out of failure - out of identifying all the myriad of ways in which EA efforts fail in real business practice, and then devising ways to prevent these sources of failure from occurring.

Pragmatic Framework

Enterprise Architecture

CONNECTING THE DOTS

In many respects Enterprise Architecture can be compared to gardening - or more accurately the MAGIC that allow a gardener to produce a pleasant garden or to grow fruit and vegetables.

A lot of people try to "sell" Enterprise Architecture with quick wins and low-hanging fruit. Whilst we will certainly not ignore such opportunities if they exist, to pursue only those quick wins is totally against the raison d'être of Enterprise Architecture.

Enterprise Architecture is concerned with creating the correct environment for the gardener and the garden to be effective and efficient. Creating the correct environment does not in itself create the garden, but as every gardener will know, that environment can have a massive positive or negative impact on the garden. This is exactly the same for Enterprise Architecture - we are creating the environment required for an Enterprise (participating in an Enterprise) to grow, to flourish, to bloom and to bear fruit - not only for this year but for next year and for many years to come. Implementing changes to become more mature in how Enterprise Architecture is utilised does not in itself do this, but provides the environment for this to happen.

Many gardeners also know you can try to create the correct environment through trial and error (and sometimes for specific reasons it is beneficial to do this), but generally speaking the best gardeners lever and utilise the tips, tricks and knowledge of other gardeners as much as possible. In this respect, they are using Frameworks.

There is a lot information about Enterprise Architecture. Much of it is conflicting, inconsistent, inapplicable or unusable. This is why PEAF was created - to provide a small and concise set of real things to use rather than long winded ivory tower opinion and explanations - knowledge that will allow the garden and the gardener to flourish.

Kevin Lee Smith

*The **Pragmatic** Gardener*

> # KEYPOINT:
>
> PEAF enables you to mature your EA capability. Pragmatically.

> # ADOPTION:
>
> Management: Instigate a project to ensure everyone related to Transformation is trained in PEAF/XEAF.

Questions to Ponder

♦ What do you use, for the Logical model for your Enterprise's EA capability?

The Adoption section of PEAF begins at Step 4. Steps 1 to 3 are contained in PEFF and are the same regardless of what part of the Transformation domain is being matured, as steps 1 to 3 define which part requires attention.

> # KEYPOINT:
>
> The Adoption section of PEAF
>
> defines 'HOW' it should be adopted
>
> and used.

Questions to Ponder

- ◆ Do you think EA frameworks should explain HOW they should be adopted?
- ◆ Which EA frameworks does your Enterprise currently use?
- ◆ Did they explain how you should adopt them, or leave you to figure it out for yourself?

Elaborating

Logical

Step 4

Design Changes

Physical

KEYPOINT:

Designing Changes allows you to decide what to change from PEAF to your own XOET.

Questions to Ponder

♦ Has your Enterprise executed this step yet?
♦ If not, would it be beneficial to do so?
♦ Who in your Enterprise is the person that can decide to execute this step and provide the mandate and resources to do so?
♦ Who in your Enterprise is the person that can execute this step?

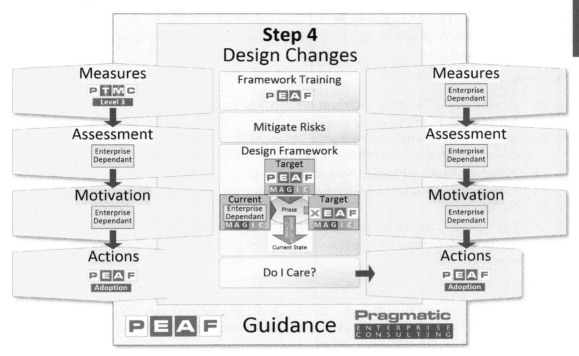

© Pragmatic 365 (2008-2021)

Here we see the basic structure for the information and process for an Adoption step.

Inputs

On the left is the input. Measures, which drove the Assessment (against those measures), which created the Motivation, to perform the Actions of this step. For all steps (Except Step 1) the input on the left comes from the previous step. For Step 1, the input on the left comes from outside the Enterprise (the Enterprise's Context).

For all steps (Except Step 0) the input on the left comes from the previous step. For Step 0, the input on the left comes from outside the Enterprise (the Enterprise's Context).

Outputs

The Actions of this step generate the outputs on the right. More detailed Measures are created, which drive the Assessment (against those measures), which drives the Motivation (or not), to perform the Actions of the next step. For all steps (except Step 6) the output on the right is passed to the next step.

Guidance

Guidance is provided by PEAF and optionally by engaging a Consultant from

Pragmatic EC.

10 - Adoption

Purpose

◆ Understand how to apply PEAF.

◆ Design the Enterprise's XEAF by starting with PEAF and modifying and augmenting it as required.

Actions

◆ **Framework Training** – Obtain the required understanding in the chosen framework (PEAF) to be able to use it. This can include reading books, attending workshops, self-study or instructor led training, or any combination thereof depending on the Enterprise and the individuals involved.

◆ **Mitigate Risks** – Mitigate risks as they occur.

◆ **Design Framework** – Using the PEAF as a base, design your Enterprise Dependant XEAF.

◆ **Do I Care?** – Based on the Assessment, what is the Motivation to proceed, and does the Motivation allow the C-Suite to care enough to warrant proceeding to the next step.

Resources

◆ It could take less than 4 weeks do this, given appropriate training and resources, however, in practice this work may be spread over many weeks due to the availability of the individuals required.

◆ Mandatory

    ◆ PEAF Knowledge.

    ◆ C-Suite:

        ▪ An appetite to execute it.

    ◆ Transformation Project Members:

        ▪ Time to expose their knowledge and views.

    ◆ Transformation Managers (PMs, Heads of, xxx Managers, etc)

        ▪ Time to expose their knowledge and views.

◆ Advisable

    ◆ **Pragmatic EC**.

    ◆ **P3** – The **Pragmatic** Publishing Platform.

Risks

◆ A reluctance by Management to allow this work to proceed (Important/Non-Urgent work aka Quality Time), due to the resources required already being maxed out on day to day work (Important/Urgent work aka Firefighting).

◆ Using PEAF without the sufficient understanding.

KEYPOINT:

Use PEAF to design your own XEAF.

ADOPTION:

EA Project Team: Follow the 4th step in PEAF for maturing your EA capability.

Adoption > Step 4 > Risks > The Brick Wall of Misconception

We don't have an EA	We don't do EA	We don't have any EAs	Ivory tower and hypothetical	Many failures
Benefits are never achieved	Invented by consultants	A large expensive team?	A large expensive project?	Losing Strategic Control
It's another silver bullet	Nothing to do with me, mate!	How much!!!	Are we there yet?	I have important firefighting to do...
We don't live in a perfect world	Oh what pretty pictures	I can't afford a modeling tool!	I don't want another maintenance nightmare	How many paperclips?
You can't define the future	Don't tell the business what to do	Don't tell IT Experts what to do	Let's model everything	Shhh! Don't mention the words EA

© Pragmatic 365 (2008-2021)

Because the field of Enterprise Architecture is very immature (we cannot call it a profession) and there is no way to know who is and is not a "real" Enterprise Architect, almost anyone can call themselves an Enterprise Architect and begin telling others about it. Negativity around EA is widespread but it is not a surprise. Most people and Enterprises have just enough knowledge to be dangerous!

A lot of people have heard of EA. Unfortunately, most of them have only heard parts of the story and from sources of varying quality and completeness. Also those parts of the story may have been heard or told at different points in time. Myths, inaccuracies and untruths abound. With this in mind it's hardly surprising that a lot of people's understanding of EA is inaccurate, incomplete, erroneous and inconsistent.

Over the years this has caused a massive amount of disinformation to build up and percolate around the business and IT communities which has lead people to have very negative views about what EA is and what it means for their Enterprise.

There are many misconceptions associated with bringing Enterprise Architecture to an Enterprise. But more than misconception, they are real risks.

Each risk defined, documents the impact and general mitigation strategies to deal with them and they are all fundamentally perception problems.

##END##

We don't have an EA

Description	EA is perceived as not existing in an Enterprise and therefore "we don't need it"

Impact	**FAILURE**
	EA is not viewed as a serious issue that management need to address and hence nothing is done to mature it.

Reality	**Every Enterprise already has an EA.** The word Architecture just means structure and so an Enterprise Architecture is really just the structure of the Enterprise. Every Enterprise definitely has structure and therefore definitely has an Enterprise Architecture. It may be good or bad. It may be documented or not. It may be understood or not. It may be what is required or not. An Enterprise may not have an Enterprise Architecture model (something documented in some way) but every Enterprise definitely already has an Enterprise Architecture.
	Every Enterprise already "does" EA. "Doing EA" is a bit of a misnomer. "Doing EA" is actually the work that happens in the Roadmapping phase of the Transformation cascade (as defined by POET) including high level project Governance. This work is already happening in every Enterprise. It may be good or bad. It may be documented or not. It may be understood or not. It may be what is required or not but every Enterprise is definitely already "doing" Enterprise Architecture.
	Every Enterprise already employs EAs. The people who currently work in the Strategising and Roadmapping phases and perform high level project Governance are EA's. They may not have that title, they may not know what EA is, but they are most definitely EAs.
	"Having" EA or "doing" EA is therefore not a question of existence or not, it's more a question of maturity - the effectiveness and efficiency by which those things exist and are done. It's a question of Maturity.

Likelihood / Impact	M / H	Mitigation	Communication

We don't do EA

Description	EA is perceived as not existing in an Enterprise and therefore "we don't need it"
Impact	**FAILURE** EA is not viewed as a serious issue that management need to address and hence nothing is done to mature it.
Reality	Yes you do - Strategy formulation and high level Transformation Planning is "doing" Enterprise Architecture

Likelihood / Impact	M / H	Mitigation	Communication

We don't have any EAs

Description	EA is perceived as not existing in an Enterprise and therefore "we don't need it"
Impact	**FAILURE** EA is not viewed as a serious issue that management need to address and hence nothing is done to mature it.
Reality	Yes you do - The Senior Management Team and Transformation planners are the Architects of the Enterprise The question is, is the MAGIC they use, mature enough.

Likelihood / Impact	M / H	Mitigation	Communication

Ivory tower and hypothetical

Description	Many people may think that EA is all a bit hypothetical and ivory tower. This is not surprising as there is no shortage of people who will wax lyrical for hours on end about EA. In fact an entire industry has built up that does just this. Seminars are frequent but never seem to offer much **Pragmatic** advice or things people can actually use. Consultancies will come and talk to you (for a large fee) about EA but getting them to actually deliver something of value, that's a different story. With all this posturing, style over substance and sound bites, it's hardly surprising that people can think EA is hypothetical and ivory tower.
Impact	**FAILURE** Senior management does not engage, meaning EA tries to move forward by driving from the bottom up and is viewed as something to be placated to "just get them off my back so I can do something more useful instead". The business and IT remain unconnected. Initiatives continue to operate in silos with short term goals.
Reality	It is precisely because we don't live in a perfect world that we need EA.
Likelihood / Impact	H / H Mitigation Communication

Many failures

Description	Many people think EA is of little practical value because they have heard (and continue to hear) stories about how people have failed at "doing" EA.
Impact	**FAILURE** EA is not viewed as a serious issue that management need to address and hence nothing is done to mature it.
Reality	It is true that many attempts at EA fail. This is largely due to EA not being well defined in the first place and then because many people do the wrong things to the wrong things at the wrong time. Bad implementation is the cause for most failures. The baby should not be thrown out with the bathwater.
Likelihood / Impact	M / H Mitigation Communication

Benefits are never achieved

Description	The benefits that EA is supposed to deliver are generally well known and yet most implementations tend not to deliver them.
Impact	**FAILURE** EA is not viewed as a serious issue that management need to address and hence nothing is done to mature it.
Reality	Apart from bad implementation another reason is that either no metrics are used or bad metrics are used. How can you know if something is successful if you do not measure it or measure it in the wrong way?
Likelihood / Impact	M / H Mitigation Communication

Invented by consultants

Description	The Head of Strategy and Architecture of a large UK Government department I worked for once said "EA - it's just something invented by consultants to get them paid more money". To be honest that view is hardly surprising considering all we have mentioned so far.
Impact	**FAILURE** EA is not viewed as a serious issue that management need to address and hence nothing is done to mature it.
Reality	In reality it is largely true that many consultancies view EA as means to more work, however EA existed long before consultants realised they could make a lot of money by exploiting it. Correlation does not mean causality. The key problem there though is a lack of understanding about what EA is actually about and how to actually do it rather than the important people in expensive suits waxing lyrical whilst charging you an arm and a leg. When the Head of Strategy and Architecture thinks that EA is useless we have really big problems. This is why education and exposing **Pragmatic** information about EA and how to do it in a **Pragmatic** way is so important.
Likelihood / Impact	M / H Mitigation Communication

A large expensive team?

Description	Do I need to employ a large team of highly paid Enterprise Architects and have a whole new set of processes, job titles and departments?
Impact	**FAILURE** Funding is not provided.
Reality	No. EA is a cultural shift. Adopting EA is to increase an Enterprise's maturity in its use of The Architecture Paradigm™ to support Strategy Development (Strategising), Transformation Planning (Roadmapping) and Project Governance. EA is therefore an adjustment to the way people do work they are currently doing, not bolting on a whole new chunk. There are some people/groups that would love you to "employ a large team of highly paid Enterprise Architects".
Likelihood /	M / H Mitigation Communication

Impact

A large expensive project?

Description	If I do utilise EA in my business, do I need to have a big EA project spanning years and costing millions of dollars?
Impact	**FAILURE** Funding is not provided.
Reality	No. It's about maturity. Adopting EA is to increase an Enterprise's maturity in its use of The Architecture Paradigm™ at the scope of the Enterprise to support Strategy Development and Transformation Planning. One step at a time. An EA project is one step and can be a large or as small as you like and is driven by understanding how mature you are, how mature you want to be, what the benefits are of moving to that level of maturity and then making the necessary adjustments. EA is a journey not a destination.

Likelihood / Impact	M / H	Mitigation	Communication

Losing Strategic Control

Description	If I do utilise EA in my business, will Enterprise Architects be making strategic decisions?
Impact	**FAILURE** .
Reality	No. The business will. EA provides the context and visibility for the business to make even better business decisions. Enterprise Architecture and Enterprise Architects are much more about exposing pertinent information for decisions to be made. Of course, if the Enterprise wishes to delegate some decision making powers to an Enterprise Architect to carry out on their behalf that's perfectly fine, but those decisions are made on behalf of the Business Management.

Likelihood / Impact	M / H	Mitigation	Communication

It's another silver bullet

Description	EA is perceived as a perfect fix for all of an Enterprise's problems, with little or no work or cost.
Impact	**FAILURE** Other associated and related activities are overlooked and stagnate while the Nirvana that EA is supposed to provide, but will not, is created.
Reality	EA is one tool in toolbox that an Enterprise uses to run efficiently. It is linked to and cooperates with other processes in the Enterprise.

Likelihood / Impact	M / H	Mitigation	Communication

Nothing to do with me, mate!

Description	EA is perceived as an IT or technology level thing.
Impact	**FAILURE** The Business does not engage with IT. The board does not see EA as something that it should discuss. It's for the IT Director to do if he wants. IT builds models and diagrams for its own purposes but does not connect them to the business level adequately thereby propagating the myth. EA is placed under the control of the IT Director or CIO. It loses visibility at the board level and descends into being seen as a cost rather than an asset.
Reality	EA is a tool to expose the relationships between the Business and IT. It is ultimately a business tool to enable the board and senior management to see and therefore understand the components of the Enterprise and the relationships between them.

Likelihood / Impact	H / H	Mitigation	Communication

How much!!!

Description	EA is perceived as large, costly and slow. EA is perceived as a huge Initiative to immediately move the Enterprise from Current to Target with associated huge costs and timescales.
Impact	**FAILURE** Similar to large EAI Initiatives in the past large sums of money are spent and time invested until the bubble bursts and someone asks "what are we getting for all this money we are spending".
Reality	The initial setup of EA should take no longer than 6 months so long as it is driven in the right way. The planning part of EA (as an integral part of the annual business planning cycle) should take no longer than 3 months. The initiatives that come out of the business planning exercise do not try to solve all problems in the first year. There is always a mixture of strategic, tactical, and temporary work in any initiative.
Likelihood / Impact	M / M Mitigation Communication

Are we there yet?

Description	EA is perceived as a destination rather than a journey, and/or as a deliverable rather than a process with deliverables.
Impact	**FAILURE** Once the principles and models are done they slowly get more and more out of date leading to distrust of them and finally resulting in Shelfware and just another set of diagrams and lists we never use.
Reality	The setup phase of EA is a destination but that is only to provide the environment to be able to perform the repetitive processes of governance and business planning.
Likelihood / Impact	M / H Mitigation Communication

I have important firefighting to do...

Description	EA is perceived as a roadblock to more important and immediate problems such as "getting the car out of the river".
	EA is perceived as purely long term & strategic and not capable of adding value in a tactical world.
Impact	**FAILURE**
	EA never gets a look in with senior management as they are solely concentrating today's, this week's, or this month's crisis.
Reality	EA never says yes or no. It provides the environment for senior management to see and understand the implications and effects of their decisions BEFORE they make them.
	EA does not preclude short term, tactical or even "throwaway" work. Having EA means that however much tactical or "throwaway" work needs to be done, it is done in the context of a wider and more strategic context.
Likelihood / Impact	H / H Mitigation Communication

Adoption

Oh what pretty pictures

Description	EA is perceived as creating static "pretty" pictures that hang on people's walls but not used by anyone.
Impact	**FAILURE** "Pictures" or models, have some value to certain people but they are mostly viewed as things to point at when saying "we have an architecture" rather than living things which aid understanding and decision making.
Reality	Models are powerful things that convey understanding and therefore then provide the basis for understanding the impacts of change). Whilst sometimes it is more beneficial to deal with lists and spreadsheets there are times where pictures show problems and inconsistencies much more clearly. EA allows access to dynamic Models.

Likelihood / Impact	H / H	Mitigation	Communication EA models should be online and navigable. EA models should consist of different and appropriate views and viewpoints targeted at specific audiences. EA Models should be actively used in business planning and projects to assess impact & risk and perform what-if analyses.

I can't afford a modelling tool!

Description	EA modelling tools are perceived as expensive and "nice to have" but not mandatory.
Impact	**FAILURE** Pictures and discrete spreadsheets are mostly produced in silos with little reuse value, with a huge information gaps and with the most important relationships missing. These pictures are, or soon become, out of date as the pictures and spreadsheets are not maintained,
Reality	Compared to the cost of paying people to manually maintain the linkages between pictures and spreadsheets, the cost of a tool is very small. Some things are not possible without a tool, e.g. managing relationships, building different views, Version control, security. federation of maintenance rights., etc.

Likelihood / Impact	H / H	Mitigation	Communication Evaluate and source a tool Expend the necessary time to understand, configure and use the tool

I don't want another maintenance nightmare

Description	EA models are perceived as being owned and updated by IT.
Impact	**FAILURE** IT does not have the bandwidth to maintain all of the information and therefore parts of the model become out of date, unconnected and subsequently unused.
Reality	Maintenance of the information within an EA model repository is performed by those most suitable and able to maintain it. E.g. IT people maintain application, Database and hardware information, Business people maintain objectives, products and business activities information.

Likelihood / Impact	H / H	Mitigation	Communication EA Models are owned by the stakeholders/users of the views. The different entities and relationships are owned and maintained as part of existing business and IT processes by the people most appropriate for that entity/relationship

How many paperclips?

Description	EA is perceived as producing Models with huge amounts of detail and will descend into analysis paralysis.
Impact	**FAILURE** The high level strategic view is lost. A huge amount of work is done for little benefit to the stakeholders
Reality	EA is all primarily about breadth rather than depth (although deep dives may be necessary occasionally). EA is interested in the entire breadth of an Enterprise but only as much depth as required for the strategic planning and governance of initiatives.

Likelihood / Impact	M / M	Mitigation	Communication Stay at the right level of granularity

You can't define the future

Description	EA is perceived as not being able to define a Future state because no one knows what that is and it's always changing anyway.
Impact	**FAILURE** The long term direction is not known and therefore work operates in a "today" silo timeframe resulting in people not even knowing if the decisions they are taking are good or bad in the long term.
Reality	All Enterprises have some idea of a future state, The fact that their view may not be complete and is probably prone to change does not detract away from this long term general vision, and it is this vision that guides the ship.

Likelihood / Impact	H / H	Mitigation	Communication Make sure the "Target" Model is defined at the correct level of granularity and well understood by the Business and IT

Don't tell the business what to do

Description	The perception is that IT is dictating to the Business.
Impact	**FAILURE** IT tells the Business how wrong it is, how stupid it has been in the past and how IT knows what to do to solve all their problems. The business stops listening to IT.
Reality	EA is all about the Business and IT working in a true partnership, where each understands the other enough to be able to co-operatively work together to achieve shared goals.

Likelihood / Impact	M / M	Mitigation	Communication.

Don't tell IT Experts what to do

Description	The perception is that EA will start dictating and restricting other work downstream. This can happen primarily with Solution Architects (as this is the primary interface between EA and Projects) but can also happen with other roles where people's autonomy and expertise can feel threatened.
Impact	**FAILURE** People who work on projects can be resistant to the setup and/or operation of an EA capability, which can derail its effectiveness.
Reality	EA is all about the Business and IT working in a true partnership, where each understands the other enough to be able to co-operatively work together to achieve shared goals. Solution Architects should not look on the EA function as constraining or restricting them, but as an enabler that acts more in a guiding role rather than a perceived policing role.
Likelihood / Impact	M / M Mitigation Communication.

Let's model everything

Description	Feverish modelling of various things without a plan for how to gather the data, how to QA it, and who will benefit from it once it is gathered.
Impact	**FAILURE** A large amount of work is done gathering data and producing diagrams for little or no benefit. Models are not connected to the sources of the information and so people continue to use the diagrams and spreadsheets they always have used or they start creating new one duplicating effort.
Reality	EA is all about being of value to the Enterprise. Models should not be created without a firm idea of who will use the information, in what way, and for what benefit.
Likelihood / Impact	H / H Mitigation Communication. Clearly Define the Version 0.1 Meta-model Clearly define the benefits to what stakeholders the model will bring

Shhh! Don't mention the words EA

Description	EA is driven in a largely covert manner, It is only known of within IT and even then only to a very select few.
Impact	FAILURE EA is only used for managing IT and usually largely from an infrastructure point of view. The business and IT remain largely unconnected.
Reality	EA is all about connecting things. EA is a cultural shift and therefore needs to be communicated, understood and bought into by the entire Enterprise.

Likelihood / Impact	H / H	Mitigation	Communication.

My bonus is based on today's share price

Description	Executive incentives reward short term investments and reduced acquisition costs.
Impact	FAILURE These incentives are in direct conflict with the stated vision, objectives and principles that EA aims to achieve.
Reality	EA is all about investment for future benefit. Executives should be incentivized to produce long terms benefit. Executives should be de-incentivized from producing short term benefits at the expense of long term strategic goals.

Likelihood / Impact	H / H	Mitigation	Communication. Change the Executive incentive scheme. Reward strategic and long term thinking

KEYPOINT:

There are many risks related to increasing your EA maturity. 99% of these are misconceptions. If you do not address them, YOU WILL FAIL.

ADOPTION:

C-Suite: Instigate an initiative to Break down the Brick Wall of Misconceptions about EA.

Questions to Ponder

- Which of these bricks of misconception exist in your Enterprise?
- What are the top 5?
- What will you do to address them?

EA is about exposing problems	EA is about exposing mistakes	EA is about breaking down silos and fiefdoms
EA is about benefit to the whole	EA is about long term benefit	EA is about inconvenient truths

Many of the things that EA aims to do will not be readily received by many people. This is because adopting EA is a paradigm shift. One could say that if there were no resistance then either you are not doing your job properly or the Enterprise is already mature enough in its use of EA. This is because the paradigm shift involves changing the culture of the Enterprise and therefore how people are motivated.

This is a (probably inexhaustive) list of problems that come up time and time again. Problems that, if not tackled will mean failure:

♦ People may not like EA exposing problems or mistakes because the Enterprises culture punishes those that do.

♦ People may not like EA breaking down silos and fiefdoms because the Enterprise's culture tends to motivate them financially and with promotions to build them.

♦ People may not like to think about the benefit to the whole Enterprise because the Enterprise's management measures them only on their small part of it, incentivising people to improve their part, to the possible detriment of the whole.

♦ People are driven to hit this years numbers, this month's targets, todays share price. This drive is completely at odds with EA as EA often means taking short term pain to achieve long term gain.

♦ Truths, if inconvenient, tend to be hidden, especially if they impact the points above. EA is built on exposing and accepting truth, even if that is painful. Progress can never be achieved if truths are ignore, however inconvenient they may be.

It is unfortunate that most of these pushbacks come from Management, because it is management that we need to convince to employ a (proper) EA, rather than the majority of "EA" work where the EA who spends his time only in IT and makes sure he does not upset anyone. A "proper" EA spends most of his days listening to people and speaking truth to power.

However…

"There are no bad people, only bad contexts. (aka bad Culture)"

- Pragmatic

And if we want to change people's behaviour, we need to concentrate on changing the context (Culture) rather than trying to change the people.

> # KEYPOINT:
>
> Many people will hate EA because: 1. It exposes problems and mistakes, 2. It breaks down silos and fiefdoms, 3. It's about long term benefits to the Enterprise, rather than short term benefits to individuals.

> # ADOPTION:
>
> C-Suite: Reward; 1) The exposing of problems and mistakes. 2) The breaking down of silos and fiefdoms. 3) Striving for long term benefits to the Enterprise, rather than short term benefits to individuals.

Questions to Ponder

- ◆ Who in your Enterprise hates EA?
- ◆ What do you need to do to stop them hating EA?

Adoption > Step 4 > Risks > Communication

Communication and knowledge transfer are the keys to mitigating most of the risks associated with EA adoption.

For this reason, good quality and continuous knowledge transfer is mandatory if an increase in EA maturity is to be a success.

If it is not done, or done badly, your EA Initiative WILL FAIL.

This is not a risk.
This is a Certainty.

© Pragmatic 365 (2008-2021)

What do we mean by Communication? We mean talking to people. Educating them. Briefing them. Putting things in their minds that change the way they think about things, the way they make decisions about things, the way they perceive things, the way they look at things.

> "We cannot solve our problems with the same thinking we used when we created them."
>
> *- Albert Einstein*

Dealing with peoples worries, fears, confusions, misinterpretations, uncertainties, delusions, mix-ups, doubts, reservations, suspicions, anxieties, apprehensions, concerns, phobias, uneasiness, etc, etc, etc.

90% of ALL EA initiatives fail because communication was either not done at all or was done at such a level that it might as well not have been done at all.

PEAF provides Books, Slidesets, Training and Toolkits to enable this communication to happen. In fact, like all frameworks in the **Pragmatic** Family (**PF2**) PEAF allows you to update and modify the content to be even more applicable to your Enterprise, and then to publish your own Books, Slidesets, Training and Toolkits to the people within your Enterprise to aid communication.

If you only take away one thing from the whole of PEAF, take this.

IF YOU DO NOT DO THIS, OR YOU DO IT BADLY, YOU WILL FAIL.

KEYPOINT:

If you do not continually

communicate, your initiative will fail.

ADOPTION:

EA Project Team: Continually

communicate.

Questions to Ponder

♦ What cultural risks, related to EA, exist in your Enterprise?
♦ What effect are they having on your EA capability and its output?
♦ Who is Accountable and Responsible for managing them?

Adoption

Constructing

Physical

Step 5

Develop Changes

Operational

> # KEYPOINT:
>
> Developing Changes allows you to
>
> create your own XOET.

Questions to Ponder

- ◆ Has your Enterprise executed this step yet?
- ◆ If not, would it be beneficial to do so?
- ◆ Who in your Enterprise is the person that can decide to execute this step and provide the mandate and resources to do so?
- ◆ Who in your Enterprise is the person that can execute this step?

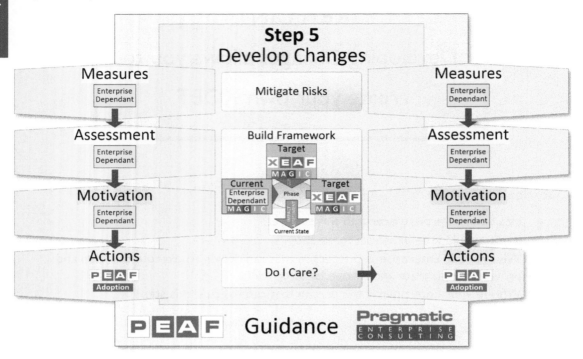

© Pragmatic 365 (2008-2021)

Here we see the basic structure for the information and process for an Adoption step.

Inputs

On the left is the input. Measures, which drove the Assessment (against those measures), which created the Motivation, to perform the Actions of this step.

For all steps (Except Step 0) the input on the left comes from the previous step. For Step 0, the input on the left comes from outside the Enterprise (the Enterprise's Context).

Outputs

The Actions of this step generate the outputs on the right. More detailed Measures are created, which drive the Assessment (against those measures), which drives the Motivation (or not), to perform the Actions of the next step. For all steps (except Step 6) the output on the right is passed to the next step.

Guidance

Guidance is provided by PEAF and optionally by engaging a Consultant from

Pragmatic EC.

Purpose

◆ Create the Enterprise's XEAF based on the Enterprise's XEAF design.

Actions

◆ **Mitigate Risks** – Mitigate risks as they occur.
◆ **Develop Framework** – Using the PEAF as a base, create your Enterprise Dependant XEAF.
◆ **Do I Care?** – Based on the Assessment, what is the Motivation to proceed, and does the Motivation allow the C-Suite to care enough to warrant proceeding to the next step.

Resources

◆ It could take less than 2 weeks do this using P3, however, in practice this work may be spread over many weeks due to the availability of the individuals required and not using P3.
◆ Mandatory
  ◆ PEAF Knowledge.
  ◆ C-Suite:
    ▪ An appetite to execute it.
  ◆ Transformation Project Members:
    ▪ Time to expose their knowledge and views.
  ◆ Transformation Managers (PMs, Heads of, xxx Managers, etc)
    ▪ Time to expose their knowledge and views.

◆ Advisable

  ◆ **Pragmatic EC**.
  ◆ **P3** – The **Pragmatic** Publishing Platform.

Risks

◆ A reluctance by Management to allow this work to proceed (Important/Non-Urgent work aka Quality Time), due to the resources required already being maxed out on day to day work (Important/Urgent work aka Firefighting).
◆ Using PEAF without the sufficient understanding.
◆ Not using P3 – The Pragmatic Publishing Platform.

KEYPOINT:

Use P3 to develop your own XEAF.

ADOPTION:

EA Project Team: Follow the 5th step in PEAF for maturing your EA capability.

Adoption > Step 5 > Actions > Setup EA Governance

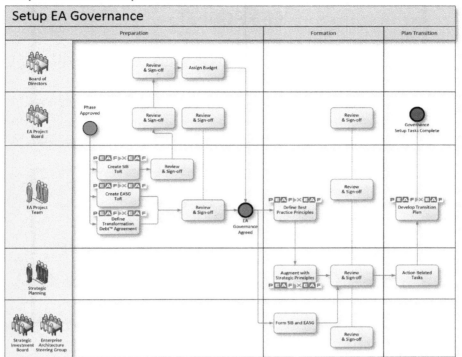

© Pragmatic 365 (2008-2021)

Preparation

- ◆ Review the SIB Terms of Reference, EASG Terms of Reference, Review Options and Solutions process and the Transformation Debt™ Agreement product that PEAF provides.
- ◆ Add, delete and modify them as necessary based on the context of the Enterprise.
- ◆ Obtain agreement and Signoff .
- ◆ Ensure Budget is assigned to the SIB.

Formation

- ◆ Review the Best Practice EA Principles that PEAF provides.
- ◆ Add, delete and modify them as necessary based on the context of the Enterprise.
- ◆ Augment the EA principles with principles that fall out of the Roadmapping phase.
- ◆ Obtain agreement and Signoff .
- ◆ Form the SIB and EASG.

Plan Transition

- ◆ Perform all actions identified in the Tasks related to the operation of the principles.

> # KEYPOINT:
>
> Without proper governance, EA will
> most likely not deliver much value.

> # ADOPTION:
>
> EA Project Team: Design and setup
> the EA Governance changes required.

Questions to Ponder

- Does this process match your Enterprises process for Preparing for Process Change?
- If not, is their anything missing?
- How would you define this process?

Adoption > Step 5 > Actions > Prepare Process Change

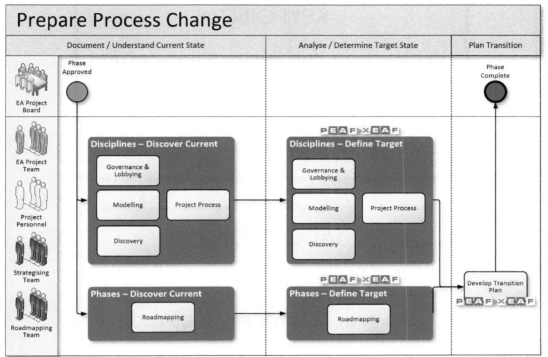

© Pragmatic 365 (2008-2021)

This process is concerned with the preparatory work required to allow us later to adjust the EA processes, aka the work going on in the Roadmapping phase and the work going on in the Disciplines uses.

Document/Understand Current State

♦ The current processes and disciplines the Enterprise Operates are understood (by modelling).

Analyse / Determine Target State

♦ Utilising the processes and disciplines provided by PEAF as a baseline, the current models are modified to reflect the target phases and disciplines we wish to operate.

Plan Transition

♦ Create a detailed plan of the things that need to be done to rollout the changes made and make them real.

KEYPOINT:

Without the fundamental processes,

EA will most likely not deliver much

value.

ADOPTION:

EA Project Team: Design and setup

the process changes required.

Questions to Ponder

♦ Does this process match your Enterprises process for Setting up EA Governance?
♦ If not, is their anything missing?
♦ How would you mature your EA Governance process?

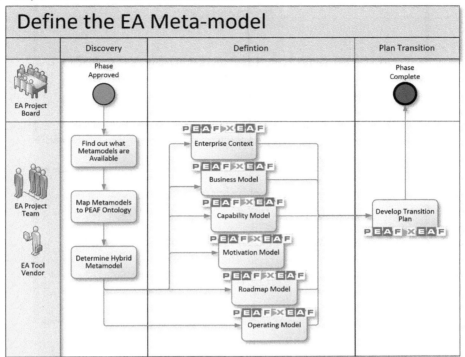

© Pragmatic 365 (2008-2021)

This process defines the Meta-model that will be used for gathering and analysing information that is to be stored in the EA Modelling Tool.

Since some EA Modelling Tools have pre-existing and somewhat static Meta-models this process may not be required. However, even if the approach is to use whatever Meta-model that comes with the Tool that will be selected, it is still a good idea to go through this process to identify the initial entities, relationships and views that are initially important to the Enterprise as beginning with a massive and detailed Meta-model can dilute the focus.

Another dimension to be aware of is that whatever Meta-model is chosen, the Meta-model will expand as times goes on and therefore consideration should be given not only to the initial Meta-model but also how that Meta-model will grow over time.

Discovery

♦ Find out what Meta-models exist and how they map to the PEAF Ontology.

Definition

♦ Using the Artefacts section of PEAF, decide what Meta-models are required.

Plan Transition

♦ Create a detailed plan of the things that need to be done to rollout the changes made and make them real.

> # KEYPOINT:
>
> Without an EA metamodel, we won't
> be able to do any sensible modelling.

> # ADOPTION:
>
> EA Project Team: Define the EA
> metamodel.

Questions to Ponder

- Does this process match your Enterprises process for Defining the EA Metamodel?
- If not, is their anything missing?
- How would you define this process?

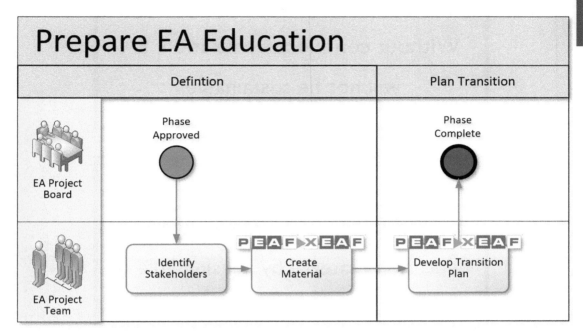

This process creates the necessary communication materials required for ongoing and continuous education and two way communications.

It is concerned with educating people about Enterprise Architecture in general and in particular the framework the Enterprise has chosen. This process, coupled with the provision of training and education in the Transitioning phase, is the most important of all the processes. Communication and education is one of the keys to mitigating many of the risks associated with adoption of EA. For this reason, good quality and continuous education is mandatory if Enterprise Architecture is to be a success.

Definition

♦ Decide who the communication will be targeted at.
♦ Using all the Material in PEAF, modify and augment it as required.

Plan Transition

♦ Create a detailed plan of the things that need to be done to rollout the communication.

IF YOU DO NOT DO THIS, OR YOU DO IT BADLY, YOU WILL FAIL.

> # KEYPOINT:
>
> Without continuous education, EA
> will not be sustainable.

> # ADOPTION:
>
> EA Project Team: Develop EA
> education material by reusing 90% of
> PEAF.

Questions to Ponder

- Does this process match your Enterprises process for Preparing for EA Education?
- If not, is their anything missing?
- How would you define this process?

Adoption > Step 5 > Actions > Prepare Culture Change

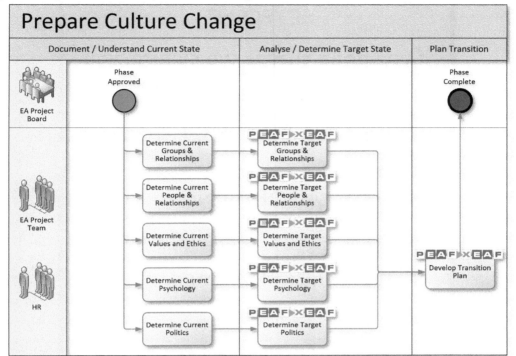

© Pragmatic 365 (2008-2021)

This process is concerned with the preparatory work required to allow us later to adjust the Culture and motivation that people operate within.

Document/Understand Current State

◆ The current culture and motivation are understood (by modelling).

Analyse / Determine Target State

◆ Utilising the processes and disciplines provided by PEAF as a baseline, the current models are modified to reflect the target culture and motivation we wish to operate.

Plan Transition

◆ Create a detailed plan of the things that need to be done to rollout the changes made and make them real.

> # KEYPOINT:
>
> If you don't change the culture, you
> will FAIL.

> # ADOPTION:
>
> EA Project Team: Design the culture
> changes required. IF you don't, you
> will FAIL.

Questions to Ponder

- ◆ Does this process match your Enterprises process for Preparing for Cultural Change?
- ◆ If not, is their anything missing?
- ◆ How would you define this process?

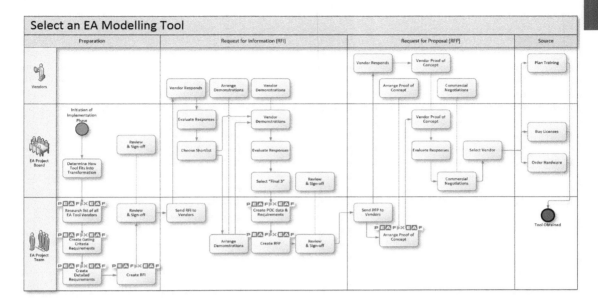

© Pragmatic 365 (2008-2021)

This process is concerned with the procurement of an EA modelling tool.

It should be noted that any information within the Enterprise is not an island and therefore (as POET prescribes) due consideration must be given to how the EA tool fits in with the landscape of other tools utilised by the Enterprise (e.g. Portfolio Planning and Management, Risk Management, Configuration Management and Change Management, etc).

Preparation

♦ Determine how this new Tool will fit into the wider Transformation Tool family.

♦ Using PEAF, create a list of all EA Tool Vendors to be considered.

♦ Using PEAF, create a set of EA Tool Requirements.

RFI

♦ Send RFI to Tool Vendors.

♦ Evaluate responses and shortlist 5-6 Tool Vendors.

♦ Organise and Attend Tool demonstrations.

♦ Evaluate demonstrations and select a "Final 3".

♦ Create the RFP.

RFP

♦ Send out RFP and arrange Proof of Concepts.

♦ Evaluate responses, perform commercial negotiations and select Vendor.

Source

♦ Plan the training, buy the licenses and order the hardware.

KEYPOINT:

Without a proper EA modelling tool,

we won't be able to do any sensible

modelling.

ADOPTION:

EA Project Team: Select an EA

modelling tool by Proof-of-Concept

comparisons.

Questions to Ponder

♦ Does this process match your Enterprises process for Selecting and EA Modelling Tool?

♦ If not, is their anything missing?

♦ How would you define this process?

Transitioning

Operational

Step 6

Rollout Changes

Physical World

KEYPOINT:

Rollout Changes allows you to

rollout your own XOET for people

to use.

Questions to Ponder

◆ Has your Enterprise executed this step yet?
◆ If not, would it be beneficial to do so?
◆ Who in your Enterprise is the person that can decide to execute this step and provide the mandate and resources to do so?
◆ Who in your Enterprise is the person that can execute this step?

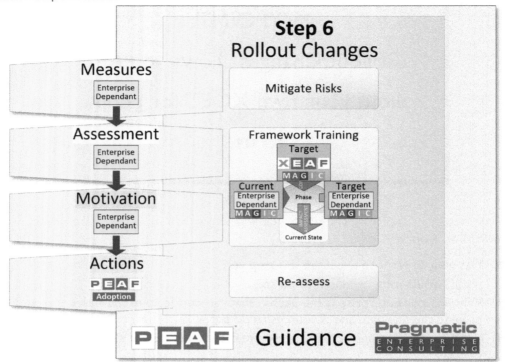

© Pragmatic 365 (2008-2021)

Here we see the basic structure for the information and process for an Adoption step.

Inputs

On the left is the input. Measures, which drove the Assessment (against those measures), which created the Motivation, to perform the Actions of this step.

For all steps (Except Step 0) the input on the left comes from the previous step. For Step 0, the input on the left comes from outside the Enterprise (the Enterprise's Context).

Outputs

The Actions of this step generate the outputs on the right. More detailed Measures are created, which drive the Assessment (against those measures), which drives the Motivation (or not), to perform the Actions of the next step. For all steps (except Step 6) the output on the right is passed to the next step.

Guidance

Guidance is provided by PEAF and optionally by engaging a Consultant from

Pragmatic EC.

Purpose

◆ Rollout the Enterprise's XEAF into operation.

Actions

◆ **Mitigate Risks** – Mitigate risks as they occur.

◆ **Framework** Training – Train the people who work in, or are accountable for, the Enterprises Transformation Capability in XEAF. This can include reading books, attending workshops, self-study or instructor led training, or any combination thereof depending on the Enterprise and the individuals involved.

◆ **Re-assess?** – After some time (6 months, 1 year, etc) the Enterprise should return to Step 1 to determine if another iteration is appropriate.

Resources

◆ It could take less than 2 weeks do this using P3, however, in practice this work may be spread over many weeks due to the availability of the individuals required and not using P3.

◆ Mandatory
  ◆ PEAF Knowledge.
  ◆ C-Suite:
    ▪ An appetite to execute it.
  ◆ Transformation Project Members:
    ▪ Time to learn and understand XEAF.
  ◆ Transformation Managers (PMs, Heads of, xxx Managers, etc)
    ▪ Time to learn and understand XEAF.

◆ Advisable

  ◆ **Pragmatic EC**.
  ◆ **P3** – The **Pragmatic** Publishing Platform.

Risks

◆ A reluctance by Management to allow this work to proceed (Important/Non-Urgent work aka Quality Time), due to the resources required already being maxed out on day to day work (Important/Urgent work aka Firefighting).

◆ Using XEAF without the sufficient understanding.

◆ Not using P3 – The Pragmatic Publishing Platform.

KEYPOINT:

Use P3 to train your staff in your

own XEAF

ADOPTION:

EA Project Team: Follow the 6th step

in PEAF for maturing your EA

capability.

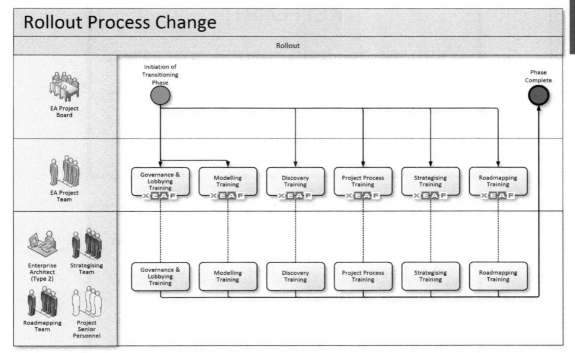

© Pragmatic 365 (2008-2021)

Rollout

♦ Provide all education and training required to rollout changes to processes.

KEYPOINT:

Without the fundamental processes,

EA will most likely not deliver much

value.

ADOPTION:

EA Project Team: Make sure key

process changes are rolled out.

Questions to Ponder

- ◆ Does this process match your Enterprises process for Rolling out Process Change?
- ◆ If not, is their anything missing?
- ◆ How would you define this process?

Setup the EA Meta-model

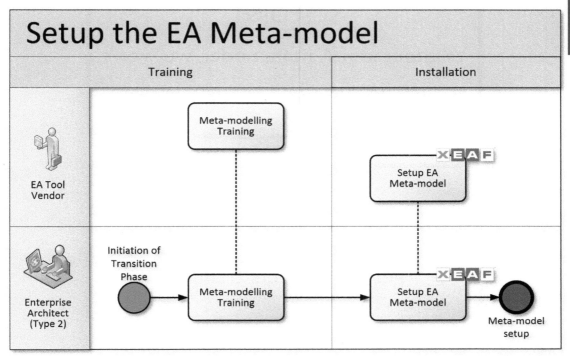

© Pragmatic 365 (2008-2021)

Training

♦ The Enterprise Architect obtains training from the EA Tool vendor regarding the maintenance, modification and development of the Meta-model.

Installation

♦ The formulated Meta-model is setup by the Enterprise Architect with support from the EA Tool vendor.

> # KEYPOINT:
>
> Without an EA metamodel, we won't
>
> be able to do any sensible modelling.

> # ADOPTION:
>
> EA Project Team: Make sure people
>
> get Meta-model training.

Questions to Ponder

- ◆ Does this process match your Enterprises process for Setting up the EA Metamodel?
- ◆ If not, is their anything missing?
- ◆ How would you define this process?

Adoption > Step 6 > Actions > Provide EA Education

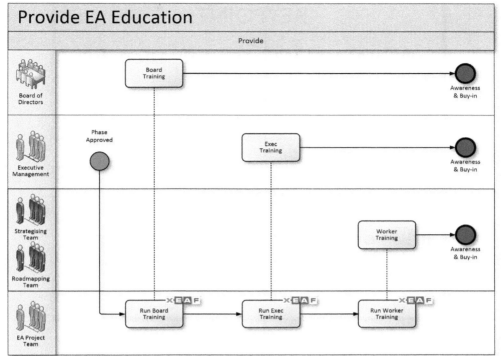

© Pragmatic 365 (2008-2021)

Here training is provided to the people working within the EA domain, regarding the Enterprise EA framework that has been developed (based on PEAF) by the EA Project Team.

It essentially consists of all of the PEAF materials that have been updated, modified and augmented from PEAF to produce that Enterprises own Enterprise Architecture Framework (XEAF).

Internal Certification can also be performed.

> # KEYPOINT:
>
> Without continuous education, EA
> will not be sustainable.

> # ADOPTION:
>
> EA Project Team: Provide continuous
> EA education.

Questions to Ponder

- Does this process match your Enterprises process for Providing EA Education?
- If not, is their anything missing?
- How would you define this process?

Adoption > Step 6 > Actions > Rollout Culture Change

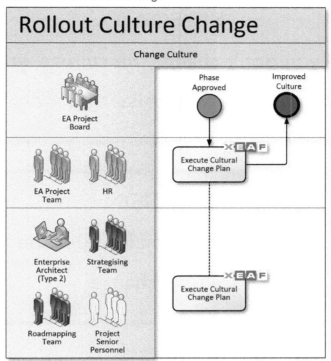

© Pragmatic 365 (2008-2021)

This process effects the cultural and human change necessary to bring about a more long term view of the management and direction of the Enterprise.

Without this, it does not matter how many principles, processes or models you adopt as the direction and management will continue to compromise the future of the Enterprise for short term (usually) financial individual gain.

IF YOU DO NOT DO THIS, OR YOU DO IT BADLY, YOU WILL FAIL.

> # KEYPOINT:
> If you don't change the culture, you
> will FAIL.

> # ADOPTION:
> EA Project Team: Roll out the
> Culture change

Questions to Ponder

- Does this process match your Enterprises process for Rolling Out Culture Change?
- If not, is their anything missing?
- How would you define this process?

Adoption

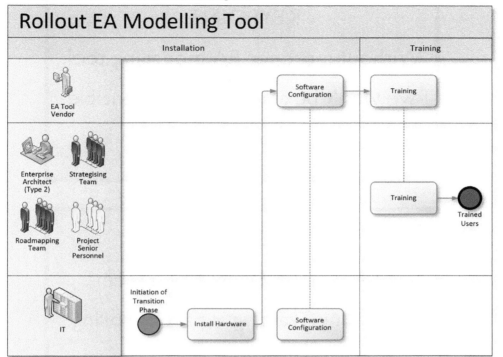

© Pragmatic 365 (2008-2021)

Installation

♦ The EA Modelling tool's hardware and software are installed and commissioned.

Training

♦ Appropriate training is performed.

> # KEYPOINT:
>
> Without a proper EA modelling tool,
> we won't be able to do any sensible
> modelling.

> # ADOPTION:
>
> EA Project Team: Make sure
> Modelling Training is part of rolling
> out the EA modelling tool.

Questions to Ponder

- Does this process match your Enterprises process for Rolling Out the EA Modelling Tool?
- If not, is their anything missing?
- How would you define this process?

Guidance

KEYPOINT:

The Guidance section of the Adoption section of PEAF defines what is used to guide people in their decision making.

ADOPTION:

C-Suite: Follow the Guidance in the Adoption Section of PEAF

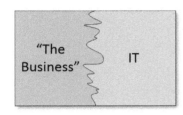

EA is not a Destination.

EA is not even a Journey.

EA is a way of Travelling.

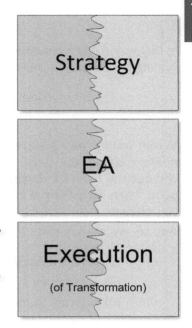

Many people believe and espouse that…

> "EA is all about - Bridging the gap between the business and IT"
>
> *Many People*

Note - use of the term "The Business" here, is used because that is how many people who talk about EA refer to "everything else in the Enterprise that is not IT". I do not necessarily subscribe to this label but since most people use these two terms together I am also using them to help explain, using terms that people currently use.

Until around 2005 I also thought that EA was all about "Bridging the gap between the business and IT". The reason I thought this was mainly because that's what everyone, including many EA's, were telling me. But having begun my quest for the truth of EA it soon dawned on me, that the idea that EA is some kind of physical thing that bridges a gap was erroneous.

In any Enterprise "The Business" and IT are inextricably linked. There is no gap. In addition, if you view EA as a kind of marriage counsellor between "The Business" and IT, helping to bring them closer together, then again EA should not be about bridging the gap, it should be about removing the gap.

In fact, the only purpose of EA is to enable and support the Transformation of the Enterprise. If the Enterprise never needed to change, there would be no reason to use EA at all.

So, since EA is all about enabling Transformation, and since EA (aka Roadmapping) is the work that is done between strategy formulation on the one hand and the execution of projects on the other, it becomes obvious that a much more valid statement was:

"EA is all about - Bridging the gap between Strategy and Execution (of change)"

- Pragmatic

In this way, EA is a continuous process of reacting to changes in the Enterprise's Strategy, and guiding the required transformation. This is where common phrase comes from...

"EA is not a destination. It's a journey"

- Many People

Which sounds very good. However, if we think more deeply, EA is not even the journey. EA is more about the **way** of making the journey. Many organisations make their journey without the use of Enterprise Architecture (yes they are all "doing" EA but there comes a point when something is being done so badly, that it ceases to be that thing. For example, if you cremate a chicken, can we still call this "cooking the dinner"?)

And so, we can say that:

"EA is not a destination.
EA is not Even a journey.
EA is a way of travelling"

- Pragmatic

KEYPOINT:

EA is about bridging the gap between Strategy and Execution

ADOPTION:

C-Suite: Accept that EA is not about bridging IT and The Business, but is about Bridging Strategy and Execution.

Questions to Ponder

- ◆ Do people in your Enterprise think EA is about Bridging the gap between the business and IT?
- ◆ Do you think that talking in terms of Business and IT in this manner is helpful?
- ◆ Do you think that the statement that EA is all about Bridging the gap between Strategy and Execution is a more helpful way of viewing the world?
- ◆ If not, why not?

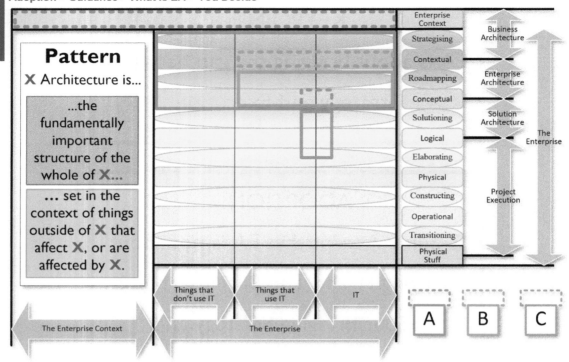

© Pragmatic 365 (2008-2021)

To borrow from the introduction to The Restaurant at the End of the Universe (a book by Douglas Adams)...

> There is a theory which states that if ever anyone discovers exactly what **EA** is for and why it is here, it will instantly disappear and be replaced by something even more bizarre and inexplicable.

> There is another theory which states that this has already happened!

This graphic shows three fundamental areas of Transformation; X, Y and Z.

Many people say it is not the labels that are important but the things that those labels represent. This is true to a certain extent, however, as POET tells us in the Introduction - language is key. Since we speak in labels all the time, it is vitally important to have a common understanding of what we mean when we use them, or at the very least, the ability to realise when we are not using the labels to mean the same thing and to act appropriately. This is especially true when a label (name or acronym) is used widely and extensively. Enterprise Architecture (EA) is definitely in that category.

There is (and has been for a long time) endless debate about what EA is. All those debates revolve around everyone putting forward their definition and then arguing about it. This approach has not taken us forward over the last 20 years, and is unlikely to do so over the next 20 years. Therefore, a more **Pragmatic** approach is needed. Instead of just stating what we believe EA to be, let's consider the question from another direction.

Before we start let's define a useful linguistic pattern, with reference to talking about eh architecture of something. We could say that...

...**X** Architecture, is the fundamentally important structure of the whole of **X**, set in the context of things outside of **X** that affect **X**, or are affected by **X**.

So that we can then easily say that

- **Application** Architecture is the fundamentally important structure of the whole of an **Application**, set in the context of things outside of the **Application**, that affect it, or are affected by it.
- **Building** Architecture is the fundamentally important structure of the whole of a **Building**, set in the context of things outside of a **Building**, that affect it, or are affected by it.
- **Aircraft** Architecture is the fundamentally important structure of the whole of an **Aircraft**, set in the context of things outside of an **Aircraft**, that affect it, or are affected by it.

So, given this pattern we have labelled the diagram with 3 things. X, Y and Z.

- **A shows** the fundamentally important structure of the whole of **the Enterprise (including but not limited to IT)**, set in the context of things outside of **the Enterprise**, that affects it, or are affected by it.
- **B shows** the fundamentally important structure of the whole of **the IT of the Enterprise**, set in the context of things outside of **the IT of the Enterprise**, that affects it, or are affected by it.
- **C shows** the fundamentally important structure of the whole of **a Project Solution**, set in the context of things outside of **a Project Solution**, that affects it, or are affected by it.

From this, it is clear to **Pragmatic** that:

- A is Enterprise Architecture (or EA for short)
- B is Enterprise IT Architecture (or EITA for short) which is what the vast majority of people wrongly think EA is.
- C is Solutions Architecture (or SA for short)

> ## KEYPOINT:
>
> X Architecture, is the fundamentally important structure of X, set in the context of things outside of X, that affect it, or are affected by it.

> ## ADOPTION:
>
> C-Suite: Understand fundamentally what the Architecture of anything is.

Questions to Ponder

- ◆ If you cannot allocate the "EA" moniker to X, Y or Z, what box would you draw on the diagram to represent it?
- ◆ What names do you use to refer to X, Y and Z?
- ◆ Does everyone within your Enterprise agree? If not, what needs to be done?

Adoption > Guidance > What Is EA > Solution Architecture

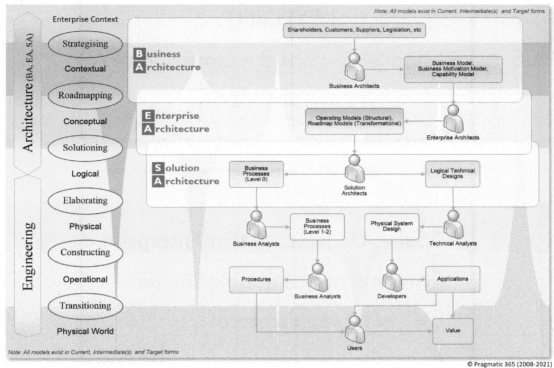

This graphic shows, at a high level, where Enterprise Architecture and Solution Architecture fits in the Enterprise in terms of:

- ◆ **Processes** - Planning, Change Projects and Operations.
- ◆ **Disciplines** - Solution Architecture, Business Architecture and Technical Architecture.
- ◆ **Levels** - The Contextual Business Vision down to an operating Enterprise.
- ◆ **Input/Output** - Shareholders and Value.

EA is a culture that pervades an Enterprise. EA does not make decisions. EA is not expensive. Implementation and operation of EA makes subtle changes to an Enterprise's existing MAGIC related to Enterprise Transformation.

The interface between EA and SA is extremely important if an Enterprise's Transformation efforts are to be Effective, Efficient, Agile and Durable.

> # KEYPOINT:
>
> EA and SA are not the same thing. EA is not just big SA.

> # ADOPTION:
>
> C-Suite: Understand that Enterprise Architecture is not big Solution Architecture.

Questions to Ponder

♦ Does this fit in with your Enterprises view of where Enterprise Architecture and Solution Architecture fits?

♦ I not, how would you show how Enterprise Architecture and Solution Architecture fit together?

♦ Is there anything in your Enterprise that you need to change?

Adoption > Guidance > What Is EA > 160 Char Challenge > Question

Kevin Smith YOU
PeaF - Cutting EA to the Bone
- www.PragmaticEA.com
See all Kevin's activity »

CHALLENGE:

Describe the purpose of EA in one 160 character SMS message
(including spaces, punctuation and carriage returns)?
Rationale: Pragmatically, if you can't describe the purpose of EA in one short
sentence, you will not get the ear of the people required to utilise it.

No rambling, ivory tower, interlectual monologues here. Just post your 160
characters.

Posted 4 months ago | Delete discussion

In October 2009, I posted what appeared to be a very simple challenge on "The Enterprise Architecture Network" LinkedIn discussion Group - Describe the purpose of EA. The discussion received more than 1,400 replies.

Many people have asked this question numerous times before (and will undoubtedly continue to ask it). Each time the question is asked the result is pages and pages of unstructured text: statements, debates, arguments, counter arguments, bun fights, fallings out, makings up, tiffs, love-ins and wars. Occasionally even peace breaks out! That's all well and good but it never seemed to solve anything or move things forward in any way.

So, I asked for only 160 character messages because I wanted to be able to take what people said, analyse them, so as to arrive at a hopefully agreeable definition that included everyone's views that people could then agree with.

The analysis was carried out during March 2010. Having not been able to find any linguistic analysis tools or anyone else to perform a more detailed analysis, it was (unfortunately for some) left to my brain to do the analysis. Whilst this "manual" analysis was very time consuming it was, I believe, worthwhile.

The downside, of course, is that this analysis can be largely subjective and therefore many people may disagree with my analysis. If so, I do not take this disagreement as an indication of failure, but more of an indication of valued discussion. The raw information is provided as part of the PEAF Toolkit and therefore people can perform any analysis on it that they wish to.

Ultimately, while anyone can disagree with the results, the only person that can disagree with the structuring of the definitions (which the results are based on) is the person who wrote the original definition.

```
┌─────────────────────────────────────────┐
│                                         │
│              KEYPOINT:                  │
│                                         │
│   If you want to know the purpose of    │
│                                         │
│         EA, ask 300+ people.            │
│                                         │
└─────────────────────────────────────────┘
```

Questions to Ponder

- ♦ Did you post an answer to this question around 2009/2010?
- ♦ If so, what answer did you post?
- ♦ If not, what would you have posted?

From over 1,400 postings there were only 374 attempts to define the purpose, the rest, whilst interesting, was the normal (mostly harmless) cut and thrust of argument, counter argument, misunderstanding, joke, etc, etc, etc.

This is a word cloud generated from the raw text of those 374 postings, before any detailed analysis has taken place. Although some things stand out it is a confusing picture. You can see why someone listening to all of those people and their postings could easily get confused about what the purpose of Enterprise Architecture was.

KEYPOINT:

300+ people use a lot of different words when describing the purpose of EA.

Questions to Ponder

♦ Do you think this word cloud helps or hinders people's understanding of EA?
♦ Are there things you think are missing?
♦ Are there things here that you believe should not be?

Adoption > Guidance > What Is EA > 160 Char Challenge > Analysis

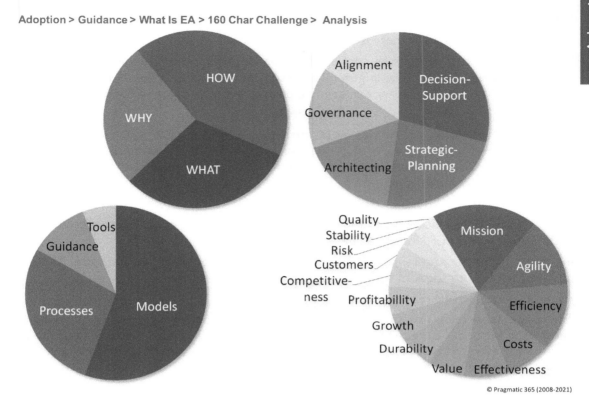

© Pragmatic 365 (2008-2021)

Overall

Although I asked people to state the Purpose of EA (the Why) the first interesting thing that became apparent was that people's responses fell into three distinct categories.

- ◆ **WHY** - These responses were a direct response to the actual question asked - the Purpose of EA - WHY do we "do it".
- ◆ **HOW** - These responses didn't explain the purpose of EA but did describe things that people do that are related to EA - HOW we "do it".
- ◆ **WHAT** - Again, these type of responses didn't explain the purpose of EA, this time they described things you would use to do things that are related to EA - WHAT is used to "do it".

As can be seen, there is generally speaking an equal split between those who define EA in terms of its purpose (WHY), those who define EA in terms of "doing it" (HOW) and those who define EA in terms of what things are produced or used (HOW).

This is the first thing that can confuse the issue when people are discussing or trying to understand what EA is because at any one time three fundamentally different things can be being discussed as if they were the same thing.

KEY FINDING

> **Any definition we create or discussion we have should always address this fact and any argument and counter argument about some of these things is futile. Let's stop arguing about which ones are addressed and agree that all of them are valid.**

WHY

All of the **WHYs** (shown in green) were reviewed and allocated to a structured list of **WHYs** that was created iteratively by analysing the **WHYs**.

In terms of why people think we do EA and its purpose, there are many different ideas.

The truth is that not one of these is correct - they all are.

This is the second thing that can confuse the issue when people are discussing or trying to understand what EA is because in general a person will list one or more of these things but never more than five. This means that any one person only has a piece of the overall picture.

KEY FINDING

Any definition we create or discussion we have should always address this fact and any argument and counter argument about some of these things is futile. Let's stop arguing about which ones are addressed and agree that all of them are valid.

HOW

All of the **HOWs** (shown in blue) were reviewed and allocated to a structured list of **HOWs** that was created iteratively by analysing the **HOWs**.

In general terms the same small number of actions are put forward time and again. There is no "clear winner" to speak of with all being tabled generally equally.

Again, it is not that one of these is correct - they all are.

This is the third thing that can confuse the issue when people are discussing or trying to understand what EA is because in general a person will list one or possibly two, maybe occasionally even three of these but never all of them. Again, this means that any one person only has a piece of the overall picture.

KEY FINDING

Any definition we create or discussion we have should always address this fact and any argument and counter argument about some of these things is futile. Let's stop arguing about which ones are addressed and agree that all of them are valid.

WHAT

All of the **WHATs** (shown in red) were reviewed and allocated to a structured list of **WHATs** that was created iteratively by analysing the **WHATs**.

It can be seen that the vast majority of people think of Models as the main artefact or thing to be used when thinking about EA. Processes are also very well represented.

Again, it is not that one of these is correct but they all are.

This is the fourth thing that can confuse the issue when people are discussing or trying to understand what EA is because in general the vast majority of people will only talk in terms of models, which only represents 50% of the whole. Again, this means that any one person only has a piece of the overall picture.

KEY FINDING

Any definition we create or discussion we have should always address this fact and any argument and counter argument about some of these things is futile. Let's stop arguing about which ones are addressed and agree that all of them are valid.

KEYPOINT:

If you ask 100 people what is the purpose of EA you will get 100 different responses that only together are likely to give you the full picture.

Questions to Ponder

- If someone asked you the purpose of EA, would your reply be an answer to WHY do EA, HOW to do EA or WHAT is used to do EA?
- How do you think it aids peoples understanding of EA to have so many different answers?

© Pragmatic 365 (2008-2021)

This word cloud was generated using the words from the analysed three perspectives combined. Looking at this cloud and letting it seep into your mind is a reasonable way of getting a flavour of EA.

> # KEYPOINT:
>
> Removing synonyms, 300+ people use a small number of different words when describing the purpose of EA.

Questions to Ponder

- ◆ Do you think this word cloud helps or hinders peoples understanding?
- ◆ Are there things you think are missing?
- ◆ Are there things here that you believe should not be?

The purpose of Enterprise Architecture is to…

enable an enterprise to realise its Vision through the execution of its Mission, whilst enabling it to respond to change and increasing its effectiveness, profitability, customer satisfaction, competitive edge, growth, stability, value, durability, efficiency and quality while reducing costs and risks

by

Strategic Planning, Architecting and Governance supported by a Decision Support framework aligning all parts of the enterprise

using

Models, Guidance, Processes and Tools.

If we take the output of the analysis and put it into a sentence we get this. Interestingly this seems to me to be a pretty reasonable definition of Enterprise Architecture. It closely matches the one PEAF defines, even though no one actually made the entire statement.

KEYPOINT:

Arranging the words of 300+ we get

a description of the Why (purpose),

How (by) and What (using) of EA.

Questions to Ponder

♦ Do you agree with this description of the Purpose of EA?
♦ If not, why not?
♦ What would you add? Take away? Change?

The purpose of Enterprise Architecture is to...

allow an enterprise to thrive

by

Strategic Planning, Architecture and Governance

using

a Framework.

© Pragmatic 365 (2008-2021)

Reducing those words to something more succinct produces this.

Having done all this analysis work I had hoped that this would unite people behind a common definition since it was they who had effectively created it - I added nothing of my own views and only took, analysed and structured what people had said.

I was wrong. So wrong!

Having arrived at this definition, I then posted a link back to the discussion to a poll where I tabled this definition and asked people if they

- ♦ Strongly Disagree
- ♦ Somewhat Disagree
- ♦ Neither Agree Nor Disagree
- ♦ Somewhat Agree
- ♦ Strongly Agree

Out of the 278 people that supplied the 374 definitions, only 15 took the time to vote in the poll. And out of those, most (82%) either disagreed or sat on the fence.

There are various possible reasons why this occurred but I think it illustrates one certain truth - people love to disagree more than they love to agree. You might disagree!

> # KEYPOINT:
>
> When asking 300+ people the question "What is EA?", the answer is surprising simple when you remove all the noise.

Questions to Ponder

- Do you agree with this description of the Purpose of EA?
- If not, why not?
- What would you add? Take away? Change?

If we wanted to be able to…

- Clearly identify the products/deliverables of projects.
- Ensure that they are produced on time and to budget.
- Focus attention on the quality of Products/Deliverables.
- Make the progress of projects more visible to management.
- Ensure that work progresses in the correct sequence.
- Involve senior management at the right time and in the right place.
- Allow projects to be stopped and, if required, re-started completely under management control, at any time in the project's life.

Can we achieve all these things without utilising a Project Management framework like PRINCE2?

Will utilising a Project Management framework like PRINCE2 guarantee we will achieve these things?

© Pragmatic 365 (2008-2021)

Let's forget EA for a moment. Let's consider something that we already know - PRINCE2 - a Project Management Framework. You can substitute PRINCE2 here for any other framework that you know of - Six Sigma, MSP, LEAN - the idea here is the same.

Here we identify the things that PRINCE2 claims to achieve. It aims to increase our maturity (Effectiveness and Efficiency) with respect to Project Management. Adopting PRINCE2 is not about **doing Project Management** - it is about **how we do Project Management**.

So, can we achieve all these things without utilising a Project Management framework like PRINCE2? The answer is, yes of course we can. If we have experienced Project Managers and they are allowed to execute their role in the way they know to be efficient and effective they would have no reason to adopt PRINCE2.

If we do get the mandate to utilise PRINCE2, will utilising it guarantee we will achieve these things? The answer is of course No. If our people are not given adequate training and time to understand it and/or if they are then driven to execute their role in ways that they then know are ineffective and inefficient then PRINCE2 adoption would fail.

So when seeking the mandate and resources to adopt PRINCE2 we would have to say - If we don't it doesn't mean we will fail and if we do it doesn't mean we will succeed.

So why would we adopt PRINCE2?

KEYPOINT:

Using a PM framework will not

guaranteed success. Not using a PM

framework will not guaranteed

failure.

Questions to Ponder

♦ Has your Enterprise adopted other frameworks?

♦ How was the mandate to do so secured?

♦ Who in your Enterprise, was Accountable for its selection and adoption?

If we wanted to be able to…

- Reduce costs, Reduce complexity, Reduce risk, Reduce cost of ownership
- Reduce the time to make valid decisions
- Increase ease of change, Increase flexibility
- Sweat the assets, Deal with Compliance
- Improve the Business IT relationship, improve IT Governance
- Identifying and implementing process improvements
- Delivering projects to enable business growth
- Linking business and IT strategies

Can we achieve all these things without utilising an EA Framework like PEAF?

Will utilising an EA Framework like PEAF guarantee we will achieve these things?

© Pragmatic 365 (2008-2021)

Here we identify the things that EA claims to achieve. It aims to increase our maturity (Effectiveness and Efficiency) with respect to Strategising, Roadmapping and Project Governance. Adopting EA is not about doing these things - it is about how we do these things.

So, can we achieve all these things without utilising an EA framework like PEAF? The answer is, yes of course we can. If we have experienced Enterprise Architects and they are allowed to execute their role in the way they know to be efficient and effective they would have no reason to adopt PEAF.

If we do get the mandate to utilise PEAF, will utilising it guarantee we will achieve these things? The answer is of course No. If our people are not given adequate training and time to understand it and/or if they are then driven to execute their role in ways that they then know are ineffective and inefficient then PEAF adoption would fail.

So when seeking the mandate and resources to adopt PEAF we would have to say - If we don't it doesn't mean we will fail and if we do it doesn't mean we will succeed.

So why would we adopt PEAF?

Like PRINCE2, PEAF is just an approach, a framework, a method for doing something. They are "tools". Using them does not guarantee we will be successful. Not using them does not guarantee we will fail. We don't have to use it - our Enterprise will not cease to operate if we do not use EA. But it is likely that we will be overtaken by those that do.

However, today's world is changing… Effectiveness, Efficiency, Agility and Durability are becoming defining characteristics of successful Enterprises. As time passes our Enterprise needs to get more Effective, Efficient, Agile and Durable with respect to how we execute Strategising, Roadmapping and Project Governance or we will be overtaken by those that do.

The 20th century was defined by a mind boggling array of new Enterprises. While new Enterprises and markets will always be created, the 21st century will be defined not by new

Enterprises or markets but by how Effective and Efficient, Agile and Durable those Enterprises are.

The question is not, can we afford to embrace EA?

The question is, can we afford not to?

> # KEYPOINT:
>
> Using an EA framework will not guaranteed success. Not using an EA framework will not guaranteed failure.

Questions to Ponder

- ◆ Has your Enterprise adopted an EA framework?
- ◆ How was the mandate to do so secured?
- ◆ If not, who in your Enterprise, is Accountable for the EA capability?

Adoption > Guidance > Where to Start? > Can I start with one Department?

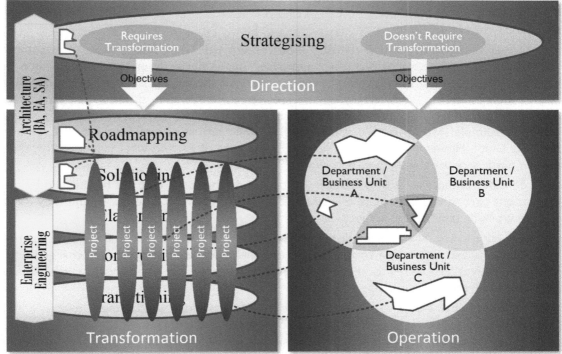

© Pragmatic 365 (2008-2021)

"Do I have to 'do' the whole Enterprise?"

"Can I start small and get some benefits first and then grow it out?"

"Can I start with one Department or Business Unit?"

These are common questions asked by management who may be "kind of sold" on the idea of EA, but don't want to spend too much time and money on. They want to dip a toe in the water rather than dive in.

In many respects, it's a bit like asking "Can I get a little bit pregnant?!"

But here's the thing… We first must understand which question is being asked, and answer it accordingly.

- ♦ Question #1 – With respect to "doing" EA (primarily Roadmapping), can I start with one Department?
- ♦ Question #2 – With respect to using PEAF to mature our EA capability, can I start with one Department"

Question #1 – "Doing" EA (primarily Roadmapping)

Aka using EA to mature the Operations capability of the Enterprise (DOTS).

Can I start with one department?

The answer is no. Why? When thinking about Enterprise Architecture, most people think about the noun - the structure of the Enterprise. This is perfectly understandable since an Enterprise Architecture is exactly that - the structure of the Enterprise. It therefore logically (albeit incorrectly) follows that you can decide to make the domain of "Enterprise Architecture" a sub-part of the whole Enterprise structure - like a Department or a Business Unit for example. Hence people often say "we will start small and just 'do' EA on one Business Unit". However, if you think about the purpose of EA and what it is used for, then this simplistic structural view breaks down.

If we consider Enterprise Strategy, there will be some Objectives that can be satisfied by the Operations part of the Enterprise. These objectives pass down to Operations and they carry out the work to satisfy these Objectives.

However, there are some objectives that the Operations part of the Enterprise cannot currently fulfil, and to be able to fulfil them, they need to be transformed or changed first. These objectives are fed into the Transformation part of the Enterprise, which initially performs the Roadmapping phase.

This Roadmapping work creates a portfolio of Projects, which then execute and change/transform various parts of the Operations part of the Enterprise.

So, the domain we choose to "do" EA on, is not determined by selecting an arbitrary part of the Enterprise like one Business Unit, but upon what needs to be Transformed, which is driven by the part of the Enterprise's Strategy that Operations cannot satisfy in its current structural state.

The only exception to this, is when a very large Enterprise (for example a government) is composed of very large parts that each have their own EA Capability. In that case, you could reduce the scope, to doing EA to one of those large parts.

Question #2 – Using PEAF to mature our EA capability

Aka using EA to mature the Transformation capability (the EA part) of the Enterprise (DOTS).

Can I start with one department?

The answer is yes. Why? Because we are only maturing one department – the EA department. We are not maturing any part of the Operation part of the enterprise.

The only exception to this, is when a very large Enterprise (for example a government) is composed of very large parts that each have their own EA Capability. In that case, you could reduce the scope, to doing EA to one of those large parts.

While Enterprise Architecture is primarily Roadmapping, we also show some changes to the Business Architecture (Strategising) and Solution Architecture (Solutioning) domains because one feeds EA and one is fed by it, meaning if we do not align BA and SA, the improvements to the EA capability can be lost.

> ## KEYPOINT:
>
> The "scope" of EA (at a point in time) is determined by the Enterprise Strategy (at a point in time) not on a Department or Business Unit level.

> ## ADOPTION:
>
> Management: Accept that you cannot arbitrarily choose to start with 1 Department or Business Unit.

Questions to Ponder

- ♦ What do people in your Enterprise think about the scope of EA?
- ♦ Are they arbitrarily trying to descope EA to a structural part of the Enterprise?
- ♦ If they are, how does this fit in with the work being undertaken by the people involved in Roadmapping?
- ♦ Does your Enterprise have more than one Roadmapping Group?

Adoption > Guidance > Where to Start? > EA Catalysts

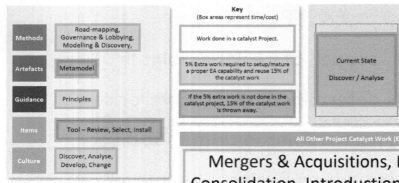

All Other Project Catalyst Work (EA Catalysts)

Mergers & Acquisitions, Business Unit Consolidation, Introduction of New Products, Services or Lines of Business, Outsourcing a Business Function, Divesting a line of Business, Operational Cost Reduction, Business Transformation, Building Relocation, Strategic Planning, Increase Business Agility, Efficiency and Effectiveness, Streamlining Business Processes, Consolidation of Suppliers, Technologies or Applications, Business Process Management, Business Process Re-engineering, Off shoring, Market/Shareholder Pressure,

© Pragmatic 365 (2008-2021)

Here we see an examples of what we call EA Catalyst Projects

- ◆ Mergers & Acquisitions
- ◆ Business Unit Consolidation
- ◆ Introduction of New Products, Services or Lines of Business
- ◆ Outsourcing a Business Function
- ◆ Divesting a line of Business
- ◆ Operational Cost Reduction
- ◆ Business Transformation
- ◆ Building Relocation
- ◆ Strategic Planning
- ◆ Increase Business Agility, Efficiency and Effectiveness
- ◆ Streamlining Business Processes
- ◆ Consolidation of Suppliers, Technologies or Applications
- ◆ Business Process Management
- ◆ Business Process Re-engineering
- ◆ Off shoring
- ◆ Market/Shareholder Pressure

They all have one thing in common. **Large** Enterprise Transformation.

When an Enterprise is faced with such a large change, they also must face a simple truth:

> "Measurement is the first step that leads to control and eventually to improvement. If you can't measure something, you can't understand it. If you can't understand it, you can't control it. If you can't control it, you can't improve it."
>
> *- H. James Harrington*

Which basically boils down to

> "You cannot change what you cannot understand and you cannot understand what you cannot see."
>
> *- Kevin Smith*

For this reason, the Catalyst Project is **forced** to start modelling things (Current State, Target State, Roadmap) and in order for them to do that, they need to acquire a modelling Tool (Review, Select, Install) and decide upon a Metalmodel.

If we add to the diagram (in green) the work to setup or mature an EA capability (maturing the Methods, Guidance and Culture), and we add the work to produce a first roadmap using that EA capability (Integrating the data loaded), it would add approximately 5% of extra cost to the Catalyst Project.

If this 5% increase in resources is added, it would enable the reuse of approximately 15% of the work done in the Catalyst Project. Namely the selected Tool and its associated Metamodel, and the Current, Target and Roadmap models that where produced.

What usually happens if this 5% additional work is not added to the Catalyst Project (which is 99.9% of the time) is that because the a) the processes to create and maintain the information in a coherent, sustainable and **Pragmatic** way and b) the information in the Tool is not kept up to date and rapidly falls out of date and therefore cannot be trusted (used). In addition, the (often expensive) licenses to use the Tool are allowed to expire or reduced to a few select people, which also prevents the data from being reused and kept up to date. Hence the Tool, Metamodel and the Current, Target and Roadmaps are effectively thrown away.

So, it is obvious that if you want to setup or mature an EA capability within an Enterprise, the perfect time to do it would be at a time where a lot of the require work has to be done anyway – known as EA Catalysts. And the bonus is you will gain the 15% that would otherwise have been thrown away.

The problem is, most Enterprises embark on a Catalyst Project only from the perspective of the objectives of the Catalyst Project (albeit large) rather than from the perspective of putting sustainable things in place that can be used in the future as well, long after this project has ceased to exist - which is the whole point of an EA model.

It is a great shame, because it is precisely at these times where you can get benefit from an investment in EA in the shorter term - since that investment will generate immediately benefit for the large Transformation "project" in question, and will serve as an immediate stress test.

It is obvious that the largest proportion of all the things that needs to be done to set up or mature an EA Capability, are being done as part of the Catalyst Project. However, because the other things in red are not done, the investments made are not sustainable as the modelling tool is limited to a few select people and the data in it becomes more and more out of date.

KEYPOINT:

If you cannot invest in an increase in EA Maturity as part of an EA Catalyst, you probably never will.

ADOPTION:

C-Suite: Mandate that large change initiatives, preserve the EA work they do and make it sustainable.

Questions to Ponder

- Have any of these catalysts existed in your Enterprise?
- What Projects that your Enterprise has executed, would you deem to be large enough to be called an EA Catalyst Project?
- Was the opportunity to adopt EA properly taken up?
- If not, why not? What needs to change so next time it will be?

Adoption > Guidance > Where to Start? > Vision

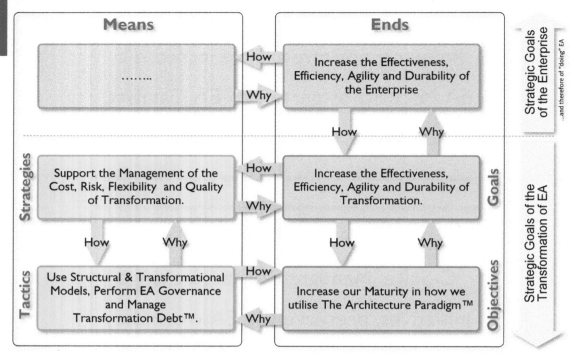

© Pragmatic 365 (2008-2021)

Without a clear vision that the Enterprise can understand, agree and believe in, any attempt to increase one's maturity will fail.

Here we set out the fundamental reasons (**Goals**) why an increase in maturity is desirable, the means by which we will achieve them (**Strategies, Tactics**) and what we must do (**Objectives**).

♦ The **Goals** of Enterprise Architecture are dependent upon and (should) support an existing Enterprise Goal (shown in grey) - to Increase the Effectiveness, Efficiency, Agility and Durability of the **entire Enterprise**. If it is not, the first thing to do is to get the Strategy creators to either explicitly add it, or explicitly state that it is not a Goal. If the Strategy creators do not believe that increasing the Effectiveness, Efficiency, Agility and Durability of the **entire Enterprise** is a goal, then they will not agree that increasing the Effectiveness, Efficiency, Agility and Durability of the **Transformation domain of the Enterprise** is a goal, and so we can stop and go and do something more interesting instead.

♦ If they do believe that increasing the Effectiveness, Efficiency, Agility and Durability of the **entire Enterprise** is a goal, then we can ask that they add a goal to Increase the Effectiveness, Efficiency, Agility and Durability of the Enterprise's **Transformation** domain.

Either way is OK. It is for the Executive Board to decide if these goals are required or not. If they do decide that these goals are valid and required, we can help to achieve them. If not, we will ignore them and therefore an increase in Enterprise Architecture maturity will not be required, for there will be no mandate to do so.

If these goals are agreed, we then can flesh out the Strategy by adding an objective of

"Increasing our maturity in how we utilise the Architecture Paradigm™"

using the Strategy of

> "Supporting the Management of the Cost, Risk, Flexibility and Quality of
> Transformation

and the Tactic of

> "Using Structural & Transformational models, Performing EA Governance
> and Managing Transformation Debt™"

> ## KEYPOINT:
>
> The Objectives that EA provides, comes from the Enterprise Strategy.

> ## ADOPTION:
>
> C-Suite: Add increasing the Effectiveness, Efficiency, Agility and Durability of your Enterprise and therefore your Transformation Capability and therefore your EA capability, to the Enterprise Strategy.

Questions to Ponder

- ◆ Are the goals of increasing the Effectiveness, Efficiency, Agility and Durability of your Enterprise defined in your Enterprises Strategy?
- ◆ If not, do you think they should?

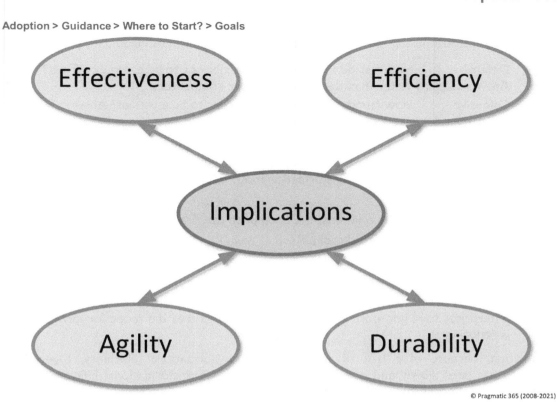

© Pragmatic 365 (2008-2021)

The rationale for increasing one's maturity in Enterprise Architecture's MAGIC comes from satisfying four key goals with respect to Enterprise Transformation:

- ◆ Effectiveness   Transforming the right things.
- ◆ Efficiency   Transforming more with less.
- ◆ Agility   Transforming faster with less.
- ◆ Durability   Be effective, efficient and agile in the future with respect to Transformation.

Most Enterprises will not have these goals in their Enterprise Strategy in relation to Transformation. They will exist in general but people tend to only think of them in terms of Operations. This is why **99%** of Enterprises spend **99%** of their time transforming the Operations part of the Enterprise and almost 0% transforming the Transformation part of the Enterprise.

The vision that EA brings, and the vision of EA, is to introduce these goals to the Enterprise Strategy with respect to Enterprise Transformation, If the C-Suite do not wish to add these goals to the Enterprises Strategy then that is their decision, but EA exposes the fact that it might be a good idea to include these goals. Therefore EA does not introduce these Goals ("Ends") per se, but it does help to provide the "Means" by which they can be effectively and efficiently achieved both for today and in the future.

The goals are closely interlinked. Achieving one goal can compromise the others. For example, increasing Effectiveness without regard to Efficiency, Agility or Durability can have severe consequences for the Enterprise Transformation and the things that Enterprise Transformation ultimately delivers. The key is to manage each of these competing goals and to make sound informed decisions having considered the impact and implications.

Effectiveness

How effective does Enterprise Transformation need to be? How do we know if we need to increase our effectiveness or not? These questions can be considered from two perspectives:

♦ Defensive   How fast do I have to run in order not to be eaten by a Tiger? Answer: Slightly faster than the slowest of your competitors.
♦ Offensive   How fast do I have to run in order to be a winner? Answer: Slightly faster than the fastest of your competitors.

EA cannot and does not determine whether an Enterprise needs to increase the effectiveness of its Transformation efforts or not - only the Management can do that. EA helps the Management to make Enterprise Transformation more effective.

Efficiency

This goal is concerned with at what cost the Enterprise can Transform.

Comparing the past with the world today…

♦ In the past, Operational Efficiency was a key business driver and differentiator. This led to production lines, mechanisation and automation.
♦ In today's business world, Operational Efficiency is still important. However, as Enterprises have got more and more efficient in this area the scope for further gains is reducing.

In addition, because of a lack of attention to Transformational Efficiency, Operational Efficiency has been slowly and quietly adversely affecting Transformational Efficiency, which then adversely affects Operational Efficiency.

Agility

This goal is concerned with how fast the Enterprise can transform itself to adapt to internal and external pressures and priorities. Let's consider some Transformation drivers:

Changes in Legislation, Competitor's strategic moves, The possibility of mergers and acquisitions, Introduction of new products and services, The wax and wane of suppliers, The creation and demise of market and customer segments, The creation and demise of market and customer Channels, Changes in scale, The introduction of new machines (and technologies)

♦ In the past all these things happened rarely if at all
♦ In today's business world these things could happen annually, monthly or even weekly and in the case of the Introduction of new products and services, could happen daily.

In general terms, if we compare the past to the world today:

♦ In the past, Agility was not really important at all because things didn't change very much. Enterprises tended to produce the same products in the same way using the same people and the same tools for long periods of time. Things that could change which would require the Enterprise to change only changed very slowly. When an Enterprise did need to change (since processes were largely carried out by people who were extremely easy to change/control) it could make those changes very quickly by telling those people to do different things, by employing more people or by sacking people.
♦ In the world today, Enterprises exist in an environment of constant and fundamental change, and therefore Enterprises need to be able to adapt and change quickly to cope with this maelstrom. They need to be more Agile. Those that can will grow and prosper. Those that don't will succumb to those that do. When an Enterprise

needs to change today it cannot rely so much on the limitless adaptability of people to effect that change. This is because so much of how an Enterprise does what it does, is now either completely or partially automated and the complexity of those automated systems and business processes is causing a severe bottleneck in the Enterprise's ability to react to change in a timely and commercially sensible fashion. Agility is becoming, and will grow even more to become, a key business driver and differentiator. This importance continues to grow year on year.

Durability

This goal is actually a component/modifier of the other three goals and can also be termed Sustainability.

An Enterprise needs to be Effective, Efficient and Agile today, but it would be unwise to unknowingly compromise how Effective, Efficient or Agile it is likely to be tomorrow.

Unless this sustainability component is built into the Enterprise's Goals, the Enterprise will be solely driven by the needs of now, above the needs of tomorrow. Effectively (and efficiently!) selling tomorrow to live today.

KEYPOINT:

EA Goals must be born from the Enterprise Strategy.

ADOPTION:

C-Suite: Add the EA Goals: To improve the Effectiveness, Efficiency, Agility and Durability of Transformation, to the Enterprise Strategy.

Questions to Ponder

♦ Are the goals of increasing the Effectiveness, Efficiency, Agility and Durability of your Enterprise Transformation capability defined in your Enterprises Strategy?
♦ If not, do you think they should?
♦ Are there others that you would add?

© Pragmatic 365 (2008-2021)

The strategies are inherently related. If too much emphasis is placed on one, things can begin to breakdown and a downward spiral of negative feedback can begin. The key is to manage each of these competing strategies and to make sound informed decisions having considered the impact and implications.

In support of the EA goals, the following Strategies are identified:

Manage Cost

♦ Reducing the cost of Transformation is important to the Enterprise but not to the exclusion of its other strategies.

♦ Reducing the cost of Transformation can and will have an impact on the other strategies.

♦ In some cases it may be to the Enterprise's benefit to increase the cost of Transformation.

Manage Risk

♦ Reducing the risks associated with Transformation is important to the Enterprise but not to the exclusion of its other strategies.

♦ Reducing the risks associated with Transformation can and will have an impact on the other strategies.

♦ In some cases it may be to the Enterprise's benefit to increase the risks associated with Transformation.

Manage Flexibility

♦ Increasing the flexibility of Transformation is important to the Enterprise but not to the exclusion of its other strategies.

- Increasing the flexibility of Transformation can and will have an impact on the other strategies.
- In some cases it may be to the Enterprise's benefit to decrease the flexibility of Transformation.

Manage Quality

- Increasing the quality of Transformation is important to the Enterprise but not to the exclusion of its other strategies.
- Increasing the quality of Transformation can and will have an impact on the other strategies.
- In some cases it may be to the Enterprise's benefit to decrease the quality of Transformation.

> # KEYPOINT:
>
> EA Strategies must be born from the Enterprise Strategy.

> # ADOPTION:
>
> C-Suite: Add the EA Strategies: By Supporting the Management of the Cost, Risk, Flexibility and Quality of Transformation, to the Enterprise Strategy.

Questions to Ponder

- ◆ Are these strategies defined in your Enterprises Strategy?
- ◆ If not, do you think they should?
- ◆ Are there others that you would add?

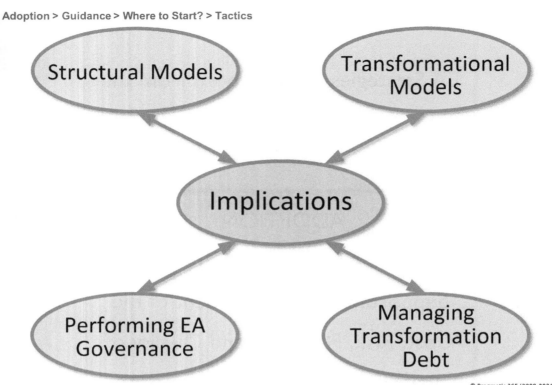

© Pragmatic 365 (2008-2021)

The tactics are inherently related. If too much emphasis is placed on one, things can begin to breakdown and a downward spiral of negative feedback can begin. The key is to manage each of these competing Tactics and to make sound informed decisions having considered the impact and implications.

Utilise Structural and Transformational Models

Maintaining Models to aid Strategic Planning by providing:

- ♦ A flexible Modelling Tool
- ♦ An extensible Meta-model
- ♦ Methods for managing the models.

Enterprises today are more complex than they have ever been. The use of technology itself brings its own level of complexities of course, but there is also increasing complexity in the business structure, process, people, etc and the context it exists within of suppliers, customers, outsourcers, media, legislation, competitors, etc, etc.

Enterprises are also in a constant state of change, whether that be to outside events or by the Board constantly searching for ways to improve the Enterprise.

A basic rule of thumb is that, if you are going to change something, you first must understand the things you are changing and how changing one part may affect other parts in potentially unwanted or surprising ways.

Therefore, in this environment of constant change and complexity it is important to understand the structure of the Enterprise (a description of its parts, but more importantly the complex relationships between those parts) so that when one part changes the management and Board can see how that affects the other parts - Enterprise Impact Assessment.

In order to properly collect, manage, and use the information, a tool is required.

It is imperative that all the entities and their associated attributes be gathered together in one place so that there is one version of the truth and so that relationships between these attributes can be defined.

The driving force, therefore, behind the use of a tool is to reduce and minimize the maintenance and management overhead of a no tool based (manual) approach.

Whilst initially a tool may not be required, there comes a time where the amount of time to continue to use a non tool based approach exceeds the cost of adopting a tool. This point tends to be reached a lot sooner than you think.

Performing EA Governance

Provide the business with governance to manage alignment to the Strategic Plan by providing:

- A governance structure
- Methods for performing governance

The purpose of governance is to ensure that as change happens on a daily basis, that change is guided in accordance with the bigger strategic and long term picture of the Enterprise.

Governance must not put up barriers and stop work from happening, but should allow decisions to be made in the context of the implications and the Transformation Debt™ that may be incurred.

Even though strategic plans are put into place, it is not long into the financial year that events can overtake an Enterprise where those plans need adjustment. In addition, by the time work gets down to the projects and programmes to carry out the work, the strategic intent can be easily lost amongst the (rightly) blinkered focus of projects.

Managing Transformation Debt™

Expose and manage Transformation Debt™ created when short term tactical choices compromise long term strategic intent by:

- Recording Transformation Debt™ as it is created (In Transformation Debt™ Agreements - TDAs)
- Exposing that as change happens so that more informed business decisions can be made at the proper time
- Taking account of it and taking opportunities to reduce it during the Strategising and Roadmapping phases.

> # KEYPOINT:
>
> EA Tactics must be born from the
> Enterprise Strategy.

> # ADOPTION:
>
> C-Suite: Add the EA Tactics: Using
> Structural and Transformational
> Models, Performing EA Governance
> and Managing Transformation
> Debt™, to the Enterprise Strategy.

Questions to Ponder

- ◆ Are these Tactics defined in your Enterprises Strategy?
- ◆ If not, do you think they should?
- ◆ Are there others that you would add?

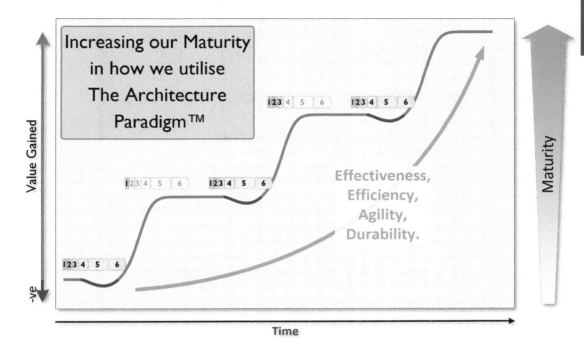

© Pragmatic 365 (2008-2021)

Our objective, to increase EA maturity, is achieved by adopting an EA Framework which is effected by following the steps of Adoption. Each iteration builds on previous iterations and leads to increased Effectiveness, Efficiency, Agility, and Durability over time.

In support of the EA tactics, the following objectives are identified:

Steps 1 to 3

♦ Determining if there is any appetite to increase EA Maturity.

♦ Setting out the business case for starting an initiative to increase EA Maturity, determining what to change and gaining the required remit, budget and resources to do so.

Steps 4 to 6

♦ Designing, developing and rolling out the necessary changes and adjustments to the Enterprise, identified in steps 1 to 3, in preparation for it to be able to utilise Enterprise Architecture.

KEYPOINT:

The Objective of using an EA Framework must be born from the Enterprise Strategy.

ADOPTION:

C-Suite: Add the Objective of using an EA Framework is to Increase your Maturity in how you utilise the Architecture Paradigm™ for defining Enterprise Strategy and Transformation planning.

Questions to Ponder

- Is this Objective defined in your Enterprises Strategy?
- If not, do you think they should?
- Are there others that you would add?

Adoption > Guidance > Tools > Types

Can we just use Visio?

Yes, but...

	Visio + Excel	Visio + Database	Custom Tool
Training	None	Some	Extensive
Entity Consistency	Manual	Automatic	Automatic
Relationship Consistency	Manual	Manual	Automatic
Cost	Minimal	Small	Medium-High

"Tools are expensive and cost a lot to procure and maintain, can't I just use Excel and Visio?"

This is a common question. The answer is - it depends!

Our Enterprise today is more complex than it has ever been, both in terms of the Enterprise MAGIC Structure and the Enterprise Context it exists within (suppliers, customer, outsourcers, media, legislation, competitors, etc, etc).

In addition we are constantly changing, Transforming either to outside events or by the Board constantly searching for ways to improve the Enterprise.

A basic rule of thumb is that, if you are going to change something, you first must understand the thing you are changing and how changing one part may affect other parts in potentially unwanted or surprising ways.

Therefore, in this environment of constant change and complexity it is important for us to understand the structure of the Enterprise (a description of its parts, but more importantly the complex relationships between those parts) so that when one part changes the people involved in Strategising, Roadmapping and Project Governance, can see how that may affect other parts.

In order for us to properly collect, manage, and use the information, a tool is required.

It is imperative that all the entities and their associated attributes be gathered together in one place so that there is one version of the truth and so that relationships between these attributes can be defined.

The driving force, therefore, behind the use of a tool is to reduce and minimize the maintenance and management overhead of a no tool based (manual) approach.

Whilst initially a custom EA tool may not be required, there comes a time where the amount of time it takes us to maintain the information increases to unacceptable levels and our ability to use the information decreases to unacceptable levels.

Most Enterprises have already reached (and gone past!) this tipping point

There are 3 basic types of tools that we could use with various pros and cons:

Visio + Excel

This entails using Visio diagrams and separate Excel spreadsheets with no linkage between them.

- In terms of Training Requirements - there are none, as most people already know how to use Visio and Excel, and if some finer points are not known, there is a huge amount of free resources on the internet.
- In terms of managing the consistency of entity information between Visio and Excel - the maintenance is purely manual. Diagrams have to be drawn manually and changing something in one application means a manual change needs to be made in the other.
- In terms of managing the consistency of relationship information between Visio and Excel - the maintenance is purely manual.
- In terms of cost – they are minimal as most Enterprises already have Visio and Excel licenses, and if more need to be acquired the costs are very low.

Visio + Database

This entails using Visio diagrams linked to a separate Database (SQL Server, Access, Excel).

- In terms of Training Requirements - some maybe needed around Database and Visio data linkage and around the use of DataGraphics.
- In terms of managing the consistency of entity information between Visio and Excel - the maintenance is automatic.
- In terms of managing the consistency of relationship information between Visio and a Database - the maintenance is purely manual.
- In terms of cost – they are small as most Enterprises already have Visio and Excel and Access licenses, although they may need to be upgraded.

Custom tool

This entails using a custom EA Modelling Tool.

- In terms of Training Requirements – extensive training is required to ensure the tool is being used effectively and efficiently.
- In terms of managing the consistency of entity information – this is automatic.
- In terms of managing the consistency of relationship information – this is automatic.
- In terms of cost – Medium to high. Possible initial cost of $40k+, with subsequent costs dependent upon the size of the Enterprise and the number of users.

KEYPOINT:

Be aware of the pros, cons and
implications of using a Visio/Excel or
a Visio/DB or a Custom Tool.

Questions to Ponder

- ◆ Which of these three types does or has your Enterprise used?
- ◆ What were the pros and cons of them?

Adoption > Guidance > Tools > Issues > Ability to Use Information

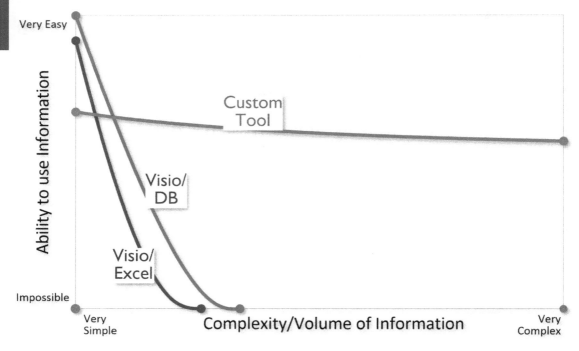

© Pragmatic 365 (2008-2021)

How easy it is to use the information in a modelling tool is very important and dependent upon the complexity and volume of the information. Here we compare how easy it is to use the information in the model as its complexity and volume increases.

While complexity and volume is low, the ability to use the information is easier for the Visio based approaches.. The Custom Tool is slightly lower due to the extra complexities of its user interface and the functions available. This is one of the reasons why many Enterprises utilise a Visio based approach. The problem is that very quickly the Visio based approaches become unusable.

Visio/Excel

As the complexity and volume of information increases, the ability to use that information quickly gets worse and worse. Very quickly a point is reached where it is impossible to continue to use the information.

Visio/DB

As with Visio/Excel the ability to use the information reduces to zero quite quickly although the decline is slightly less severe due to the connection with a structured database providing slightly better use.

Custom Tool

As the complexity and volume of information increases, the ability to use the information increases due to more functionality being used such as multi person access and data integration, presentation and dissemination features.

KEYPOINT:

As the complexity and volume of information grows, the ability to use the information can quickly become impossible unless a custom EA modelling tool is used.

Questions to Ponder

♦ How easily can you currently use the information in your EA Modelling Tool?

♦ What is the current level of complexity/volume of information it contains?

♦ What will the level of complexity/volume of information be in 1 year? 2 years? 5 years?

♦ How will the ease of using the information change over time?

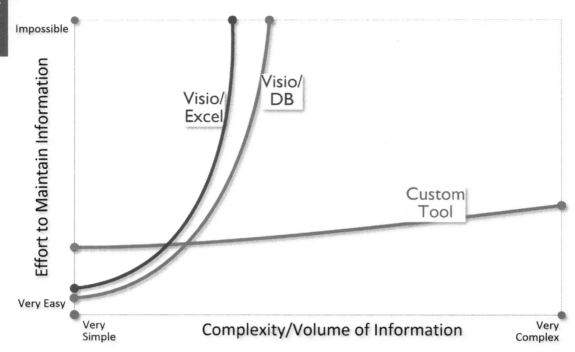

© Pragmatic 365 (2008-2021)

How easy it is to maintain models in a modelling tool is very important and dependent upon the complexity and volume of the information. Here we compare how much effort it takes to maintain the information in the model as its complexity and volume increases.

While complexity and volume is low, the effort to maintain the information is generally low but disproportionally large for a Custom Tool due to the user interface and the conformity it enforces.

Visio/Excel

As the complexity and volume of information increases, the effort to maintain the information quickly grows exponentially to impossible levels due to the effort to keep the drawings in Visio and the data in Excel in sync, the difficulty in maintaining the relationships between the differing Domains, and the consistency of the data.

Visio/DB

As with Visio/Excel the effort to maintain the information quickly becomes impossible although the inevitable is slightly delayed due to the linkages between drawings and the database being automatic.

Custom Tool

As the complexity and volume of information increases, the features of referential integrity, linked drawings, multi-user access and dissemination of information keeps the effort to maintain the information at a manageable level.

KEYPOINT:

As the complexity and volume of information grows, the effort to maintain it can quickly become impossible unless a custom EA modelling tool is used.

Questions to Ponder

- How easily can you currently maintain the information in your EA Modelling Tool?
- What is the current level of complexity/volume of information it contains?
- What will the level of complexity/volume of information be in 1 year? 2 years? 5 years?
- How will the effort required to maintain the information change over time?

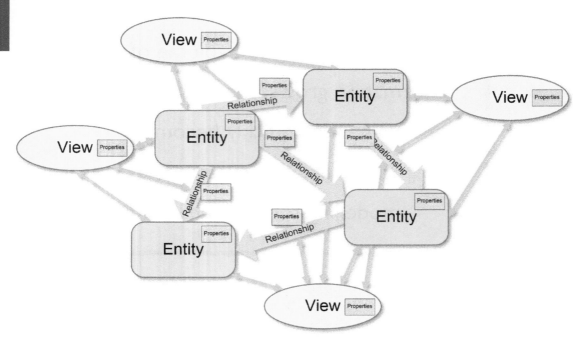

There are essentially three fundamental types of data we need to maintain and manage in an EA tool:

- **Entities** - These are the "things" that we gather information about such as Objectives, Business processes, Applications, Goals, Locations, Departments, Databases.
- **Relationships** - There are the "linkages" between the entities such as relating Business Processes to Departments or applications
- **Views** - These are the illustrations of one or more Entities and one or more Relationships drawn in a particular kind of notation. Views can also be assembled into dashboards. Note that a diagram could be pictorial, tabular or text based.

> "The value is in the lines, not the boxes."
>
> ### *- Kevin Smith*

While Entities and Views are very important, it is the Relationships that provide us the real value and power, and it is the Relationships that are the primary reason for us adopting a tool. Without relationships, all we have is lists.

People can cope with a small number of Relationships between a small number for Entities but the human brain reaches its limit at maybe three Entities and 5 Relationships. Anything more than that and you just cannot keep it in your brain. With literally thousands of relationships, our brains need help!

A Tool will allow us to keep all these relationships and give us the ability to surf through them depending on the task at hand. A kind of Just-In-Time-Intelligence.

> # KEYPOINT:
>
> Modelling tools should be architected and built on 4 fundamentals: 1) Entities. 2) Relationships. 3 Properties. 4) Views.

> # ADOPTION:
>
> EA Project Team: Favour modelling tools that are architected and built on 4 fundamentals: 1) Entities. 2) Relationships. 3 Properties. 4) Views.

Questions to Ponder

- ◆ Which models does your Enterprise have?
- ◆ Can you indicate on a few, those things that are Entities, Relationships, Properties and Views?
- ◆ How do you determine if something is a View or an Entity?
- ◆ How do you determine if something is a Property or a Relationship?

EA Model		CMDB
Planning	Purpose	Operational
Strategising, Roadmapping	Phases	Construction / Transitioning
Conceptual / Logical	Type	Physical / Operational
Low	Detail	High
Management / Architects	Used By	Developers / Change Managers

© Pragmatic 365 (2008-2021)

Some people may believe that we already have all the information for an EA Model already in our Configuration Management Database (CMDB). After all, it contains lots of information about applications, databases, etc. However, although related and linked, these two repositories of information are different in many ways.

In order for us to realise why using our CMDB is not a good idea - it is important to understand how an EA Model relates to our CMDB.

Here we see a comparison of various fundamental aspects.

> # KEYPOINT:
>
> You cannot use your CMDB as you EA modelling tool because their purpose and content are totally different.

Questions to Ponder

- Are there people in your Enterprise that think a CMDB can double up as an EA Model?
- Can you think of any more differences between an EA Model vs a CMDB?

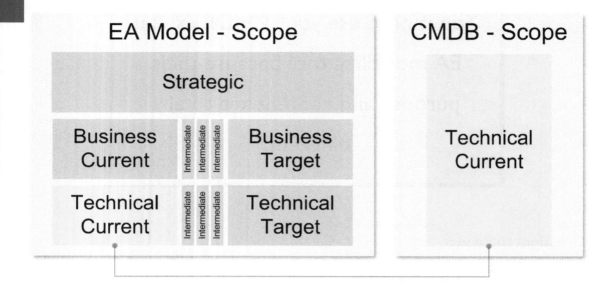

In terms of content, our CMDB only contains technical information about the current state of our Enterprise.

While our EA Model would need to contain information about the current state of our IT - our EA model also needs to contain:

- The target and intermediate states of our IT (but at higher levels of abstraction).
- The target and intermediate states of our Business information (Methods, Artefacts and Culture).
- The Strategic information required to support and drive Roadmapping.

> # KEYPOINT:
>
> ## CMDBs Only contain a subset of information you need to work with in an EA modelling tool.

Questions to Ponder

- ◆ Do you integrate Current Technical Data from your CMDB into your EA Model?
- ◆ What other things are in your EA Model that are not in your CMDB?

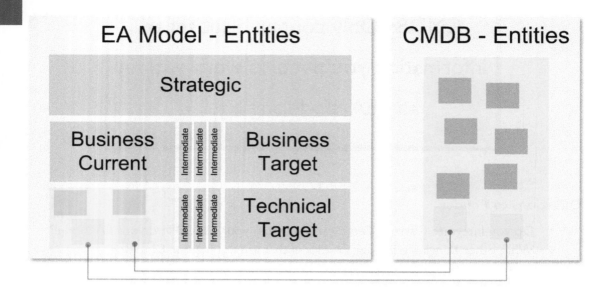

If we then consider only the technical content, it can be seen that although there are many entities stored in our CMDB, only some of them would be required in our EA Model. E.g. our CMDB contain entities relating to network switches but our EA Model would not.

In addition our EA Model will need to contain more entities that are sourced from other places. E.g. Logical Applications.

KEYPOINT:

CMDBs Only contain a subset of Current Technical information you need to work with in an EA modelling tool.

Questions to Ponder

♦ Do you integrate all Entities from your CMDB into your EA Model?
♦ What Entities are in your EA Model that are not in your CMDB?
♦ What Entities are in your CMDB that are not in your EA Model?

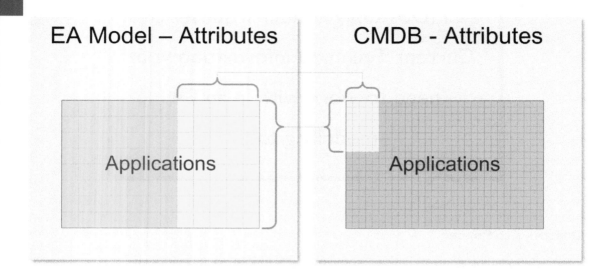

If we then consider only one of the entities that are shared between our EA Model and our CMDB, it can be seen that although there are many attributes (columns) stored in our CMDB, only some of them would be required in our EA Model. E.g. our CMDB contains attributes relating to the IP addresses of servers but our EA Model would not.

Also, although there are many records (rows) stored in our CMDB, only some of them would be required in our EA Model. E.g. our CMDB contains records relating to all the applications in use but our EA Model would only contain records relating to the most important applications.

In addition our EA Model will need to contain more attributes that are sourced from other places. E.g. The cost of an application.

KEYPOINT:

CMDBs Only contain a subset of Current Technical Attributes you need to work with in an EA modelling tool.

Questions to Ponder

- Do you integrate all Attributes, from all Entities from your CMDB, into your EA Model?
- What Properties are in your EA Model that are not in your CMDB?
- What Properties are in your CMDB that are not in your EA Model?

Methods

Methods

KEYPOINT:

The Methods section of PEAF defines 'WHAT' should be done, 'HOW' and 'WHEN'.

ADOPTION:

C-Suite: Instigate a review of the Methods used for Enterprise Architecture, to determine if their maturity is appropriate.

Questions to Ponder

- ◆ With respect to your Enterprises EA capability, what Methods are employed?
- ◆ Are those Methods documented? Understood?
- ◆ Are they fit for purpose?
- ◆ Are they followed? All the time? Only when it suits?
- ◆ Which of them are Good? Why? Bad? Why?

Methods > Phases > Overview

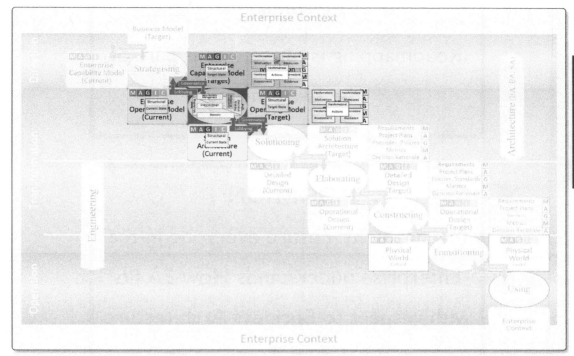

Here we consider the Methods for the whole Transformation domain (as defined by POET) and highlight the Phase which constitutes our EA domain.

Although our Primary domain is Roadmapping, we should also consider Strategising because the work that goes on in that phase and its outputs have deep and profound impacts on the work being undertaken in Roadmapping. We should also consider the Solutioning phase because the work that goes on in Solutioning can have deep and profound impacts if it does not follow the work produced in Roadmapping.

We also show the fundamental Disciplines required to perform the core work of Enterprise Architecture including the Governance and Lobbying Disciplines required to link that work up to Strategising and down to Solutioning.

Methods

KEYPOINT:

Roadmapping is phase that is part of the EA domain.

ADOPTION:

Management: Ensure everyone in the Enterprise understands How EA fits with respect to Business Architecture and Solution Architecure.

Questions to Ponder

- Do you agree that this phase can be broadly deemed to be the scope of EA work?
- Where would others in your Enterprise draw the line?

Methods

Strategising
(aka Business Architecture)

Sometimes called Business or Enterprise Strategy

e.g. Value Propositions, Cost Structure, Revenue Streams, Partners, Channels, etc, Mission, Vision, Strategies, Tactics, Goals and Objectives

---

KEYPOINT:

EA supports the Strategising phase.

ADOPTION:

Management: Ensure everyone in the Enterprise understands how EA supports Strategising.

Questions to Ponder

- Does your Enterprise recognise Roadmapping as a phase?
- Does your Enterprise recognise how this work it fits into the whole Transformation domain?
- If not, how does it make sure that it works coherently with the phases around it?
- What does your Enterprise call this phase?
- Who in your Enterprise is accountable for this work being performed?
- Who do they hand the output of their work over to?

Methods > Phases > Strategising > Process

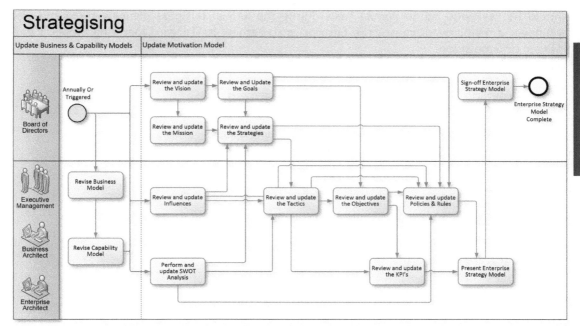

© Pragmatic 365 (2008-2021)

Update Business Model

The exact definition and process required is not shown here as it is outside the scope of the Transformation capability. However, it is listed for completeness as it is an important input to the Business Motivations model. More information can be found in POED.

Update Motivation Model

The exact definition and process required is not shown here as it is outside the scope of the Transformation capability. However, it is listed in some detail as it is an important input to the Roadmapping (EA) work. More detailed information can be found in POED.

Why

The Business Motivation Model defines the driving forces behind where it is moving to in the future and why. It is important because it creates the overall context for any analysis and definition of what needs to change in the Enterprise, over what time period and why. The more people that understand the business environment and the Vision, Goals, and Objectives, the more likely it is that they will be achieved.

In addition, once the Enterprise Strategy Model is populated, the information in the other models can be related to it. This allows a clear line-of-sight back to the Vision, Goals and Objectives of the Enterprise, and ultimately to the part of the Business Model impacted.

Scope

Its scope is the Entire Enterprise.

Source

The most common source of this information is in published documents and the Enterprise's Intranet.

When

Much like the Target Model, once defined the Enterprise Strategy Model is not set in stone. It should be reviewed on an annual basis during the annual business planning cycle and also whenever a major event causes the Enterprise to rethink its Target Operating Model. E.g. A Merger or acquisition.

Who

- ◆ Provision: The Board & Executive Management
- ◆ Sign-off: The Board.
- ◆ Modelling: Anyone trained in the tool being used.
- ◆ Update: Senior Management.

How

- ◆ Collect the Information
- ◆ QA the information
- ◆ Load the information
- ◆ Integrate the Information

> # KEYPOINT:
>
> If Enterprise Strategy is not captured in a structured way, we can't use it.

> # ADOPTION:
>
> Enterprise Architect: Ensure that Enterprise Strategy is captured in a structured way.

Questions to Ponder

- Does this process match your Enterprises process for producing their Enterprise Strategy?
- If not, is their anything missing?
- How would you mature your Enterprises Strategising process?

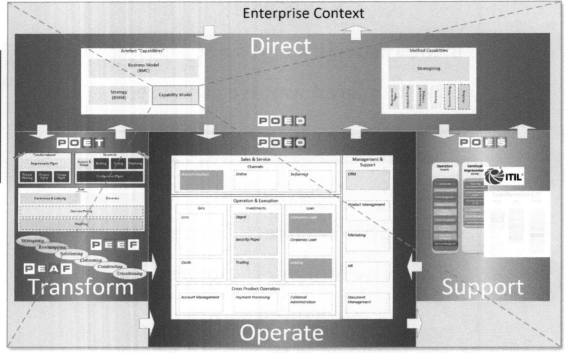

© Pragmatic 365 (2008-2021)

The Sales & Service, Operation & Execution, Cross Product Operation, and Management & Support boxes show a typical example Capability Model. Obviously, the actual Capabilities are different depending upon the actual Enterprise.

Operate

However, this example, like most Capability models, only considers Capabilities associated with the Operate Capability of the Enterprise, and completely or partially misses three other strategically important domains.

These domains are the other domains defined by DOTS, namely Transform, Direct and Support. While these domains (Macro Capabilities?) are not at the core of what an Enterprise does to fulfil its reason to exist, they are nonetheless strategically important to its continued existence, and therefore require Capability Models to define them.

The great news is that, while Operation requires different Capability Models for different industry verticals, these other three domains are not so constrained, as the fundamentals of Direct, Transform and Support are identical, regardless of the business vertical the Enterprise operates in.

Transform

This domain is the one that is most often missing from an Enterprise's Capability Model. The reasons are varied, but some pertinent ones are:

- ♦ There is no board level representation (aka CXO), unlike Operation (aka COO).
- ♦ It is not core to the Enterprise, unlike Operation.
- ♦ It rarely Changes, unlike Operation.

POET provides the overall Capability Model (and a lot more) for this domain, and we show its highest level here. We also show how the lower level capability models for the Architecture (PEAF) and Engineering (PEEF) domains.

Direct

This domain is very often missing from Capability Models, although it does sometimes get one box called "Strategy". Some boxes say "The magic happens here" and I would have to agree that's a really good name, because while there are hundreds if not thousands of frameworks and books written on the subject, its largely a dark art! Never has the phrase "The MAGIC happens here" been more correct, since MAGIC is the fundamental ontology that Pragmatic defines, for getting stuff done.

POED (which has not been written yet) would provide the Capability Model for this domain, but until it does POET defines the Artefacts and Methods we see here, as they are the key Artefacts needed for Transform to be able to do its work.

In fact, it turns out that many of the Capabilities used in Transform, are also used in Direct, for example, Requirements Management, Analysis & Design, Governance and Lobbying, Discovery, Decision Making and Modelling....

Support

POES (which has not been written yet) would provide the Capability Model for this domain, but it's just a placeholder at this stage. The main reason for this is that there is already a very good and well known (not always easy to find both things being good and well known at the same time!!!) Capability Model for the Support domain ITIL. ITIL is good but is more IT support focussed, whereas Pragmatic advocates using the Support Capability for other types of support too, such as Business, HR and Finance support.

Of course, ITIL has grown into the Transform domain too with its Strategy, Design and Transition Capabilities - so that's nice and confusing!!!!

Finally, we can see that the Capability Model that is created in the Direction part of the Enterprise (Artefact "Capabilities") is the Capability Model of the Enterprise, which is what the whole of this diagram shows.

> # KEYPOINT:
>
> Many Enterprises only create Capabilitiy Models for Operate and miss the strategically important Direct, Transform and Support domains.

> # ADOPTION:
>
> Enterprise Architect: Use DOTS as your highest level Capability Model.

Questions to Ponder

- Considering the Capability Models you have seen, do they include Capabilities for Direct, Transform and Support as well as Operate?
- What Capabilities would you define for Direct, Transform and Support?
- Does your Enterprise define capabilities for Direct, Transform and Support as well as Operate?
- If not, who will you tell? What will you do?

Methods > Phases > Strategising > Capability Modelling > With MAGIC

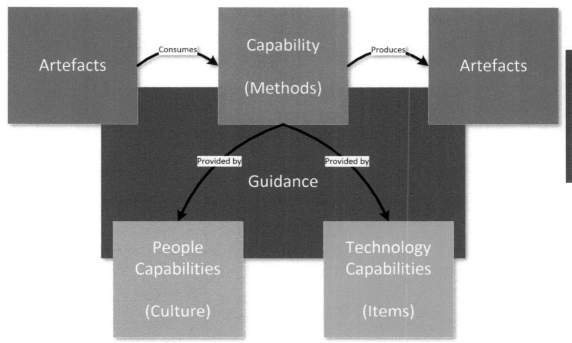

Essentially what people normally think of, when thinking about Capabilities, map to the Methods of MAGIC. Essentially, the highest level of a Capability is defined in terms WHAT it is required to do, without any thought as to HOW it will be done. Having defined WHAT the Capability needs to do, we can then move on to defining HOW a Capability will achieve its ends.

This is where Culture and Items come into play, by considering whether they are carried out by People (Culture in MAGIC) or by Technology (Items in MAGIC). Hence, we define People Capabilities and Technology Capabilities to support the Method Capabilities.

Artefacts (the A in MAGIC) are rarely defined in a Capability Model, but they jolly well should be! The Artefacts are the key things that the Capabilities consume and produce, and while it could be argued that Artefacts are not capabilities because they don't do anything, they are very helpful in defining and understanding what the Capabilities actually do.

You can think of them as the flow between capabilities.

The relationships between them.

Aka Architecture.

That just leaves Guidance (the G in MAGIC). Guidance is what generally guides the Capabilities. Again, while not strictly a Capability in itself, Guidance is nonetheless important to consider when defining or working on Capabilities.

Methods

> # KEYPOINT:
>
> Many Enterprises only consider the capabilities from the point of view of Method Capabilites.

> # ADOPTION:
>
> Enterprise Architect: Use MAGIC to create Pragmatic Capabilities.

Questions to Ponder

- ◆ Considering the Capability Models you have seen, do they include Capabilities for Direct, Transform and Support as well as Operate?
- ◆ What Capabilities would you define for Direct, Transform and Support?
- ◆ Does your Enterprise define capabilities for Direct, Transform and Support as well as Operate?
- ◆ If not, who will you tell? What will you do?

Roadmapping
(aka Enterprise Architecture)

Sometimes called Annual Business Planning or Transition Planning

Creates a portfolio of projects and roadmaps to be initiated over the coming year(s)

Methods

> # KEYPOINT:
>
> Roadmapping is "doing" EA.

> # ADOPTION:
>
> Management: Ensure everyone in the Enterprise understands that the core of EA work is Roadmapping.

Questions to Ponder

- Does your Enterprise recognise Roadmapping as a phase?
- Does your Enterprise recognise how this work it fits into the whole Transformation domain?
- If not, how does it make sure that it works coherently with the phases around it?
- What does your Enterprise call this phase?
- Who in your Enterprise is accountable for this work being performed?
- Who do they hand the output of their work over to?

Methods > Phases > Roadmapping > Process

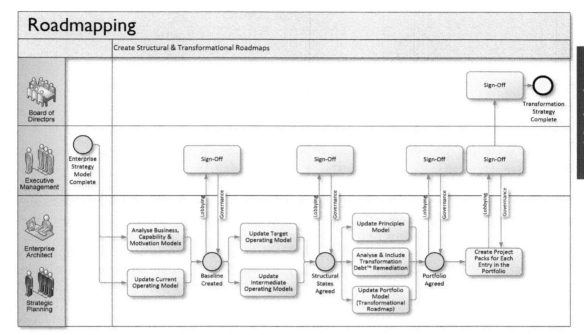

© Pragmatic 365 (2008-2021)

Although the process laid out here is step by step, it should be understood that many iterations of this work may need to be done, and that these steps only provide an overall outline of the work required and the probably order of its execution.

When

The process is usually conducted once per year although can be executed on an ad-hoc basis whenever a major event causes the Enterprise to rethink its Intermediate or Target Model. E.g. A Merger or acquisition. In addition, it should be understood that when Solutioning and Engineering projects execute, they may (via Lobbying) expose problems or opportunities that cannot be solved or exploited unless the roadmap is revisited.

Methods

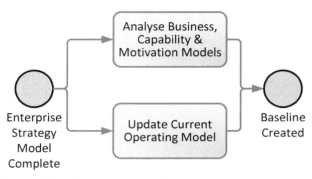

Analyse Business Capability & Motivation Models

Here we confirm that the Business Capability & Motivation models are of the required standard for us to use them, and we understand them. This is easily said, but in practice could take an appreciable amount of time, especially if the Business Capability & Motivation Models are not of the required quality. Many Enterprises create these "Models" but they are often incomplete, incoherent, and stored in unstructured storage such as word documents. There is nothing "perfect world" about wanting to have this information in structured storage (aka a Modelling Tool). Doing so easily exposes any inconsistencies or incompleteness, allowing them to be corrected before more expensive work is carried out based on them.

For many Enterprises who do not express their Business Capability & Motivation Models in a Modelling Tool, this is the first thing that needs to be done. Its not all doom and gloom though! Although it is essentially extra work (extracting the information from Word documents and placing it into a Modelling Tool) it is a great way for the EA to really understand what the Business Capability & Motivation Models are saying.

Obviously, if this is the first time this has been done, it will take more time. For subsequent times, it should be easier since a lot of the information should already exist, and we can spend more time understanding the differences between the old Business Capability & Motivation Models and the new ones.

Update Current Operating Model

Here we ensure we have an update baseline of the Current Operating Model. If this is the first time, this will need to be created and could take an appreciable amount of time. If not, it comes from the last Roadmaps Target Operation Model and should be simply to confirm that it still represents reality.

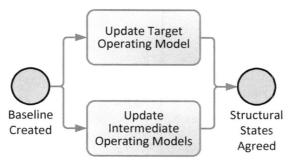

Update Target Operating Model

The Target Operating Model largely aspirational. It represents what some people may call "a perfect world". If the definition of "a perfect world" is "something that is impossible to achieve" then the Target Model is NOT "a perfect world" Model. The Target Model should be attainable given enough resource and time, and while it MAY never be achieved, it is POSSIBLE.

The Target Model is also inspirational. It provides a reasonably clear statement as to what the Enterprise would look like in the future. The more people who understand that in an Enterprise, the more chance the Enterprise has of attaining it. Documenting, understanding, and distributing a clear statement of the Target state, provides everyone with a goal to aim at in principle.

Because it is defining the Enterprise in the future (5 to 10 years) its scope, depth and detail is not as high as the Current Model. It is meant to contain a broad brush definition of the target with only enough detail to convey what is important about the target.

Update Intermediate Models

Here we create one or more Intermediate Models. These Models correspond to Objectives defined in the Motivation Model, although the relationship between the two does not have to be one to one. The decision regarding what these states are and their timing in relationships to the Objectives is part of the art and science of Architecture.

The further these models are in the future, the less detail (certainty) they are likely to contain.

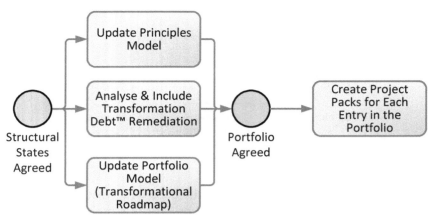

Update Principles Model

Here we Update the Principles that the Transformation Capability will use for Governance & Lobbying as the project portfolio executes. As stated in other places, while many of these principles are born from general Best Practice, some of them Enterprise specific, having been born from the Target and Intermediate models that have been defined for this Enterprise.

Analyse & Include Transformation Debt™ Remediation

Here we look at the current Transformation Debt™ which exists and try to include its remediation at the same time as work that is satisfying the Objectives and the resulting Target and Intermediate Operating Models. While having specific Remediation projects to remove Transformation Debt™ is not out of the question, it is more likely (efficient) that any reduction is carried out by including the necessary remediation work in other existing projects that are "touching" that part of the Enterprise.

Update Portfolio Model (Transformational Roadmap)

Here we construct a set of projects, programs, and initiatives (Roadmap) required to move the Enterprise from its Current Operating Model towards its Target Operating Model, through the required Intermediate Operating Models, including the remediation of Transformation Debt where reasonable.

Create Project Packs for Each Entry in the Portfolio

Here we flesh out each of the projects, programs and initiatives we have formulated with the conceptual designs for each, along with high-level scoping documents and Business Problem Definitions. It is this information that will be handed to Solution Architects later when the next phase of work (Solutioning) begins.

Methods

> ## KEYPOINT:
> ## Accumulated Transformation Debt™
> ## is reviewed during Roadmapping.

> ## ADOPTION:
> ## Enterprise Architect: Feed
> ## outstanding Transformation Debt™
> ## into Roadmapping.

Questions to Ponder

- ◆ Does this process match your Enterprises process for doing Roadmapping?
- ◆ If not, is their anything missing?
- ◆ Does it feed currently existing Transformation Debt into the mix?
- ◆ How would you mature your Enterprises Roadmapping process?

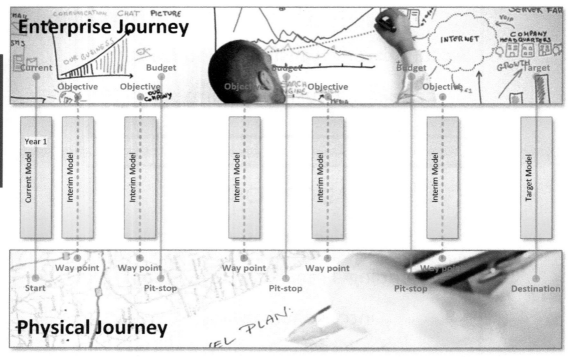

© Pragmatic 365 (2008-2021)

Although it is important to understand where you are (Current Model), where you are going (Target Model) and why you are going there (Strategy Model), it is usually impossible and/or not desirable to create a huge plan of work to move there in one step.

As in planning a very long journey, you will need to make "Pit-stops" on the way, and you may have to visit various other "Way-points" on the way. "Pit-Stops" equate to the request for and provision of annual budgets providing the fuel to continue the journey.

Pit stops can also equate to knowledge. As we move along the Enterprise's journey, there is learning. At the next pit stop, more knowledge than before is available and this knowledge will impact, favourably, the journey's execution (either by facilitating achievement of the next objective, reducing consumption of resources or speeding up decision-making and change throughout the journey. {{Pedro Correa}}

"Way-points" equate to the business objectives which must be accomplished along the road to the "Destination" or Target Model.

An Intermediate Model is a statement of intent for some time in the future. The time it relates to usually equates to a particular objective although Intermediate Models can also be time based such as yearly, quarterly, etc.

Methods

> ## KEYPOINT:
>
> EA is not a destination. EA is not a journey. EA is a way of travelling.

> ## ADOPTION:
>
> Management: Ensure everyone in the Enterprise understands that EA is not a destination. EA is not a journey. EA is a way of travelling.

Questions to Ponder

- ◆ Would you agree that an Enterprise's Transformation journey can be compared to a physical journey?
- ◆ If not, what would you compare your Enterprise's Transformation journey to?

Methods > Phases > Roadmapping > Create/update Intermediate Models

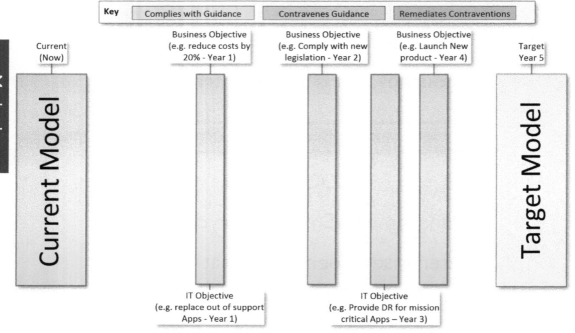

© Pragmatic 365 (2008-2021)

Scope

Depending on which Intermediate Model is being defined, its scope, depth and detail is really a function of how far that model is in the future. If it's the next intermediate model in terms of time, then it will be almost as detailed as the current model. For Intermediate Models that are further in the future, their depth and detail get less and less as they become more aspirational the more into the future they project.

Note that for Roadmapping, we are referring here to the Conceptual layer. The Logical, Physical and Operational layers get populated and filled out as the projects in the roadmap execute.

Source

The information to populate the intermediate model(s) should be provided by an analysis of the Strategy, Current and Target Models. However some Intermediate Model(s) may already exist in the Enterprise in terms of diagrams, drawings and spreadsheets.

When

Populating the Interim Model(s) is usually done when sufficient clarity is known about one or more objectives.

This usually occurs during Annual Business Planning but can also occur at any time during the year dependent upon the timescales related to the Objectives.

Who

- ◆ Provision: Strategic Planning Team.
- ◆ QA: The Board & Senior Management.
- ◆ Modelling: Anyone trained in the tool being used.
- ◆ Update: Strategic Planning Team.

How

Populating the Intermediate Model(s) is the result of analysing the Strategy Model, the Current Model (if it exists) and the Target Model (if it exists).

- ◆ Analyses Strategy, Current & Target Models
- ◆ Determine the number of Intermediate Models
- ◆ For each Intermediate Model
  - ◆ Analyse its Objective(s)
  - ◆ Load the information
  - ◆ QA the information

Methods

> # KEYPOINT:
>
> Intermediate models satisfy Business and Technical Objectives from the Enterprise Strategy.

> # ADOPTION:
>
> Enterprise Architect: Create intermediate models to satisfy Business and Technical Objectives from the Enterprise Strategy.

Questions to Ponder

- ♦ How would you describe your Enterprises long term Target?
- ♦ What are some of your Enterprises short and mid term business objectives?
- ♦ What are some of your Enterprises short and mid term IT objectives?
- ♦ Do people working on projects know what these objectives are?

Methods > Phases > Roadmapping > Create/update Portfolio Model

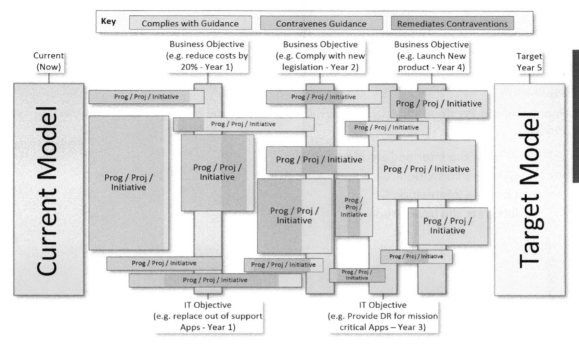

© Pragmatic 365 (2008-2021)

Why

The Intermediate Model(s) defines WHERE the Enterprise wants to get to and WHEN. The Strategy Model defines WHY they want to get there. The Portfolio Model(s) defines HOW the Enterprise will achieve that transition, by defining the Programmes, Projects and Initiatives that are required.

Scope

The scope, depth and detail of the Portfolio Model(s) is not meant to provide detailed project plans. The Portfolio Model(s) should provide only enough detail to be able to organise all of the change required to move from one state (Current or Intermediate Model) to another state (Intermediate or Target Model).

In addition, the scope, depth and detail of the Portfolio Model(s) will get less and less the further into the future they get.

Source

Initially an Enterprise will almost certainly already have one or more Portfolio Models in spreadsheets, documents and/or in portfolio analysis tools. Therefore, initially, the Portfolio Models may not be the optimum mix depending upon the Intermediate state the Enterprise wishes.

In this situation the Portfolio Model and the resultant linkages back to an Intermediate Model may well illustrate shortcoming of the existing portfolio.

As time progresses however, the Portfolio Model(s) will increasingly get their information and become much more dependent upon the Intermediate Model(s).

When

Predominantly during the Annual Business Planning cycle, although adjustments may need to be made as the year progresses.

Methods

Who

- ◆ Provision: Strategic Planning Team.
- ◆ QA: The Board & Senior Management.
- ◆ Modelling: Anyone trained in the tool being used.
- ◆ Update: Strategic Planning Team.

How

Populating the Portfolio Model is the result of analysing the Strategy Model and the Current Model.

- ◆ Analyse the Intermediate Model
- ◆ QA the information
- ◆ Load the information
- ◆ Integrate the Information

> ## KEYPOINT:
>
> The Project Portfolio effects transformation between the intermediate models.

> ## ADOPTION:
>
> Enterprise Architect: Create a project portfolio to effect transformation between the intermediate models.

Questions to Ponder

- What does your Enterprise's project portfolio roadmap look like?
- Is it multi year and moving towards a strategic structural goal?
- Is the amount of working being done in a strategic way increasing over time?
- Is the amount of working being done in a tactical way increasing over time?

Methods

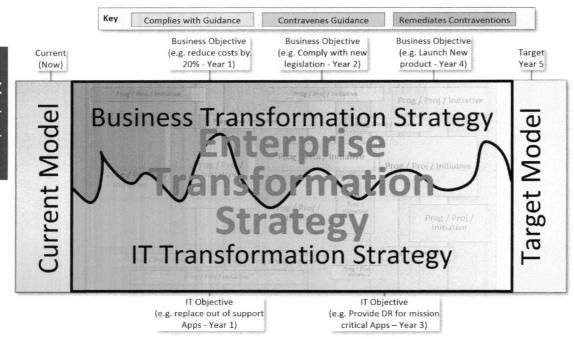

© Pragmatic 365 (2008-2021)

And so, we effectively have a **Business Transformation Strategy**, which defines the current, target and intermediate states of Business entities, and the roadmap of projects and programmes required to effect the transformation of them over time.

And we have an **IT Transformation Strategy**, which defines the current, target and intermediate states of IT entities, and the roadmap of projects and programmes required to effect the transformation of them over time.

However, as we have seen, the business and IT are inextricably linked and the line between the two is very blurred. Therefore what we really end up with, is an integrated **Enterprise Transformation Strategy**, which defines the current, target and intermediate states of integrated Business and IT entities, and the integrated roadmap of projects and programmes required to effect the transformation of them over time.

KEYPOINT:

The Enterprise Transformation Strategy is composed of interlocking Business and IT Transformation Strategies.

ADOPTION:

Enterprise Architect: Create the Enterprise Transformation Strategy by creating interlocking Business and IT Transformation Strategies.

Questions to Ponder

- ◆ Does your Enterprise have an integrated business and IT Transformation strategy?
- ◆ Does your Enterprise use these terms?
- ◆ Who is Accountable and Responsible for producing it?

Methods > Phases > Solutioning

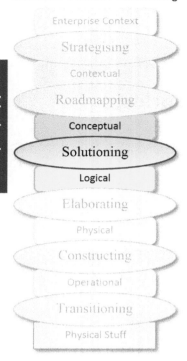

Solutioning
(aka Solution Architecture)

Sometimes called Initiating

e.g. Logical Designs for particular parts of the Enterprise focussed on particular Business Objectives

KEYPOINT:

Solutioning is "doing" Solution
Architecture.

ADOPTION:

Management: Ensure everyone in the
Enterprise understands what the
term Solutioning refers to.

Questions to Ponder

- ◆ Does your Enterprise recognise Solutioning as a phase?
- ◆ Does your Enterprise recognise how this work it fits into the whole Transformation domain?
- ◆ If not, how does it make sure that it works coherently with the phases around it?
- ◆ What does your Enterprise call this phase?
- ◆ Who in your Enterprise is accountable for this work being performed?
- ◆ Who do they hand the output of their work over to?

Methods > Phases > Solutioning > Process

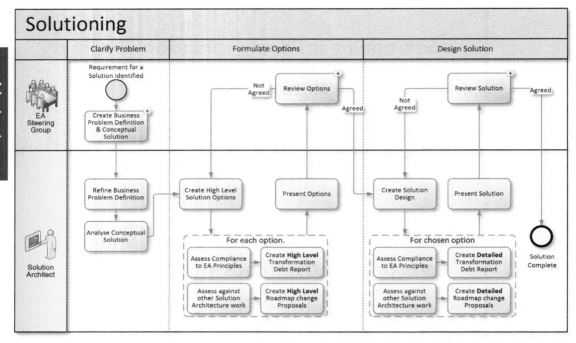

Solutioning is not part of PEAF and does not prescribe what this phase does, (that is the job of PEEF - The **Pragmatic** Enterprise Engineering Framework) but we need to document it so we can show how Governance & Lobbying fits in, and also to make sure it fits in, in the correct way.

The key things here are:

- The process starts out with a clear business problem and conceptual solution produced by the Enterprise Architecture work.
- All options that can be envisaged are documented, evaluated and presented to the EASG . Each option must be accompanied by:
  - An evaluation of Transformation debt incurred
  - Any suggested changes to the roadmap.
- A logical design is produced for the chosen option, accompanied by:
  - An evaluation of Transformation debt incurred
  - Any suggested changes to the roadmap.

Methods

> # KEYPOINT:
>
> If Solution Architecture is not carried out properly, any EA will be seriously compromised.

> # ADOPTION:
>
> Enterprise Architect: Ensure that Solutioning is carried out in a structured way.

Questions to Ponder

- ♦ Does this process match your Enterprises process for performing Solution Architecture work?
- ♦ If not, is their anything missing?
- ♦ How would you mature your Enterprises Solution Architecture process?

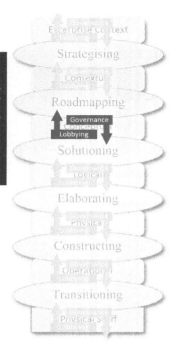

Governance & Lobbying

Aka Risk Management

The work that happens to guide project execution ensuring compliance looking down (Governance) and raising issues and problems looking up (Lobbying)

> ## KEYPOINT:
>
> EA performs Governance down to projects, and accepts Lobbying up from Projects.

> ## ADOPTION:
>
> Enterprise Architect: Perform Governance down to projects.
>
> Accepts Lobbying up from Projects.

Questions to Ponder

- ◆ Does your Enterprise recognise that EA Governance is imperative to Transformation?
- ◆ Does your Enterprise recognise that EA Lobbying is imperative to Transformation?
- ◆ Does your Enterprise recognise that EA Governance and Lobbying is the glue which keeps Project execution in line with the strategic goals?
- ◆ If not, what does it do to keep Project execution in line with the strategic goals?

Methods > Governance & Lobbying > Process

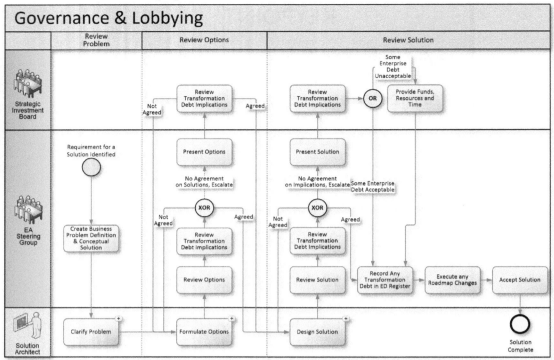

© Pragmatic 365 (2008-2021)

The steps in the bottom part of this process (in grey) are there to illustrate what work should be going on in a project as part of the Solutioning phase. PEAF does not prescribe what these are (that is the job of PEEF - The **Pragmatic** Enterprise Engineering Framework) but we need to document them so we can show how Governance & Lobbying fits in, and also to make sure it fits in, in the correct way.

> ## KEYPOINT:
>
> Reviewing Options and Solutions is the heart of Governance.

> ## ADOPTION:
>
> Enterprise Architect: Make sure EA Governance reviews: 1. The Business Problem. 2. Solution Options. 3. Solution.

Questions to Ponder

- Does your current Project Process start with a clear definition of the Business Problem?
- Does your Governance ensure that all options have been considered?
- Do you expose Transformation Debt™ as it is being created?
- If you do not do one or more of the above, does that cause issues and problems?
- If so, what are the effects of those issues and problems?
- What will you do to solve them?

Methods > Governance & Lobbying > Overview

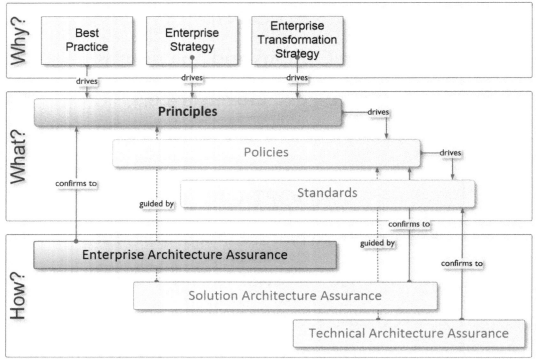

© Pragmatic 365 (2008-2021)

The purpose of governance is to ensure that as change happens on a daily basis, that change is guided in accordance with the bigger strategic and long term picture of the Enterprise.

Governance must not put up barriers and stop work from happening, but should allow decisions to be made in the context of understanding the implications of the Transformation Debt™ that may be incurred.

Even though strategic plans are put into place, it is not long into the financial year that events can overtake an Enterprise where those plans need adjustment. In addition, by the time work gets down to the projects and programmes to carry out the work, the strategic intent can be easily lost amongst the (rightly) blinkered focus of projects.

Principles	Over-arching statements that convey the philosophy, direction or belief of an Enterprise. Serves to "guide" people in making the right decisions for the Enterprise.
Policies	Focus on desired results, not on means of implementation. Policies always state required actions, and may include pointers to standards.
Standards	A mandatory action or rule designed to support and conform to a policy. A standard should make a policy more meaningful and effective.

> # KEYPOINT:
>
> # EA Governance is the highest level of Transformation Governance.

Questions to Ponder

- ◆ What types of Assurance does your Enterprise have?
- ◆ Are there different levels?
- ◆ Who is Accountable and Responsible for creating the Principles, Policies and Standards?
- ◆ Who is Accountable and Responsible for operating your levels of Assurance?

Methods > Governance & Lobbying > Dovetailing with the Project Process

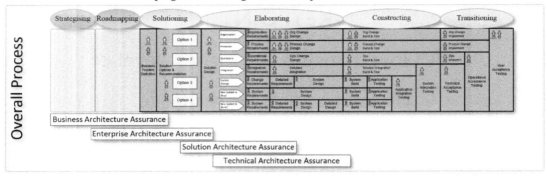

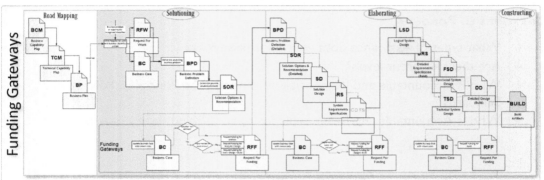

© Pragmatic 365 (2008-2021)

EA Governance comes into play before any projects are initiated and continues as those projects execute.

Here we illustrate a generic project process (phases do not negate the possibility of utilising Agile and iterative methodologies). The purpose of the diagram is not necessarily to define the project process as every Enterprise will already have its own project process, but to illustrate where Enterprise Architecture Governance begins and ends in that lifecycle.

Enterprises can utilise the **Pragmatic** Enterprise Engineering Framework (PEEF) in order to increase their maturity in that area, namely Solutioning, Elaborating, Constructing and Transitioning.

> ## KEYPOINT:
>
> EA work has to integrate with your project processes (SDLC).

> ## ADOPTION:
>
> EA Project Team: Ensure that EA Governance/Lobbying work dovetails with your project processes (SDLC).

Questions to Ponder

- ◆ What is the Project Lifecycle of your Enterprise?
- ◆ Where does EA Governance fit into it?

Methods > Governance & Lobbying > Strategic vs Tactical

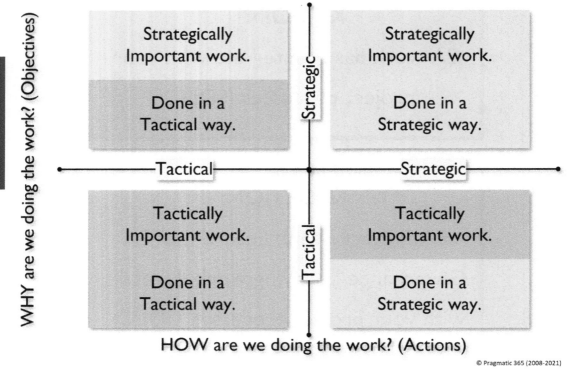

© Pragmatic 365 (2008-2021)

The words Strategic and Tactical are used frequently in Enterprises in relation to Transformation. However, these words are normally ill defined, and as such, different groups tend to use them in different ways, while assuming they are being used in the same way.

"The Business"

"The Business" tends to talk in terms of WHY work is required. Objectives.

- ◆ Strategic – Achieves long term objectives.
- ◆ Tactical – Achieves short term objectives which may or may not contribute to Strategic Objectives.

These definitions seem reasonable. But, in my experience, "The Business" tends to call everything they want Strategic - In 40 years, I cannot recall "The Business" ever saying something they wanted was Tactical. In some ways you could say that this is correct, since even Tactical work (should) contribute to Strategic objectives. However, I suspect calling everything Strategic is more to do with politics:

- ◆ To increase the likelihood of the work being chosen ("We must do this – it's a strategic project").
- ◆ To drive the work on after it has been started ("Full steam ahead – it's a strategic project")
- ◆ To prevent work stopping ("We can't stop now! – it's a strategic project").

"IT"

"IT" tends to talk in terms of HOW work is performed. Actions (to achieve Objectives).

- ◆ Strategic – Done in a way that maximises long term value, by following best business practice principles, which will cost more in the short term, compared to Tactically.
- ◆ Tactical – Done in a way that maximises short term value, by ignoring best business practice principles, which will cost more in the long term, compared to Strategically.

Arguments

Something that happens a lot in Enterprises when projects are executing, is a discussion (or rather an argument) about whether a project is Strategic or Tactical.

 "IT" may be raising red flags saying "This is a Tactical Project" while "The Business" may be saying "This is a Strategic Project". They are both right, but for different reasons. WHY we are doing the project is Strategic, but HOW we are doing the project is Tactical. This is why many "Tactical Projects" end up being the "Strategic Solution"

This disconnect between "The Business" and "IT" can often lead "The Business" to ignore "IT" when it says "Its Tactical" and just chalk it up to "IT" complaining again, try to live in a perfect world

Quadrants

The diagram shows a quadrant diagram with all possible permutation of the Strategic vs Tactical conundrum. The red boxes denote states that logically should not exist. If the reason for doing something is because it is strategically important (Achieves long term objectives) why would it be done in a Tactical way (Done in a way that maximises short term value, by ignoring best business practice principles, which will cost more in the long term, compared to Strategically).

Similarly, If the reason for doing something is because it is tactically important (Achieves short term objectives which may or may not contribute to Strategic Objectives) why would it be done in a Strategic way (Done in a way that maximises long term value, by following best business practice principles, which will cost more in the short term, compared to Tactically.)

The green boxes denote states that logically should exist. If the reason for doing something is Strategically important (Achieves long term objectives) it is reasonable (even desirable) that the work should be done in a Strategic way (Done in a way that maximises long term value, by following best business practice principles, which will cost more in the short term, compared to Tactically).

Similarly, If the reason for doing something is Tactically important (Achieves short term objectives which may or may not contribute to Strategic Objectives) it is reasonable (even desirable) that the work should be done in a Tactical way (Done in a way that maximises short term value, by ignoring best business practice principles, which will cost more in the long term, compared to Strategically.).

Of course, there may be exceptions, but the general rule is that if you find yourself in the red boxes, serious thought should be given to the reasons for that.

Methods

KEYPOINT:

Don't confuse the Tactical/Strategic

reasons for doing projects, with the

Tactical/Strategic methods of

executing them.

ADOPTION:

Management: Ensure everyone in the

Enterprise understands the difference

between a Strategic/Tactical project,

vs a project executed in a

Strategic/Tactical way.

Questions to Ponder

- ◆ Does your Enterprise confuse Strategic Projects and Tactical work?
- ◆ If so, does that cause any problems?
- ◆ What needs to change to alleviate those problems?
- ◆ Can you think of an example of Tactically Important work, done in a Strategic way?

Methods > Governance & Lobbying > Transformation Debt™

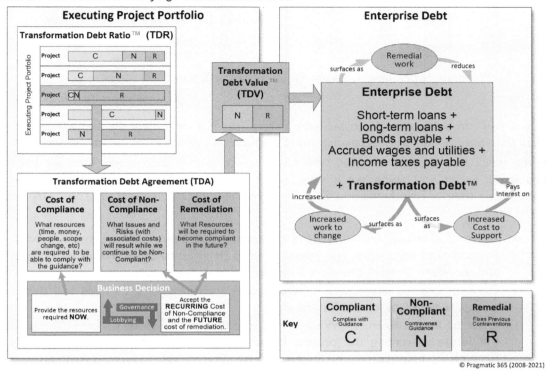

© Pragmatic 365 (2008-2021)

The work undertaken in any project can be thought of consisting of three fundamental types:

- ◆ **Compliant Work** - Work that complies with Guidance. Generally the most effective, most efficient and least risky manner of achieving an end.
- ◆ **Non-Compliant Work** - Work that contravenes Guidance. Generally less effective, less efficient and more risky manner of achieving an end.
- ◆ **Remedial Work** - Work that exists to correct previous Tactical Work (i.e. changing previous Tactical work into Strategic Work)

Guidance here refers to the Guidance of the Structural (MAGIC) and Transformational (MAGMA) information, dependant on the phase of the Transformation cascade we are in.

Here we see the Transformation Debt Ratio™ (TDR) for the projects in the currently executing Project Portfolio. TDR is the ratio (adding up to 1.0 or 100%) of Compliant vs Non-Compliant vs Remedial work in any project. Each project has a different ratio of Compliant vs Non-Compliant vs Remedial work.

Non-Compliant work is essentially a shortcut, and while a dictionary definition of a shortcut sounds quite positive and inviting:

1 : a route more direct than the one ordinarily taken

2 : a method or means of doing something more directly and quickly than and often not so thoroughly as by ordinary procedure <a shortcut to success>

- Merriam-Webster

In the business world the following is more true:

Methods

"A shortcut is the longest distance between two points."

- Issawi's Law of the Path of Progress

Add to this the following…

"Nothing is permanent, except for temporary solutions."

- Jeroen van de Kamp

…and you can perhaps begin to see why Enterprises not only naturally decay into entropy over time but how uninformed management decisions actively encourage and hasten it.

If the work in a project complies with all Guidance (aka is Compliant) then we have no problems. If not and some work does not comply with some Guidance (aka is Non-Compliant) then a Transformation Debt™ Agreement (TDA) is created. The TDA details three things:

- ♦ **Cost of Compliance** - What is preventing the project from complying with the guidance and what does the project need to be given to allow the project to comply and therefore convert the work from Non-Compliant to Compliant.
- ♦ **Cost of Non-Compliance** - What issues and risks going forward will this Non-Compliance create for the Enterprise.
- ♦ **Cost of Remediation** - What will it cost the Enterprise to become Compliant in the future (assuming the project is not allowed to do what is required now to become Compliant).

In simple terms:

- ♦ The **Cost of Compliance** - What will it cost the project to do the right things now.

If the project is not granted the Cost of Compliance:

- ♦ The **Cost of Non-Compliance** - What pain will the Enterprise have to endure going forward, until we incur
  - ♦ The **Cost of Remediation** - What will it cost the Enterprise later to fix it.

But why is it called an "Agreement" rather than an "Assessment" or "Waiver" or something else?

Originally, **Pragmatic** called it a "Waiver", but that word did not truly reflect what it was. The reason we call it a Transformation Debt™ Agreement, is because it really is an agreement! An agreement by management that they agree to provide the resources required to satisfy the guidance, or that they agree to accept the recurring cost of non-compliance and potentially the future cost of remediation. Another way to think about it, since it is possibly incurring debt, it is similar to a loan agreement, where you detail the loan amount, what the interest is, and what it will cost to pay off the loan in the future.

Having defined this information, a business decision can then be made to either provide what is required now or accept the pain we will have to endure going forward AND the costs of fixing it later. This is what sits at the heart of **Governance** and **Lobbying**.

Since a project that is Non-Compliant with guidance while the project is executing could become Compliant at any time before the project ends, only when a project completes will we know how many TDAs have been issued and the Transformation Debt™ being created in the form of the **Cost of Non-Compliance** that the Tactical work created and the **Cost of Remediation** to correct that Tactical work in the future.

At that point in time the Cost of Non-Compliance that the Non-Compliant work created and the Cost of Remediation to correct that Non-Compliant work in the future can be added to the Transformation Debt™ for the whole Enterprise.

In effect the Cost of Non-Compliance is akin to paying interest on the Debt we have incurred, while the Cost of Remediation (if spent) is akin to paying off the Debt.

When you incur Transformation Debt™, you are selling tomorrow, to get through today.

Methods

KEYPOINT:

Transformation Debt™ Agreements expose Transformation Debt™ Value.

ADOPTION:

Management: Ensure that Transformation Debt™ Agreements to expose: 1) The cost of Compliance. 2) The cost of Non-Compliance. 3) The cost of remediation, are raised.

Questions to Ponder

♦ Does your Enterprise think about how Transformation work is carried out in terms of Compliant vs Non-Compliant vs Remedial?

♦ When projects currently do not comply with guidance, what happens?

♦ Does your Enterprise keep track of how much Transformation Debt™ your Transformation projects are creating?

♦ When projects currently do not comply with guidance, is some kind of Transformation Debt Agreement (TDA) issued?

♦ If not, how are valid and sound business decisions made?

Transformation Debt Ratio ™ (TDR)

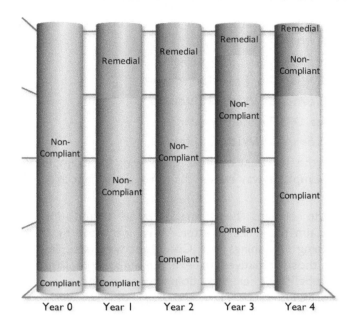

If you never **PLAN** to do Transformation in a way that complies with guidance,

you will never **DO** Transformation in a way that complies with guidance.

© Pragmatic 365 (2008-2021)

Although Transformation Debt Ratio™ is defined for each project, it can also be combined to produce an TDR for a group of projects in a program or an overall TDR for the entire Project Portfolio. Of course, when combining TDR you need to weight each individual TDR to get a balanced view.

While TDR for the entire Transformation Portfolio provides a useful metric at a point in time, it is more useful to track it over time. A sensible view might be that over time, an Enterprise might like to see the amount of work that is Compliant increase and the amount of work done in a Non-Compliant way decrease - since doing work in a Compliant way is generally the most effective, most efficient and least risky manner of doing it.

- ♦ In Year 0 - the year of adopting PEAF (and hence Transformation Debt™) it is more than probable that a lot of work will still have to done in a Non-Compliant way. However we make the necessary plans to do a decent amount of Remedial work the following year.
- ♦ In Year 1, while still having to do a lot of work in a Non-Compliant way, we perform the Remedial work we planned the year before, which lays the groundwork for Year 2.
- ♦ In Year 2, we can now start to do more work in a Compliant way (because of the remedial work we did in the previous year) and less work in a Non-Compliant way, while still doing some Remedial work, both of which lays the groundwork for Year 3.
- ♦ In Year 3, doing work in a Compliant way is now beginning to outweigh doing work in a Non-Compliant way (because of the remedial and Compliant work we did in the previous year) and this, in addition to a little Remedial work, lays the groundwork for Year 4.
- ♦ In Year 4 we are doing most work in a Compliant way and only do work in a Non-Compliant way when really necessary.

Methods

This is only an example of course and will vary from Enterprise to Enterprise and will be influenced by many factors such as the fiscal climate and current Enterprise Strategy.

However, the examples provided illustrate one of the indicators of increasing EA Maturity in that Enterprises that are more "mature" are the ones who spend a greater proportion of their resources doing work in a Compliant way rather than a Non-Compliant way and therefore need to spend little on remedial work.

The key point is:

If You Never PLAN To Do Transformation
In A Way That Complies With Guidance,
You Will Never DO Transformation
In A Way That Complies With Guidance.

Unless you planned for it, time pressures (the incessant need for quick wins for example) will always force you to do work in a Non-Complaint way rather than in a Compliant way. The key is breaking the cycle.

Another thing to consider is that the choices being made when formulating the Transformation Portfolio should perhaps aim to do less, better. What we mean by that is that it might be a better approach to doing less things in a Compliant way (spending the money and time you save on allowing those initiatives to execute in a Compliant way (thereby incurring no Transformation Debt™) rather than doing more things in a Non-Compliant way (thereby incurring Transformation Debt™).

Methods

> ## KEYPOINT:
> Over time, increase the ratio of Strategic to Tactical work.

> ## ADOPTION:
> Management: Over time, increase the amount of Transformation work done in a Compliant fashion, while decreasing the amount of Transformation work done in a Non-Compliant fashion.

Questions to Ponder

- ◆ What is the TDR for your currently executing Transformation Portfolio?
- ◆ How do you want that to change going forward?
- ◆ What do you need to do to make that happen?
- ◆ What will you do to break the cycle?

Methods > Disciplines > Modelling

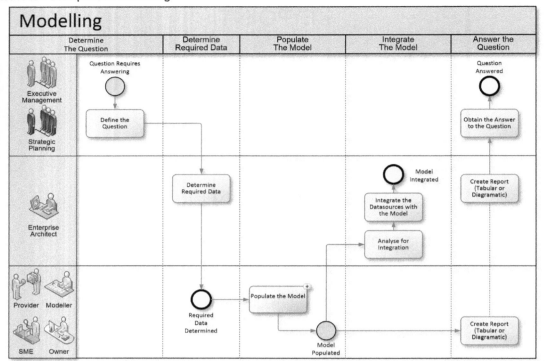

© Pragmatic 365 (2008-2021)

Stage 1 - Determine the Question

Identity a question (and who is asking the question {{Anders W. Tell}}) that we want an answer to, that we either:

- ◆ Currently cannot answer, or
- ◆ Can get an answer but the quality and confidence in that answer is too low to be useful.

Stage 2 - Determine Required Data

Having understood what the question is, this stage identifies what information will be required to answer it. It should be noted that the temptation to try to answer the question should be resisted.

Stage 3 - Populate the Model

The third stage of the iteration is to find and populate the model with the information identified. This sub-process is described in detail in the next section.

Stage 4 - Integrate the Model

This phase ensures that the work that has been done and the information loaded into the model is sustainable. For each of the Datasources there are two alternatives (which were identified in the Analysis Phase):

- ◆ The Datasource is removed - The processes and people using the original Datasource will stop using it and will use the information in the model.

♦ The Datasource is preserved - The necessary interfaces are built to enable the synchronisation and management of the data going forward.

If this stage is not performed or is done badly it makes the entire exercise utterly pointless. Most Enterprises ignore this stage which may go somewhere to explain why many modelling efforts fail.

Stage 5 - Answer the question

Having populated the model, it is now possible to use the model in concert with the tools and analyses provided by the modelling tool to answer the question. After this, another iteration is possible.

Methods

KEYPOINT:

Modelling anything must follow a

pragmatic process, if it is to be of

value.

ADOPTION:

Enterprise Architect: When

Modelling: 1. Define the Question. 2.

Determine the Data. 3. Populate the

Model. 4. Integrate Datasources. 5.

Answer the Question.

Questions to Ponder

♦ Does your Enterprise only model things when there is a clear reason to do so?
♦ When things are modelled are the sources correctly removed or integrated?
♦ Do you federate the maintenance of the information that has been modelled?
♦ If you do not do one or more of the above, does that cause issues and problems?
♦ If so, what are the effects of those issues and problems?
♦ What will you do to solve them?

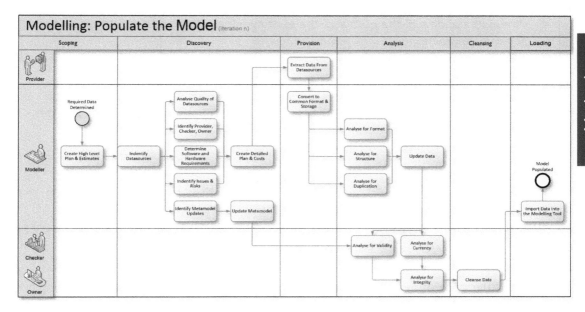

Populating the model should be approach as any other data migration exercise - for that is exactly what it is.

Phase 1- Scoping

This phase should be a very short initial piece of work to provide a first level assessment of the scope and cost of the data migration.

It is where the source data is analysed, the scope of the work is determined and the overall risk is evaluated in terms of the complexity of the work involved.

The primary deliverables from the Scoping phase are:

- ♦ A high-level estimate of the number of days and cost to complete the data migration.
- ♦ A high-level statement of any major issues identified at this stage that may affect the delivery of the migration.
- ♦ A high-level work plan for the migration and estimated timeframes.
- ♦ An estimate of the resources required to support the migration.
- ♦ Provides a specific estimate of the number of days and cost for the subsequent Discovery phase.
- ♦ Provides a budgetary anticipated final cost estimate for subsequent phases.

Phase 2 - Discovery

This phase comprises the detailed work necessary to determine the exact costs and plan for doing the migration exercise. It ensures the Enterprise understands the scope of what is being undertaken, including detailed plans and costing's.

The primary deliverables from the Discovery phase are:

- ♦ Agreement of the Meta-model to be populated.

- A detailed understanding of the scope of the migration activity that is to be undertaken, including identification of the Datasources (source files, locations, formats, etc that are being migrated from).
- An understanding of the quality of the existing information and the options available for data cleansing.
- Identification of any hardware and software that will be required.
- Documentation of the issues and risks with the proposed migration.
- Identification of the key resources from each of the parties involved, who will be required to ensure success, including an assessment of resource capability and the training that may be required.
- Production of realistic plans and costs for the work.

Phase 3 - Provision

This phase comprises the work required to gather together all of the information that currently exists into one place in preparation for the analysis phase.

It is likely that as this phase progresses other information sources previously unknown will be discovered.

Phase 4 - Analysis

This phase is the core of the work that needs to be undertaken which invokes analysing and understanding the information gathered. This analysis will consider the following:

- **Format** - The format for fields may not be consistent. E.g. a field meant to indicate the cost of maintenance may be expected to contain values in thousands (10), but may contain the actual value (10,000).
- **Structure** - There may be structured data in free-format fields which therefore contain information that should be structured but are not.
- **Duplication** - This is the most common area where problems can exist. There may be two, three, or even more "lists" of the same information. E.g. more than one group has a list of applications.
- **Validity** - The values that are contained in fields may or may not confirm to what was originally meant. E.g. a field meant to indicate the importance of an application to the business may be expected to contain values such as "C" for Critical, "I" for Important, "N" for No important, but may contain unexpected values such as "X" or "-"
- **Currency** - The information may be recent or may be out of date.
- **Integrity** - There may be related information that should exist but does not. E.g. An application may say it utilises a database but the database may not be defined.
- **Integration** - Will the information in the tool replace the information in its current form or require integration and synchronisation. (To be carried out in Stage 4 of the Modelling discipline).

Phase 5 - Cleansing

Having analysed the information in the previous phase, this phase takes this knowledge and uses it to manipulate and process the information into valid, current and consistent data suitable for importing in the Model.

This is where difficult decisions regarding which information is "correct" or not are made and therefore the time and resources required to perform this critical phase should not be underestimated.

If this phase is not performed or is done badly it makes the entire exercise utterly pointless. Most Enterprises ignore this phase which may go somewhere to explain why many modelling efforts fail.

Phase 6- Loading

This phase is concerned with loading the information into the tool's repository and the associated checks and testing to ensure correctness completeness and consistency.

KEYPOINT:

Populating a model is a Data

Migration exercise.

ADOPTION:

Enterprise Architect: Treat the

Population of Model Data as a Data

Migration exercise.

Questions to Ponder

- ♦ Does your Enterprise approach modelling as a Data Migration exercise?
- ♦ Are there clear responsibilities with respect to Scoping, Discovery, Provision, Analysis, Cleansing and Loading?
- ♦ If you do not do one or more of the above, does that cause issues and problems?
- ♦ If so, what are the effects of those issues and problems?
- ♦ What will you do to solve them?

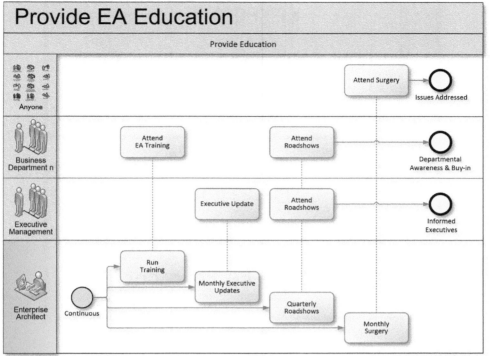

© Pragmatic 365 (2008-2021)

Communication and education is one of the keys to mitigating many of the risks associated with adoption EA. For this reason, good quality and continuous education is mandatory if Enterprise Architecture is to be a success.

IF YOU DO NOT DO THIS, OR YOU DO IT BADLY, YOU WILL FAIL.

Education and Training consists of two main areas:

- Formal classroom based information and knowledge transfer.
  - This is kind of education is required to be able to present and transfer key knowledge and information about Enterprise Architecture, what it is consists of and the mechanics of how to adopt and operate it.
- Informal discussions, workshops and round tables.
  - This kind of education is required because there will be many questions and reticence on the part of some groups or individuals consisting of worries, misunderstandings and existing "baggage" that, if not tackled and tackled successfully, will totally undermine and erode an EA initiative.

Methods

> # KEYPOINT:
> ## Without continuous EA Education,
> ## EA will die.

> # ADOPTION:
> ## Enterprise Architect: Provide
> ## continuous EA Education.

Questions to Ponder

- ◆ Does your Enterprise provide EA Training?
- ◆ Do new hires get introduced to your EA framework?
- ◆ If not, does this have an effect on how effective your EA capability is?
- ◆ If so, what are the effects of those issues and problems?
- ◆ What will you do to solve them?

The artefacts defined in PEAF constitute the EA Meta-model and some of its content such as Principles.

There are many Meta-models that already exist (for the reasons defined above) and the lack of a Meta-model has never really been a reason why EA initiatives fail. For this reason, PEAF does not concentrate on defining a complete and detailed Meta-model (no point reinventing the wheel). However, PEAF does defines some important things that are usually missing and also exposes a higher level structure that people can use to understand how the detailed Meta-models they wish to use fit and relate.

Unfortunately, this is not an easy task because all the myriad Meta-models out there do not share any common backbone or structure (such as MAGIC and MAGMA). Even if you can figure out which parts of which Meta-models you wish to use, integrating them into a whole is also fraught with difficulty, again because there is no common meta-meta-structure (such as MAGIC and MAGMA).

This is exacerbated by Tool Vendors not providing facilities for the importation and separate management of different Meta-models from different sources along with the functionality to then present and manage and use them as a coherent whole.

This whole problem area is an area that **Pragmatic** is currently working on, driving Meta-model providers to structure their Meta-models around a Structural Ontology

(MAGIC), a Transformation Ontology (MAGMA), all expressed at different levels of abstraction (Enterprise Context, Contextual, Conceptual, Logical, Physical, Operational) and driving Tool Vendors to think about how to then use them and allow people to use and manipulate them.

This will be a long and hard road (some say impossible), but one that will reap fantastic benefits for Enterprises globally. These 2 things (doing the impossible and fantastic rewards for customers) are the things that mean it's something that **Pragmatic** has a passion to do.

In the meantime, **Pragmatic** will continue to map existing Meta-models to MAGIC and MAGMA to provide Enterprises with, at least, a starting point to understand how they relate and therefore how to adopt them.

KEYPOINT:

The Artefacts section of PEAF defines 'WHAT' information is consumed and produced and 'WHEN'.

ADOPTION:

C-Suite: Instigate a review of the Artefacts used for Enterprise Architecture, to determine if their maturity is appropriate.

Questions to Ponder

- ◆ With respect to your Enterprises EA capability, what Artefacts are used?
- ◆ Are those Artefacts documented? Understood?
- ◆ Are they fit for purpose?
- ◆ Are they used? All the time? Only when it suits?
- ◆ Which of them are Good? Why? Bad? Why?

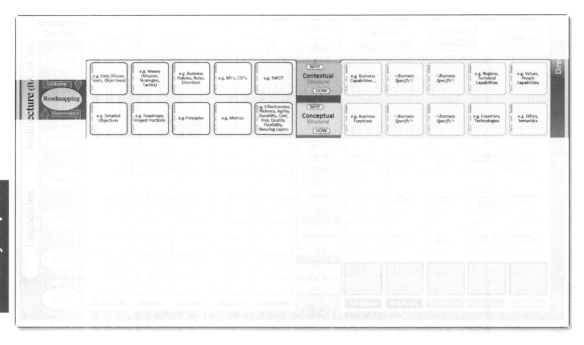

In this section, we look at the Artefacts of EA. The artefacts deal with the structures required for Structural (WHAT) and Transformational (WHY & HOW) description.

Most frameworks and ontologies focus only on Artefacts and within Artefacts only the Structural (WHAT). When you see the MAGIC that **Pragmatic**'s frameworks expose, it might make you wonder how much value they contain wile missing so much.

It is understandable however, that people concentrate on Artefacts as they are very "tangible" - the things being produced and consumed - but also because many frameworks come from IT departments and IT people, and IT people love datamodels, ontologies and Meta-models, and those types of things are reasonably easy to produce. Methods, Guidance, Items and Cultural things are much harder to produce and therefore tend not to be.

Here we consider the Artefacts for the whole Transformation domain (as defined by POET) and highlight the Artefacts within the EA domain.

Essentially, we are concerned with the Transformational and Structural information utilised by the Roadmapping phase (as defined in the Methods section) and the associated Governance/Lobbying work down to projects.

The structural information (MAGIC) and transformational information (MAGMA) that is produced, is represented at the Conceptual level.

We also show the Contextual information, not because it is produced by EAs (although EAs do contribute to it) but because it forms the input for the EA (Roadmapping) work.

> ## KEYPOINT:
>
> Enterprise Context, Contextual and Conceptual information levels are part of the EA domain.

> ## ADOPTION:
>
> Management: Ensure everyone in the Enterprise understands which levels of information relate to EA.

Questions to Ponder

- In what way does your Enterprise consider Transformational and Structural models at these levels?
- What ontologies and Meta-models are you using?
- How do they map to, and fit into this Ontology?
- Are they any gaps or overlaps?
- If there are gaps and or overlaps, is it useful to know that?
- What will you do to fill the gaps and remove the overlaps?

Artefacts > Ontology > Models

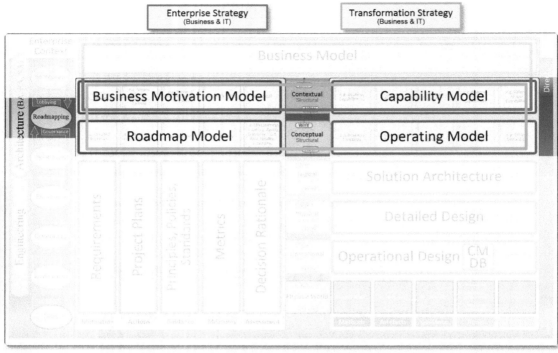

Here we show the common names for the various domains in the EA Ontology.

Many people use these terms (and others) but what they are exactly, and more importantly how they relate to each other, tends not to be clear. This is very worrying since they are all interrelated and depend on each other in complex ways. Not knowing or realising these relationships exist, causes Enterprises to try to create one or more of them without the required input information to do so. Or, if that information exists, to not relate one to the other and hence mistakes of monumental importance can remain hidden until much later when their impact is great, which tends to drive people to minimise or ignore them until something catastrophic happens. Not a good way to manage anything.

KEYPOINT:

Enterprise Strategy is the Business Motivation and Capability models, set in the context of the Business Model. Transformation Strategy is the Roadmap and Operating models, set in the context of the Capability and Business Motivation models.

> # ADOPTION:
>
> Enterprise Architect: Support the creation of the Enterprise Strategy, by modelling the Business Model, Business Motivation Model and Enterprise Capability Mode.
> Enterprise Architect: Create the Transformation Strategy, by creating the Roadmap Model and Operating Model.

Questions to Ponder

- ♦ Do people in your Enterprise understand what these terms are?
- ♦ Do they understand how they relate?
- ♦ Do you have any of these things defined despite the input information for their creation was not available?
- ♦ Do you have any of these things defined and not related to each other?
- ♦ What do you need to do to improve this situation?

Artefacts > Ontology > Models > Relationships

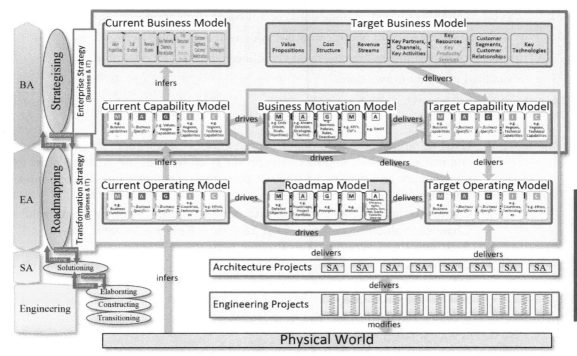

© Pragmatic 365 (2008-2021)

Here we see an outline of the information required to perform the roadmapping phase that constitute "doing" Enterprise Architecture and forms the basis for a project to perform the required work. The information flows into the portfolio of projects that effect the change defined by the roadmap. We also include the Business, Capability and Motivation model work (Business Architecture) because if this work is not done to the required standard, and/or its output is no represented and accessible in a reasonable way, the EA work is likely to produce far from optimum results. (aka pants!).

Working up from the bottom:

- ♦ The Physical World, essentially defines what the current capability model is.
- ♦ Projects defined by the Transformational Roadmap, modify this real world, and by doing so, deliver the Target Operating Model.
- ♦ The Target Operating Model, in turn, delivers the Target Capability Model and the Objectives from the Business Motivation Model, both of which are driven by the Current Capability Model.
- ♦ Thus, the Target Capability Model, ultimately delivers the Target Business Model.

To initiate the work. a Project Brief (PRINCE2) or Project Charter (PMBOK) is required.

PMBOK's definition of a Project Charter is:

> "...the document issued by the project initiator or sponsor that formally
> authorizes the existence of a project and provides the project manager with
> the authority to apply organizational resources to project activities.

PRINCE2's definition of a Project Brief is:

"… used to provide a full and firm foundation for the initiation of the project. Nothing should be done until certain base information needed to make rational decisions about commissioning of the project is defined, key roles & responsibilities are resourced and allocated, and a foundation for detailed planning is available."

Lets define what we mean by these things:

- ◆ **Business Models**
    - ◆ Used to discuss and document how the Enterprise will generate revenues and make a profit. It explains what products or services the business plans to manufacture and market, and how it plans to do so, including what expenses it will incur.
    - ◆ Comprises information such as Customer Segments, Customer Relationships, Channels, Value Propositions, Cost Structure, Revenue Streams, Key Activities, Key Resources, Key Partnerships.
    - ◆ Created by the board supported/facilitated by the EA offering structures to capture the information and ensuring the result is complete and consistent and raising Technology catalysts where appropriate.
    - ◆ Industry standard used - Business Model Canvas
- ◆ **Business Motivation Model**
    - ◆ Used to discuss and document the Enterprises business plan in terms of what it wants to achieve, how it will achieve those ends and what will guide the business
    - ◆ Comprises information such as Vision, Goals, Objectives, Mission, Strategies, Tactics, Business Principles, Policies, Rules and Standards.
    - ◆ Created by the board supported/facilitated by the EA offering structures to capture the information and ensuring the result is complete and consistent and raising Technology catalysts where appropriate
    - ◆ Industry standard used: OMG - Business Motivation Model
- ◆ **Capability Models**
    - ◆ Describes the complete set of capabilities an Enterprise requires to execute its Business Model and fulfil its mission.
    - ◆ Comprises information such as organizational level skills embedded in people, processes, and technology.
    - ◆ Created by the EA with the C-Suite.
    - ◆ Industry standard used: PEAF – MAGIC (Methods, Artefacts, Guidance, Items and Culture)
- ◆ **Operating Models**
    - ◆ An abstract or visual representation of how an organization delivers value to its customers or beneficiaries as well as how an organisation actually runs itself. It is the highest level structural view of the Enterprise.
    - ◆ Comprises information such as Business Functions, Products, Information, Ethics, Roles, Countries, Technologies (including but not limited to Information Technology).
    - ◆ Created by the EA with the C-Suite.

- ◆ Industry standard used: PEAF – MAGIC (Methods, Artefacts, Guidance, Items and Culture)
- ◆ **Roadmap**
  - ◆ Describes the programs, projects and initiatives needed to change the Methods, Artefacts, Guidance, Items and Culture of the Enterprise from the Current state to the Target state in order execute the Enterprise Strategy.
  - ◆ Comprises an interrelated set of projects programs and initiatives related to the Target Capability model Principles, Policies and Standards used to guide them.
  - ◆ Created by the EA.
  - ◆ Industry standard used: PEAF – Principles.

Since the way "doing" Enterprise Architecture (aka Roadmapping) is the same regardless of the Enterprise type, **Pragmatic** provides a default Project Brief document and PowerPoint briefing presentation, that contains 95% of what is required to initiate the work.

Artefacts

KEYPOINT:

Make sure you have the correct input

information for the model you are

building.

ADOPTION:

Management: Ensure EAs have the

information required to do their job.

Questions to Ponder

- ◆ Do these models and relationships agree with those used by your Enterprise?
- ◆ What does your Enterprise use to express each of these models?
- ◆ Is it clear to the people in your Enterprise, what these models are and the dependencies between them?

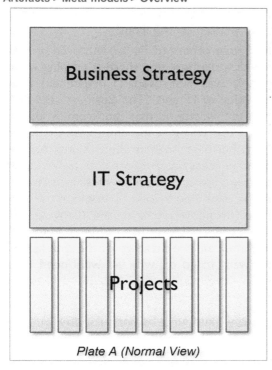

Plate A (Normal View)

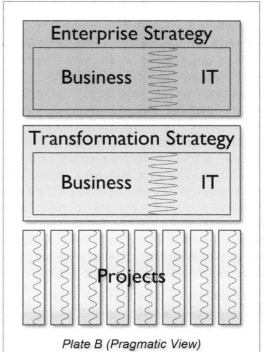

Plate B (Pragmatic View)

- ◆ **Plate A** illustrates the "normal" but flawed mental model, that many Enterprises have. It takes the view that the Business Strategy is written and then thrown over a wall to those IT bods to figure out the IT strategy, and out of that there then comes projects - Generally IT projects, because most transformation is all or mostly, about changing IT. Effectively the proper Roadmapping phase (the core of EA) is lost or, if not lost, is limited to and conflated with IT Strategy.

- ◆ **Plate B** illustrates the **Pragmatic** view where the Business and IT strategies are formulated together. They are (should be) inextricably linked and must be formulated together as each feeds on the other. The IT Strategy is shown smaller because the Business Strategy is much bigger! The Business Strategy includes, Methods, Artefacts, Guidance, Culture and part of Items (IT - which is itself a sub domain of the larger Technology domain) while the IT Strategy only covers the IT part of the Technology Part of the Items domain. Thus, the Business Strategy and IT Strategy come together to make the Enterprise Strategy which then flows into the Transformation Strategy (the high level plan of how the required Enterprise Transformation will be undertaken)

Enterprise Strategy (aka Business Strategy)

A strategy is really just a high level plan and answers four basic questions:

1) Where are we?
2) Where do we want/need to go?
3) Why do we want/need to go there?
4) How will we get there?

I say "should" because many "Strategy" documents produced by Enterprises are not Strategy documents at all based on this definition. The only thing that makes a lot of them "Strategy" documents is because they have the word "Strategy" written on the front!

Although we use the term Enterprise Strategy (and urge others to do so) many Enterprises refer to this as Business Strategy. The term is in widespread use and there is nothing wrong with that per se. But as time has passed since it was first used, IT happened! More importantly people have begun (unfortunately) to refer to IT and "The Business" (as PEAF does - because you cannot ignore reality however wrong it may be from a purist's perspective). The word Business has come to mean "everything in the Enterprise that is not IT". This distinction is reinforced with terms such as Business Analysis and Business Analysts who work 99% of the time purely on the people and process issues of a solution, leaving the IT issues to someone else. So the term Business Strategy would seem to intimate that there is a separate IT Strategy (another slight misnomer as explained below). In addition the term Business is not very general to refer to the whole (do people refer to the Army as "The Business"?) and so we prefer to use the word Enterprise hence we use the term Enterprise Strategy instead of Business Strategy because it is, after all, the Strategy of the Enterprise - aka a high level plan of where we are, where we want to go to, why we want/need to go there and how we are going to get there.

Transformation Strategy (aka IT Strategy)

Although we use the term Transformation Strategy (and urge others to do so) many Enterprises refer to this as IT Strategy. This has happened because most of the Transformation happening in any Enterprise is IT Transformation. The difference between Transformation and IT has become blurred and confused.

It should be noted here that we are walking a fine line between the words I would like to use and the words I have to use because of history and the way people generally use them (rightly or wrongly).

> ## KEYPOINT:
>
> The Business Strategy and IT Strategy are inherently linked and cannot be thought of separately.

> ## ADOPTION:
>
> Enterprise Architect: Develop the IT Strategy at the same time as the Business Strategy in an integrated way, not after the Business Strategy is thrown over the wall.

Questions to Ponder

- ◆ Do you agree with the definition of a "Strategy" above? If not, how would you define a "Strategy"?
- ◆ Does your Enterprise define an integrated Enterprise Strategy (Business and IT)?
- ◆ Does your Enterprise define an integrated Transformation Strategy (Business and IT)?
- ◆ If not, does this cause any issues or problems?
- ◆ If so what do you need to do to alleviate them?
- ◆ What Meta-models do you currently use?
- ◆ Do they have limitations?
- ◆ How do you integrate them?

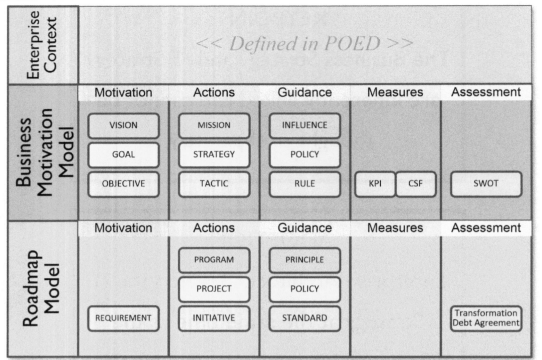

© Pragmatic 365 (2008-2021)

Business Model

The Business Model Meta-model is loosely based on the Business Motivation Model (BMM) that was developed by The Object Management Group (OMG) although various changes have been made - most notably being that it is structured using MAGMA.

- ◆ Motivation
    - ◆ **Vision** - A statement about the enduring value the Enterprise will deliver without regard to how it is to be achieved.
    - ◆ **Goal** - Statements about a state or condition of the Enterprise to be brought about or sustained through appropriate means. Compared to an Objective, a Goal tends to be: ongoing, qualitative (rather than quantitative), general (rather than specific), longer term.
    - ◆ **Objective** - Statements of a specific time-targeted, measurable, attainable target that an Enterprise seeks to meet in order to achieve its Goals. Compared to a Goal, an Objective is: short-term, not continuing beyond its timeframe (which may be cyclical).
- ◆ Actions
    - ◆ **Mission** - The ongoing operational activity of an Enterprise.
    - ◆ **Strategy** - Courses of action that is one component of a plan for a Mission. It is accepted by the Enterprise as the right approach to achieve its Goals, given the environmental constraints and risks. Compared to a Tactic: longer-term, broader in scope.
    - ◆ **Tactic** - Courses of action that represents part of the detailing of Strategies. Compared to a Strategy: shorter term, narrower in scope.
- ◆ Guidance

- ◆ **Influence** - An act, process, or power of producing an effect without apparent exertion of tangible force or direct exercise of command, and often without deliberate effort or intent.
- ◆ **Policy** - Guides the Enterprise. Compared to a Rule it is less structured, less discrete or not atomic, less carefully expressed in terms of standard vocabulary.
- ◆ **Rule** - Influences or guides business behaviour, in support of a Policy. Compared to a Policy it is highly structured, discrete or atomic, carefully expressed in terms of standard vocabulary.

◆ Measures

- ◆ **CSF** (Critical Success Factor) - are the causes of our success. Measures the things we must do to be successful and used to measure and track Actions.
- ◆ **KPI** (Key Performance Indicator) - Measures the effects of our success. They are indicators that we are winning and used to measure and track Motivation.

◆ Assessment
- ◆ **SWOT** (Strengths, Weaknesses, Opportunities, Threats) - An assessment that indicates an area of advantage or area of excellence, an area of inadequacy, something that can have a favourable impact, something that can have an un-favourable impact to the execution of the Means or achievement of Ends.

Roadmap Model

◆ Motivation
- ◆ **Requirement** - Conceptual representation of requirements. More detailed than an Objective.

◆ Actions
- ◆ **Program** - A grouping of Projects and Initiatives.
- ◆ **Project** - A grouping of Initiatives.
- ◆ **Initiative** - A piece of work.

◆ Guidance
- ◆ **Principle** - Conceptual guidance.
- ◆ **Policy** - Logical guidance.
- ◆ **Standard** - Physical guidance.

◆ Assessment
- ◆ **Transformation Debt Agreement (TDA)** - An assessment of the impact and implications of not following a Principle, Policy or Standard.

Artefacts

KEYPOINT:

Specific Entities are required to define the Business Motivation and Roadmap models

ADOPTION:

EA Project Team: Define the Motivation, Actions, Guidance, Measure and Assessment entities, you need to create the Business and Roadmap Metamodels.

Questions to Ponder

- What entities does your Enterprise use to model this information?
- Are they well known and consistently used from person to person?
- If not, what problems does that create and what can you do to alleviate them?

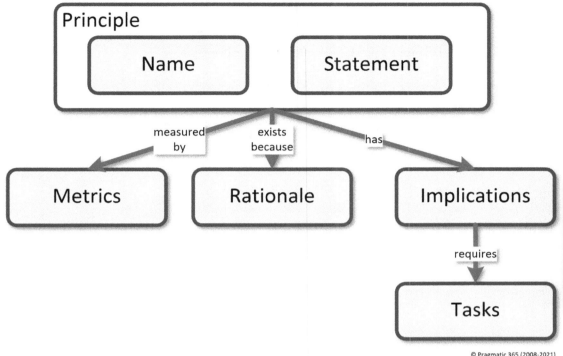

© Pragmatic 365 (2008-2021)

Artefacts

◆ **Name** - The name of the Principle.
Represents the essence of the Principle as well as being easy to remember.

◆ **Statement** - Succinctly and unambiguously communicates the fundamental rule.
For the most part, the principles statements for managing information are similar
from one Enterprise to the next. It is vital that the principles statement be
unambiguous.

◆ **Rationale** - Highlights the reasons why this Principle exists.
Describing why this principle exists is important. If people understand why a principle
exists, they are more likely to "buy-into-it" and adoption is greatly enhanced.
Principles usually exist to solve a particular problem or to guide change in a particular
fashion.

◆ **Implications** - Highlights the implications, both for the Business and IT, for
operating the principle - in terms of resources, costs, and activities/tasks.
Without implications, principles are just words that management can agree to but
can then fall into disrepair due to the implications as they occur. Defining and then
getting agreement on the implications is a key step in principle agreement and
adoption.

◆ **Metrics** - Lists the measures that must be in place in order to monitor whether the
positive results that each principle is meant to achieve are being achieved.
It is imperative to understand and know whether the principles are having the
desired effect or not and to what degree. The metrics given for each principle define
how well that principle is achieving its desired result and not the number of
Transformation Debt™ Agreements produced. Whilst counting the number provides
a simple metric for all principles, this is akin to measuring the input rather than the
output. E.g. Measuring how fast we are pumping water, not how much water we are

pumping. For this reason, these metrics measure the desired outputs of each principle.

- ♦ **Tasks** - Lists the tasks that must be executed to be able to operate the Principle. If the associated tasks for a principle are not undertaken, it will be impossible to utilise and therefore gain the benefit from that principle.

KEYPOINT:

The purpose of a Transformation Debt™ Agreement is to expose Transformation Debt™.

ADOPTION:

EA Project Team: Define the Transformation Debt Agreement entities, you need to be able to record Transformation Debt™

Questions to Ponder

♦ What entities does your Enterprise use to model this information?
♦ Are they well known and consistently used from person to person?
♦ If not, what problems does that create and what can you do to alleviate them?

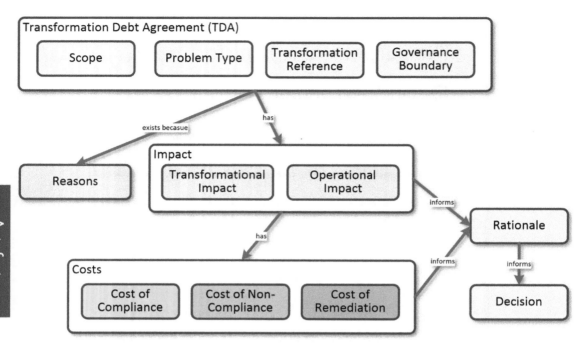

© Pragmatic 365 (2008-2021)

Artefacts

Summary

Scope	The information that is causing the problem. Transformational (Motivation / Actions / Guidance / Measures / Assessment) or Structural (Methods / Artefacts / Guidance / Items / Culture)
Problem Type	The type of problem. (Cannot Comply / Insufficient or Inadequate Input)
Transformation Reference	The Program, Project or Initiative experiencing the problem
Governance Boundary	The governance level that is experiencing the problem. (Strategising-Roadmapping / Roadmapping-Solutioning / Solutioning-Elaboration / Elaboration-Construction / Construction-Transitioning)
Reasons	A high level description of why this problem exists.
Transformational Impact	The general impact non-compliance will have on the Effectiveness, Efficiency, Agility and Durability of how the transformation is being performed.

Operational Impact	The general impact non-compliance will have on the Effectiveness, Efficiency, Agility and Durability of the **result** of the transformation.
Cost of Compliance	A summary (**Capital**, **Revenue**, **People**, **Time**, **Scope**, **etc**)
Cost of Non-Compliance	A summary (**Capital**, **Revenue**, **People**, **Time**, **Scope**, **etc**)
Cost of Remediation	A summary (**Capital**, **Revenue**, **People**, **Time**, **Scope**, **etc**)
Decision	The result of the decision. (**Compliance** / **Non-Compliance**)
Rationale	The reasons why the decision was taken

Artefacts

Cost of Compliance

Capital Costs	What money (Capital) do you need that you do not have budget for?
Revenue Costs	What money (Revenue) do you need that you do not have budget for?
People	What People do you need that you cannot get access to?
Time	What time is required that has not been budgeted for and how does that impact the project milestones?
Scope	What change in scope is required?
Process	What changes to the project plan are required? (tasks to be removed, changed or added)

Cost of Non-Compliance

	Description	A description of the issue.
Issues	Actions	How the issue will be resolved.
	Costs	What it will cost us to deal with the issue or the impact of the Issue (Money (Capital/Revenue), People, Time, Scope, Reputation, Loss of Ability to Innovate, Reduced Agility, etc).

Artefacts	**Risks**	Date	A target date of when the issue will arise.
		Owner	Who owns/is responsible for ensuring the Issue is resolved as specified.
		Description	A description of the risk.
		Effect	A description of the effect to the Enterprise if the risk occurs.
		Proximity	An indication of how imminent the risk is to occurring (months).
		Likelihood	Likelihood that the risk will occur. (Low, Medium, High).
		Impact	An Indication of the impact to the business if the risk occurs. (Low, Medium, High).
		Mitigating Actions	How the risk will be mitigated with respect to Likelihood and/or Impact.
		Costs	What must be provided to mitigate the risk (Money (Capital/Revenue), People, Time, Scope).
		Target Date	A target date of when the remedial work will be undertaken by.
		Owner	Who owns/is responsible for ensuring the Issue is resolved as specified.

Cost of Remediation

Capital Costs	What money (Capital) will you need, to remove the issues and risks and be compliant, and how that will change (probably increase) over time?
Revenue Costs	What money (Revenue) will you need, to remove the issues and risks and be compliant, and how that will change (probably increase) over time?
People	What People will you need, to remove the issues and risks and be compliant, and how that will change (probably increase) over time?
Time	What time will you need to remove the issues and risks and be compliant, and how that will change (probably increase) over time?
Process	What tasks will you need to execute, to remove the issues and risks and be compliant, and they will change (probably increase) over time?

> # KEYPOINT:
>
> The purpose of a Transformation Debt™ Agreement is to expose Transformation Debt™.

> # ADOPTION:
>
> EA Project Team: Define the Transformation Debt Agreement entities, you need to be able to record Transformation Debt™

Questions to Ponder

- What entities does your Enterprise use to model this information?
- Are they well known and consistently used from person to person?
- If not, what problems does that create and what can you do to alleviate them?

Artefacts > Meta-models > Structural

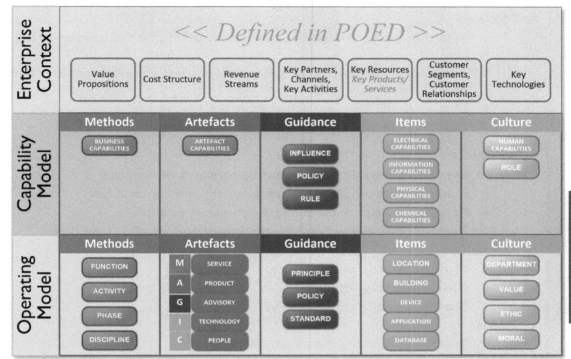

© Pragmatic 365 (2008-2021)

Capability Model

- ◆ **Methods**
    - ◆ **Business Capabilities** - Core business functionality (with inputs/outputs – Artefacts) required to effect the Business model
- ◆ **Artefacts**
    - ◆ **Artefact Capabilities** – Core business supplies or production
- ◆ **Guidance**
    - ◆ **Influence** - An act, process, or power of producing an effect without apparent exertion of tangible force or direct exercise of command, and often without deliberate effort or intent.
    - ◆ **Policy** - Guides the Enterprise. Compared to a Rule it is less structured, less discrete or not atomic, less carefully expressed in terms of standard vocabulary.
    - ◆ **Rule** - Influences or guides business behaviour, in support of a Policy. Compared to a Policy it is highly structured, discrete or atomic, carefully expressed in terms of standard vocabulary.
- ◆ **Items**
    - ◆ **Physical/Mechanical Capabilities** – e.g. Buildings, Tables,
    - ◆ **Electrical Capabilities** – e.g. Motors, Servers,
    - ◆ **Chemical Capabilities** – e.g. Oxidation, Hydrolysis
    - ◆ **Information Capabilities** – e.g. storage, processing, display
- ◆ **Culture**
    - ◆ **Human Capabilities** – Skills
        - ▪ **Role** - A group of behaviours

- **Methods**
    - **Function** - A hierarchical list of Business functions that the business carries out.
    - **Activity** - A high Level logical grouping of business processes carried out by one or more departments.
    - **Phase** - A step ion a Function or Activity.
    - **Discipline** - A type of work performed in one or more Phases.
      {{Murambwa Clever Haparari}}
- **Artefacts**
    - **Service** - The services the Enterprise consumes or produces.
    - **Product** - The products the Enterprise consumes or produces.
    - **People** - The people the Enterprise consumes or produces.
    - **Technology** - The technologies the Enterprise consumes or produces.
- **Guidance**
    - **Principle** - Conceptual guidance.
    - **Policy** - Logical guidance.
    - **Standard** - Physical guidance.
- **Items**
    - **Location** - Physical geographical locations.
    - **Service** - A Technology Service used by Functions and activities.
    - **Application** - The main applications in use.
    - **Datastore** - The main groups of data in use.
    - **Device** - A generic piece of hardware provided as or part of a service to the business.
- **Culture**
    - **Value** - Defines what is fair and unfair.
    - **Ethic** - Rules of behaviour based on Morals.
    - **Moral** - Relates what is right and wrong.
    - **Department** - The departmental structure of the Enterprise.

> ## KEYPOINT:
>
> Specific Entities are required to define the Enterprise Context, Enterprise Capability and Operating models.

> ## ADOPTION:
>
> EA Project Team: Define the Method, Artefact, Culture and Environment entities, you need to create the Enterprise Context, Capability Model and Operating Model Metamodels.

Questions to Ponder

- ♦ What entities does your Enterprise use to model this information?
- ♦ Are they well known and consistently used from person to person?
- ♦ If not, what problems does that create and what can you do to alleviate them?

Guidance

KEYPOINT:

The Guidance section of PEAF defines what information is used to guide people in their decision making.

ADOPTION:

C-Suite: Instigate a review of the Guidance used in the Enterprise's EA Capability, to determine if their maturity is appropriate.

Questions to Ponder

- With respect to your Enterprises EA capability, what Guidance is used?
- Is the Guidance documented? Understood?
- Is it fit for purpose?
- Is it used? All the time? Only when it suits?
- Which part of the Guidance is Good? Why? Bad? Why?

Best Practice...

- **Reuse before Buy before build**
- **Reduce complexity**
- **Sound business case**
- **Avoid over engineering**
- **Open integration, etc, etc, etc.**

Enterprise Strategy...

- **E.g. Outsource non core business processes**
- **E.g. Consolidate to 2 data centres**

© Pragmatic 365 (2008-2021)

There are two types of Principles.

Best Practice Principles are the type that PEAF provides, which apply to the majority of Enterprises.

The other type, are born from your Enterprises Strategy and its resulting Enterprise Transformation Strategy.

The purpose of these principles is not to constrain, but to provide a broad cultural framework in which work will be carried out.

As work progresses, these principles should be augmented with principles arising from considering the Enterprise Strategy Model.

Guidance

> ## KEYPOINT:
>
> Principles come from Best Practice and your Enterprise's Strategy.

> ## ADOPTION:
>
> EA Project Team: Create Principles from Best Practice and your Enterprise Strategy.

Questions to Ponder

- ◆ What Best Practice Principles does your Enterprise operate?
- ◆ What Enterprise specific Principles does your Enterprise operate?

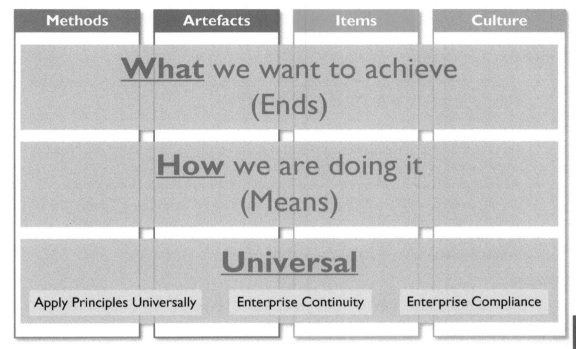

Most people think of principles in terms of Business, Data, Application and Technology – or some other similar categorisation. **Pragmatic** considers principles from a more **Pragmatic** perspective. We use MAGIC as a primary categorisation approach. Since the Guidance part of MAGIC is where the Principles sit, Guidance is not listed itself, as a category.

In addition, we can also consider principles in terms of those which guide outcomes or **What** we want to achieve (Ends), or those that guide how the outcomes are achieved or **How** we are doing it (Means).

We Therefore have 8 types of principles:

- ◆ What (we deliver)
    - ◆ Principles that guide the Methods we deliver.
    - ◆ Principles that guide the Artefacts (a lot of which is data) we deliver.
    - ◆ Principles that guide how the people we deliver to (Culture).
    - ◆ Principles that guide the IT and other technologies we deliver (Items).

- ◆ How (we transform)
    - ◆ Principles that guide how we transform (Methods).
    - ◆ Principles that guide the things that are consumed and produced (Artefacts - a lot of which is data) as we transform.
    - ◆ Principles that guide people as we transform.
    - ◆ Principles that guide the IT and other technologies we use (Items) as we transform.

Although principles can be categorised, some apply universally, namely:

Universal Principles

Apply Principles Universally

We apply principles to all parts of the Enterprise.

Rationale:

♦ If parts of the Enterprise are exempt from these principles, this will undermine and reduce the benefits gained to an unacceptable level.

Implications:

♦ Parts of the Enterprise may react negatively and resist the removal of the "flexibility" to pick and choose which principles to adopt.

♦ All change initiatives will be reviewed for their compliance with the principles.

♦ An unresolved conflict with a principle will be resolved by issuing a Transformation Debt™ Agreement (TDA) which will then be analysed, costed and managed.

♦ Any deviation from these principles will be documented and managed as Transformation Debt™ Agreements (TDAs).

Metrics:

♦ Raw: % of Initiatives that have been examined for compliance with the principles.

♦ Raw: Per project: Number of TDAs issued

♦ Raw: Per project: Number of TDA issues.

♦ Raw: Per project: Total Cost of TDA issues.

♦ Raw: Per project: Number of TDA risks

♦ Raw: Per project: Total impact cost of TDA risks

♦ Raw: Per project: Number TDAs avoided

♦ Derived: Total: Number of live TDAs

♦ Derived: Total: Number of TDAs issued

♦ Derived: Total: Number of TDAs closed

♦ Derived: Total: Number of TDAs issues

♦ Derived: Total: Total Cost of TDAs issues

♦ Derived: Total: Number of TDA risks

♦ Derived: Total: Total impact cost of TDAs risks

♦ Derived: Total: Number TDAs avoided (At which level)

Enterprise Compliance

We comply with all relevant laws, policies and regulations.

Rationale:

♦ The Enterprise is not viable unless it complies with appropriate laws and regulations.

Implications:

♦ A programme of training is required to make appropriate people aware of appropriate laws, policies and regulation and when, where and how to apply them.

♦ Non-Functional Requirements need to identify the laws, polices and regulations (internal and external) that solutions must comply with.

Metrics:

♦ Raw: % of systems which have been formerly reviewed and deemed compliant.

Enterprise Continuity

We maintain appropriate levels of Enterprise Continuity.

Rationale:

♦ The impact to the Enterprise if it is unable to conduct its business is not only measured in terms of lost revenue and wasted employee time, but can also have an impact on the Enterprise's reputation with its suppliers and its customers.

♦ The impact of any disruption can continue long after the actual disruption has been corrected.

Implications:

♦ The component parts of the Enterprise and the MAGIC they use must be assessed in terms of the importance and criticality to the business.

♦ The level of business continuity to be put in place is dependent upon the importance or criticality to the business.

♦ The Business continuity plan and measures put in place will be adequately tested periodically.

♦ The Business continuity plan will be reviewed periodically.

♦ Appropriate levels of availability, disaster recovery, and security for all systems (not just IT systems) will be addressed in their design.

Metrics:

♦ Raw: Existence of a BC Risk Log.
♦ Raw: Number of open risks.
♦ Raw: % of risks with mitigation tasks.
♦ Raw: % of mitigation tasks planned for action.
♦ Raw: % of mitigation tasks in progress.
♦ Raw: % of mitigation tasks completed.
♦ Raw: Existence of a BC test plan.
♦ Raw: Execution of the BC test plan every 12 months
♦ Raw: % of applications that have been assigned a business criticality.
♦ Raw: % of applications that meet the level of business criticality assigned.

> ## KEYPOINT:
>
> Don't think in terms of Business and
> IT principles. Use MAGIC to
> categorise them.

> ## ADOPTION:
>
> EA Project Team: Categorise
> Principles using MAGIC.

Questions to Ponder

- What categories does your Enterprise use to group related principles?
- Do your categories cover the Methods and Artefacts and Culture and Environment used for Transformation?
- If not, what problems does that create and what can you do to alleviate them?

Methods	Artefacts	Items	Culture
• Reduce Manual Processes • Consolidate • Open Integration	• Treat Data as Assets • Do Not Duplicate Data • Make Data Accessible • Define Data • Secure Data	• Ease-of-Use • Common Use • Security • Minimise Customisation • Replace Legacy Appropriately • Increase Independence • Reduce Diversity • Increase Interoperability	

© Pragmatic 365 (2008-2021)

Here we see a set of Principles related to WHAT we want to achieve (Ends). It is interesting to note that the Cultural Principles are blank. This is because most Transformation/Change that happens within an Enterprise does not change or guide the Culture.

If this sounds like a bad thing to you, you are not alone! In **Pragmatic** 's opinion, while Cultural change is easily the most difficult thing to effect, it is usually the thing that has the most profound impact, not only in terms of its outcome, but also in terms of whether the outcome is positive or negative. Interestingly, it seems to be true that effecting a bad culture is much more easily done than effecting a good culture!

Method Principles

Reduce Manual Processes

We reduce and remove manual processes - but only when there is a clear business reason for doing so.

Rationale:

♦ The benefit of manual processes are that they are immeasurably flexible, can be easily changed (on a daily basis if necessary) with little cost and without any of the problems associated with changing electronic software systems. This is the reason, manual processes tend to grow and grow through an Enterprise. However, manual processes require people to operate them, office space, desks, HR, or not scalable, etc, etc Therefore straight through processing (STP) is a valid target aim.

♦ There are places where manual processes should and/or must be used as systems and technology cannot currently replace them or they are more cost effective.

- ♦ Cost is only one aspect though, people are good at non-repetitive highly complex tasks rather than repetitive simple tasks and so it makes sense to use one of the most important assets of the company (i.e. its people) in the best way possible.

Implications:

- ♦ People rarely ask the question "why do you do it that way". Even if they do, the usual answer is "because that's the way we've always done it". It takes a determined and concentrated effort to research, investigate and identify processes that can be reduced or removed.
- ♦ People can believe that removing or reducing manual processes will make them less worthwhile to the company, give them less job satisfaction and/or could ultimately lead to loss of jobs. This is a misnomer in that what usually happens is that people feel more worthwhile and get better job satisfaction and job losses do not materialise as people are freed up to do more productive and less repetitive work.
- ♦ Usually the people best suited to spot where improvements could be made are the people on the coal face who have to follow and work within these processes on a day to day basis.

Metrics:

- ♦ Raw: The number of manual, semi-automatic and automatic process.
- ♦ Raw: The cost of manual, semi-automatic and automatic process.
- ♦ Derived: The total cost of manual, semi-automatic and automatic process.
- ♦ Derived: The ratio of the number of manual to semi-automatic to automatic processes.
- ♦ Derived: The ratio of the cost of manual to semi-automatic to automatic processes.

Consolidate

We consider consolidation at all times and we proactively drive towards reducing proliferation and complexity.

Rationale:

- ♦ Anything which is complex costs more to produce and maintain.
- ♦ This increase in cost tends to increase in an exponential manner - initially not having much impact on costs and timescales, but as complexity grows there comes a point whereby costs become prohibitive.
- ♦ Consolidation is concerned across the board e.g. Processes, Applications, Vendors, Hardware, Software, Services.

Implications:

- ♦ Consolidation is not something that happens overnight and usually consolidation projects do not make economic sense.
- ♦ Consolidation should become part of all projects remits and the Business should provide the resources to effect consolidation as opportunities arise.
- ♦ Consolidation should become part of the Roadmapping phase, allowing for pieces of consolidation work to be included in the project portfolio.

Metrics:

♦ Raw: % of programmes, projects and initiatives that include a consolidation component.

Open Integration

We view and manage the integration of IT systems as a strategic capability separate to each individual system and project, rather than something that is thought of as part of each individual system.

Rationale:

♦ One of the key capabilities to IT successfully supporting the Business is Integration.

♦ Integration is the glue and the key to flexibility - Open, configurable, scalable, resilient, secure.

♦ Integration is the cornerstone and backbone of any agile Enterprise in this world of constant change (business model's technologies, environmental, regulatory, commercial, etc).

♦ Integration should not be thought of as something secondary that just connects various things, it needs to be thought of as the heart of IT and the Business, connecting packaged applications with legacy, bespoke and external systems.

Implications:

♦ In the same way as Enterprises have teams responsible for networks, servers and databases the Enterprise also should have an integration team which creates new integrations or replaces old integrations and is driven by the Business and project need.

♦ In this way integration is considered, guided and architected on a strategic and infrastructural level and implementation is carried out on a system by system or interface by interface level.

♦ This approach removes the problems associated with a "big bang" approach, but still allows a big picture to be the driving force behind individual integration work carried out as part of other projects. Systems, parts of the Enterprise and individual links can be brought into this systemic integration environment gradually as time, money and business pressures dictate.

Metrics:

♦ Raw: An integration group exists within IT with its own budget.

♦ Raw: Number of shared integration points, systems, technologies, interfaces being used.

Artefact Principles

Treat Data as Assets

We accept that Data are assets that have value to the Enterprise.

Rationale:

- Data is the blood of most Enterprises, and its value can be huge.
- Data, like anything else of value, needs to be maintained if its use is to be preserved.
- Collecting and storing data can be very time consuming and resource intensive, and so to not maintain data (so it can be used in the future) is extremely inefficient.
- Data exists in two fundamental categories:
  - **Production**: These data are the product (for a data based Enterprise - like a bank). They are the crown jewels of the Enterprise.
  - **Business**: These data aids decision-making. Unless this data is accurate, current and available when it is needed bad decisions can be made with far reaching consequences to the entire Enterprise.

Implications:

- Each major data entity will have an associated data steward assigned responsible for managing the data.
- Data Stewards are responsible for the quality of the data they are responsible for.
- Procedures must be created to monitor data quality and correct any errors. A set of Data Management Policies are required.
- A Metadata repository is required.
- Common tools are required for creating, maintaining and managing data.

Metrics:

- Raw: Does a Business Data Model exist?
- Raw: % that have an assigned business data steward.
- Raw: % that have defined data quality procedures.
- Raw: Per Entity: Data Quality score.
- Derived: Total Data Quality score.

Do Not Duplicate Data

We ensure that Data are shared across organisational and technical boundaries.

Rationale:

- The Enterprise holds a large amount of data, but it is stored in multiple physical databases.
- Duplication of data costs money in effort to maintain it and to synchronise its copies.
- Duplication means there are many versions of "the truth" making decision making very haphazard.
- Duplication adds un-needed complexity.

Implications:

- Data Sharing and Data Security can be contradictory - It is important to recognise that data stored in the same place can have different security requirements.
- A set of Data Management Policies are required.
- A Metadata repository is required.
- Common tools are required for creating, maintaining and managing data.

Metrics:

- Raw: Do Data Management Polices and Standards exist?
- Metrics for measuring the adherence and effectiveness of these are defined in the associated policies/standards.

Make Data Accessible

We ensure that people have access to the data required to perform their duties.

Rationale:

- Data which is accessible increases efficiency and effective decision making.
- Access to data must be considered for an Enterprise wide perspective otherwise data silos are likely to grow.

Implications:

- Different levels of access need to be defined for all data entities - Create, Read, Update, Delete.
- An Enterprise wide access framework is required to manage access based on Enterprise role rather than individual persons.
- A set of Data Management Policies are required.
- A Metadata repository is required.
- Common tools are required for creating, maintaining and managing data.

Metrics:

- Raw: A Data Accessibility user survey has been created.
- Raw: % of entities that have had a Data Accessibility user survey carried out.
- Raw: % Data Accessibility score for each entity.
- Derived: Total % Data Accessibility.

Define Data

We define and use Data consistently.

Rationale:

- For the Enterprise to come together and work in a partnership there must be a common and well understood definition for all the important data entities within the Enterprise.

Implications:

- A Metadata repository is required.
- Whenever there is disagreement over the use of an existing definition or when new definitions are required the Architecture Review Board will ensure consistency and completeness.

Guidance

Metrics:

- Raw: % complete Business Data Dictionary.

Secure Data

We protect Data from unauthorized use and disclosure.

Rationale:

- In the same way access to applications is controlled through role based security, so must access to data.
- It is all too easy to have an application provide elaborate security access control and restrictions but if the data that the application uses can be accessed directly in a relatively easy fashion then that data is not sufficiently protected.
- This is especially pertinent to integrations across Enterprise boundaries where different data in a data set may be considered differently in terms of security.

Implications:

- It is possible that to gain data security, data is physically separated into different database. This may not be the optimal method of securing the data since it needlessly fragments the data and can cause maintenance issues.
- A Data security policy and standards are required.
- Existing data sources will need assessing and evaluating.
- Like applications, security must be designed into data entities and attributes at design time, not by adding it later.

Metrics:

- Raw: % of Databases that have had a security assessment.
- Raw: Do Best Practice Data Security Policies and Standards exist?
- Metrics for measuring the adherence and effectiveness of these are defined in the associated policies/standards.

Items (Technology) Principles

Ease-of-Use

We ensure that technology is easy to use. The underlying technology is transparent to users, so they can concentrate on tasks at hand.

Rationale:

- The more a user has to understand the underlying technology, the less productive that user is.
- Ease-of-use is a positive incentive for use of applications. It encourages users to work within the integrated information environment instead of developing isolated systems to accomplish the task outside of the Enterprise's integrated information environment.
- Most of the knowledge required to operate one system will be similar to others therefore training is kept to a minimum, and the risk of using a system improperly is reduced.
- Using different applications should be as intuitive as driving different cars.

Implications:

- Applications will be required to have a common "look and feel" and support ergonomic requirements. Hence, the common look and feel standard must be designed and usability test criteria must be developed.
- Guidelines for user interfaces should not be constrained by narrow assumptions about user location, language, systems training, or physical capability. Factors such as linguistics, customer physical infirmities (visual acuity, ability to use keyboard/mouse), and proficiency in the use of technology have broad ramifications in determining the ease-of-use of an application.
- It is accepted that increased use of COTS applications may mean this principle is not met as much as would be if purely bespoke applications are used.

Metrics:

- Raw: An Ease-Of-Use satisfaction survey has been created.
- Raw: % of services/applications that have had an Ease-Of-Use satisfaction survey carried out.
- Raw % Ease-Of-Use satisfaction score for each service/application.
- Derived: Total % Ease-Of-Use satisfaction.

Common Use

We ensure that technology that can support and/or be reused by multiple parts of the Enterprise are favoured over those that are only point solutions.

Rationale:

- Technology that only solve one problem or support one part of the Enterprise exacerbate the proliferation of Technology that cause increased cost and complexity.

Implications:

Guidance

- Existing point solutions may need to be replaced.
- Careful management of projects is required to identify possible synergies as early as possible.
- Projects may need extra investment to allow their scope to be expanded in order to procure a broader application or service.

Metrics:

- Raw: Number of applications providing essentially the same functionality or services

i3. Security

We ensure that technology will be secured from unauthorized access.

Rationale:

- Malicious intrusion, viruses, and terrorism increasingly threaten the Enterprise's systems.
- The Enterprise has a duty to maintain its customer's and supplier's trust in its systems from unauthorized access and to preserve confidentiality where required.
- Secure systems ensure the continuity of the Enterprise's business.

Implications:

- Systems must be secured with application security best practices.
- Application security assessments being conducted on a regular basis.
- Must identify, publish, and keep applicable policies current.
- Security must enable not impede business.
- Security must be designed into the Enterprise, its structure, processes and systems from the beginning. Adding it later seriously compromises quality and/or seriously increases costs.

Metrics:

- Raw: % of Systems, Applications, Departments that have had a security assessment.
- Raw: Do Best Practice Application Security Policies and Standards exist?
- Metrics for measuring the adherence and effectiveness of these are defined in the associated policies/standards.

Minimise Customisation

We only allow the customisation of COTS packages when there is a clear and burning business advantage for doing so.

Rationale:

- One of the benefits of buying a COTS package is the reduced maintenance burden and the easy acceptance of updates from the manufacturer.
- The more a COTS package is Customised (as opposed to Configured) the more these basic benefits are lost.
- A heavily customised COTS package effectively becomes a built application.

Implications:

- The Business may have to forego some functionality and settle for "what the product can do out-of-the-box" rather than have all their requirements fully satisfied.
-

Metrics:

- Raw: Number of Customisations done.

Replace Legacy Appropriately

We will replace legacy systems only when there is a valid business case for doing so.

Rationale:

- Legacy systems are not inherently bad and a wholesale approach to replace them with the latest technology will be avoided.
- Replacement of existing/legacy systems will only be done if there is a sound value proposition to do so and if the risks have been properly evaluated.

Implications:

- Legacy systems will continue to exist in the Enterprise and it should be noted that this position will not change much over time.
- Only the specifics of which systems are legacy will change. i.e. the systems introduced today will be deemed to be "legacy" at some point in the future.

Metrics:

- Raw: Number of legacy systems in place.
- Raw: A legacy system evaluation framework exists
- Raw: % of legacy systems that have been evaluated.

Increase Independence

We ensure that applications and services should be independent of specific technologies.

Rationale:

- Technologies (Hardware and software) change and evolve over time. As time passes some technologies are favoured over others due to security concerns, scalability, costs, or other important drivers.
- Applications which are independent of the technologies they require to operate provide the business with an increased level of flexibility to change technologies when required based on business drivers.

Implications:

- Technology Standards are required.
- This principle may be difficult to comply with because Commercial Off-The-Shelf (COTS) applications can tend to be platform dependent.

Metrics:

- Raw: For each application and service, the number of alternative Technologies that could be used.

Guidance

◆ Derived: Average number of alternative Technologies per application/service.

Reduce Diversity

We aim to reduce the number of technologies wherever possible.

Rationale:

◆ The higher the number of technologies used the higher the cost of supporting and maintaining them.

◆ If many technologies are in use, it becomes a necessity for IT resources to have to concentrate on a subset of technologies thereby reducing the flexibility of the workforce.

Implications:

◆ Technology Standards are required.

◆ This principle may be difficult to comply with because Commercial Off-The-Shelf (COTS) applications can tend to increase technology diversity.

Metrics:

◆ Raw: For each Technology, the number of different types in use.

◆ Derived: Average number of instances per Technology.

Increase Interoperability

We aim to increase the level of interoperability between disparate technologies wherever possible.

Rationale:

◆ Where disparate technologies have to be utilised, interoperability provides the best way of enabling them to work together coherently.

◆ Interoperability reduces the cost of integration and maintenance.

Implications:

◆ Interoperability Standards are required.

◆ This principle may be difficult to comply with because Commercial Off-The-Shelf (COTS) applications may or may not adopt open standards.

Metrics:

◆ Raw: For each Technology, the number of different types in use.

◆ Derived: Average number of instances per Technology.

Culture Principles

> ## KEYPOINT:
>
> When categorising Principles, think in terms of those that guide WHAT we want to achieve (Ends).

> ## ADOPTION:
>
> EA Project Team: Create Principles that guide WHAT we want to achieve (Ends).

Questions to Ponder

- ◆ Has your Enterprise defined principles that guide WHAT you want to achieve (Ends)?
- ◆ If not, what problems does that create and what can you do to alleviate them?

Methods	Artefacts	Items	Culture
• Plan Ahead and Organise • Refactor Where Possible • Manage Transformation Debt™ Value • Manage Transformation Debt™ Ratio • Be Architecture Centric • Be Service Oriented • Avoid Under/Over Engineering • Reuse • Buy (for reuse) Before Build	• Artefacts Must Be Complete, Sufficient and Comprehensible • Structured Modelling • Relationships & Traceability • Have a Sound Business Case		• Disagreement <> Confrontation • Explain Decisions • Record Decisions • Consider Context & Implications • Work Smart not Hard • Consider Efficiency • Consider Important Non-Urgent Work • Consider Things of Fundamental Importance • Consider the True Value of Things • Prioritize Substance over Style • Consider Future Benefit • Expose Individual and Contrary Opinion • Change Actions and Beliefs over Perceptions • Don't Jump to Conclusions • Think Strategically • No Bullying • Expose Problems • Proactive Business Leadership • Recognise Responsibilities

© Pragmatic 365 (2008-2021)

Here we see a set of Principles related to HOW we effect Transformation (Means). It is interesting to note that the Items Principles are blank. This is because most Transformation/Change that happens within an Enterprise only considers the Items (Technology) that is being delivered, rather than the Items (Technology) being used to deliver them.

If this sounds like a bad thing to you, you are not alone! In **Pragmatic**'s opinion, Items (Technology) that are being delivered are always to the fore largely because a) delivering new or changed Items (Technology) is the purpose of many (IT) projects and b) there is no one Accountable for the Items (Technology) being used by Transformation. Thus, all focus is on the Items (Technology) being delivered rather than the Items (Technology) being used to deliver them.

Method Principles

Plan Ahead and Organise

We ensure we plan to work in a Strategic way in order to allow us to do work in a strategic way.

Rationale:

♦ Most companies tend to find themselves in a fire fighting spiral, where problems and priorities are focussed on just keeping the Business running.

♦ This is a spiral because work that should be done to head off the next potential problem or panic is not done resulting in the potential problem becoming a real problem to such an extent that it makes it onto the panic sheet.

♦ If you do not plan to do any strategic work, you will never do any strategic work.

Implications:

◆ The firefighting spiral needs to be broken and the only way to do that is to plan ahead and organise work not only based on short term objectives but also from the point of view or stopping things becoming a crisis in the future.

◆ Therefore, a proportion of budget and effort needs to be directed towards preventing things becoming a crisis in the future rather than exclusively performing crisis management and firefighting activities.

◆ Only by planning ahead will the crisis management spiral be broken.

Metrics:

◆ Raw: % of budget spent on strategic work.

Refactor Where Possible

We always consider refactoring and improvement whenever anything is changed.

Rationale:

◆ Improving something whilst already "having your fingers on it" costs a lot less in terms of time and resources than doing so at a later time.

◆ If you don't improve things as a normal part of "work" (continuous improvement) they will potentially never be improved.

Implications:

◆ Requires time and resources.

◆ People need an environment that allows then to refactor and improve things "as they go"

◆ Management needs to create that environment.

Metrics:

◆ Raw: Amount of refactoring work undertaken.

Manage Transformation Debt™ Value

We expose, document, and manage Transformation Debt™ Value (TDV).

Rationale:

◆ Transformation Debt™ exists. It is created every day. This principle recognises its existence and therefore the requirement to expose and manage it.

◆ Transformation Debt™ incurs interest. This interest is paid as long as the interim change (debt) exists in the form of maintenance and other costs that would not exist otherwise. Remedial change is like paying off a (portion of a) loan and as such reduces overall debt and subsequent interest.

◆ Transformation Debt™ is not inherently a bad thing. It is an important tool for an Enterprise to achieve its goals and objectives. Like financial debt, Transformation Debt™ needs to be visible & managed. If Debt is not managed it will inevitably only increase.

◆ Like any debt, Transformation Debt™ is bad when you:

    ◆ Don't know you are incurring it.

Guidance

◆ Don't know how you will pay off the debt.
◆ Don't know the interest rate.
◆ Don't know how long you will have to pay interest for.

Implications:

◆ Changes are required in process and culture to enable identification of Transformation Debt™ to be an acceptable and appropriate thing to do.
◆ A Strategic Investment Board (with budget) is required to sit above all projects and programs.

Metrics:

◆ Raw: The Transformation Debt™ (cost of the issues and risks created) of each programme, project and initiative.
◆ Derived: The total cost of Transformation Debt™.

Manage Transformation Debt™ Ratio

We classify all change in terms of the Transformation Debt™ Ratio (TDR - Strategic vs Tactical vs Remedial)

Rationale:

◆ **Strategic**: Changes that take you directly from where you are to where you want to be. (May or may not also satisfy a short term need.)
◆ **Tactical**: Changes that satisfy a short term need, but does not take you from where you are to where you want to be in the most effective and/or efficient way.
◆ **Remedial**: Changes that correct previous Tactical change. This remedial change will also consist of Strategic and Tactical change.
◆ All projects have a Business and a Technical change component. The Transformation Debt Ratio™ for each can be very different. E.g. The Business change component of an initiative may be 90:10:0, whereas the IT change component of the same initiative may be 10:30:60.
◆ Strategic changes do not increase Transformation Debt™ but could reduce it as a side effect.
◆ Tactical changes, by definition, increase Transformation Debt™.
◆ Remedial changes decreases Transformation Debt™.
◆ When budgets and timescales are constrained, the bias is more likely to be towards Interim change (taking on more debt) whereas when budgets and timescales are more relaxed the bias is more likely to be towards Strategic and Remedial change (paying off the debt).

Implications:

◆ All Programmes, Projects and Initiatives need to be classified in terms of Strategic vs Interim vs Remedial ratios, for the Business change component and for the IT change component.
◆ It should be also noted that the Transformation Debt Ratio™ is a ratio of how change is effected not why. E.g. Change may be driven by a strategic imperative but if the way that change is effected is interim then the Debt Ratio would be 0:100:0 and not 100:0:0

Guidance

Metrics:

- Raw: The % of programmes, projects and initiatives that have the Transformation Debt Ratio™ identified.
- Derived: The total %'s of Strategic vs Interim vs Remedial ratios (Business & IT)

Be Architecture Centric

We adopt Architecture Best Practice

Rationale:

- Architecture is about structure, reuse, cost reduction and flexibility.
- An architecture centric approach to delivering services to the Business is a widely accepted and adopted best practice for success.
- Currently there are limited architecture resources, groups, documentation, principles, policies, standards, governance.
- Work undertaken tends to be tactical rather than strategic in focus.
- IT systems are diverging in terms of technology and applications and point solutions are proliferating. IT finds it difficult to provide a good service to the Business. This results in IT being viewed as a cost rather than a positive value. IT has a tactical reactive focus rather than a proactive strategic focus.
- This will allow the Enterprise to be in control of its IT capabilities and fully understand how they are related to each other and the Business.
- Projects produce good quality, fit for purpose solutions.

Implications:

- Define an architecture framework.
- Introduce/improve and integrate Enterprise, Solution and Technical architecture processes and products.
- Introduce a Best Practice project management approach.
- Introduce Business/IT planning and Project Portfolio Management.

Metrics:

- Utilise the Metrics (part of the Maturity Model) defined in the Adoption section of the Framework you have adopted.

Be Service Oriented

We adopt a service based approach instead of an application based approach.

Rationale:

- The traditional application based approach to providing functionality does not promote reuse and flexibility at the Business level. i.e. it is difficult to rearrange and re-connect applications as business needs change.
- Adopting a Service based approach to providing services to the Business will increase Business agility enabling it to respond faster and more efficiently to internal and external change .

Implications:

◆ We need to identify and provide reusable business level services that can be linked together and easily changed to increase business agility.

◆ A Service based approach is not a product that can be bought and installed. It is more a way of thinking and structuring things. This can be difficult to grasp although the benefits can be substantial.

◆ Vendors of packaged applications (COTS) may not be as mature as the Enterprise would like and may require work to define and wrap various functionality as services.

Metrics:

◆ Raw: Number of internal facing Functional Services defined.

◆ Raw: Number of external facing Functional Services defined.

◆ Raw: Number of internal facing Data Services defined.

◆ Raw: Number of external facing Data Services defined.

◆ Raw: % of programmes, projects and initiatives which are defining new services.

◆ Raw: % of programmes, projects and initiatives which are using existing services.

Avoid Under/Over Engineering

We will not under or over engineer solutions.

Rationale:

◆ If solutions are under engineered there is a danger that Enterprise will not reap the benefits associated with an architecturally driven approach i.e. reuse and flexibility is not free and has to be designed appropriately into solutions.

◆ If solutions are over engineered there is a danger that projects and systems can drown in the drive to achieve the perfect solution or the increased costs and timescales do not warrant the perceived benefit created.

◆ A balance needs to be achieved.

Implications:

◆ Costs, timescales, how the solution is constructed, the functionality it provides and how that functionality is provided need to be considered as a whole in the context of the four EA Strategies (aka the spinning plates of Cost, Flexibility, Risk and Quality).

◆ The key to allow this to occur is the three party partnership behind the successful adherence to this principle, represented by:

- ◆ Project Manager   - Cost & timescales.
- ◆ Architect   - How the solution is engineered.
- ◆ Business Analyst   - What functionality the solution contains.

◆ These roles should exist as a true partnership with no one partner being able to overrule the other and with each role being equally concerned and mindful of the 4 EA Goals. Where common agreement cannot be reached, this principle will be violated and the Transformation Debt™ Agreement process will begin.

◆ This will require considerable discussion and agreement to break down the usual "The Project Manager rules the roost" mentality and to provide the environment where this important cultural change can happen.

Metrics:

- ◆ Survey of PM's, BA's and TA's - "Do you think that PM's, BA's and TA's are working together as an equal partnership or does one role seem to have more power than the other? If so which ones?"
- ◆ The number of answers where one role is shown to have more 'power' than the others.

Reuse

We consider and favour the reuse of existing people, processes, locations and technology over buying, adopting or creating anything new.

Rationale:

- ◆ Reuse is the key to low costs.
- ◆ Must be balanced against increase complexity that reuse introduces.

Implications:

- ◆ A repository of what exists and the relationships between them needs to be maintained.
- ◆ This can be difficult and can be viewed as introducing complexity, risk and cost. However, if these risks and costs are weighed against the longer term benefits and costs it usually is in the best interests of the Business to reuse wherever possible.
- ◆ Reuse of standard things is favoured over reuse of bespoke things.
- ◆ Reuse of bespoke things should only occur when there is a compelling business expediency to do so.

Metrics:

- ◆ Raw: The number of times things are reused.

Buy (for reuse) Before Build

We buy Services (for reuse) before buying packages (for reuse) before building (for reuse) .

Rationale:

- ◆ There is no reason to re-invent the wheel.
- ◆ Where possible, the Enterprise should lever existing and future functionality offered by IT companies instead of bespoking IT.
- ◆ Please see the sub principles for more detailed Rationale.

Implications:

- ◆ Buying (for reuse) means that whenever an individual programme, project or initiative identifies the need to purchase, the requirements and the eventual decision on what is purchased is considered from a more holistic strategic perspective.
- ◆ The individual programme, project or initiative may encounter a higher cost (both in terms of evaluation as well as licensing and ongoing cost) than it would have if it only considered its own scope.

- For selection, the 80/20 rule applies, favouring Services/Packages which satisfy 80% or more of requirements as opposed to a built Services/Package which satisfies near to 100%.
- A best of breed approach should generally be followed. However, the numbers of existing vendors, services and packages already in use should be taken into account. i.e. One solution may not be best in breed but is favoured because the vendor is already being used to provide other services or packages.
- Vendors supplying other Services/Packages which may be of interest at a later time should be favoured. Services/Packages that have the capacity to be extended or additional modules purchased should be favoured.
- Please see the sub principles for more detailed Implications.

We buy Services (for reuse) before Building.

Rationale:

- Externally supplied services managed through SLAs tend to be cheaper and make an Enterprise more agile.
- This should be tempered by the commodity vs specialist nature of the system being sourced and the security, resilience of the service and the company providing it.
- Services that can also provide programmatic access (e.g. using web services technologies) should be favoured over those which provide a purely user interface.

Implications:

- Vendors supplying other services which may be of interest at a later time should be favoured. Services that have the capacity to be extended or additional modules purchased should be favoured.
- Procurement processes may have to change radically to enable this.
- Integration aspects need to be carefully considered.

We buy Packages (for reuse) before Building.

Rationale:

- Packaged applications tend to be far cheaper to produce and to support and maintain than bespoke applications.
- However, this should be tempered by the commodity vs specialist nature of the system being sourced.

Implications:

- Vendors supplying other capabilities which may be of interest at a later time should be favoured. Systems that have the capacity to be extended or additional modules purchased should be favoured.

We Build (for reuse).

Rationale:

- Bespoke development tends to be the most costly option in terms of up-front costs and support and maintenance costs.
- Bespoke developments tend also to be the most risky for non-software house based companies.

Guidance

♦ Bespoke development can produce significant competitive advantage and so tends to be only considered for USP type functionality or when the functionality required does not exist in the market place. If this is the case, it may be prudent to consider a partnership with a software house to jointly develop a new package that can subsequently be sold.

Implications:

♦ Where a requirement cannot be satisfied by a COTS system or where the requirement for competitive advantages dictates a build solution, a build should be adopted.

♦ The 80/20 rule applies regarding the scope and complexity of the solution.

♦ The system being built should (as much as practicable) allow for easy extension and additions, and also allow the potential to be re-used by other parts of the Business.

♦ A generic and/or data driven application that can easily be extended and re-used should be favoured.

♦ Should adhere to defined quality standards. For example the system should be fully documented to enable it to be supported or changed up by other developers at a later date.

Metrics:

♦ Raw: The number of COTS services in use.
♦ Raw: The number of COTS packages in use.
♦ Raw: The number of bespoke systems in use.
♦ Derived: The ratio of COTS Service to COTS Package to Bespoke.

Guidance

Artefact Principles

Artefacts Must Be Complete, Sufficient and Comprehensible

We ensure that all artefacts used are of the quantity, quality and format required by the person using the artefact.

Rationale:

- Artefacts are used by one process to perform an action.
- Artefacts used by a process that are not of the required quantity, quality and format, greatly increases the risk of that process producing bad outputs.
- If those artefacts are decisions, bad decisions can end up being piled upon bad decisions.

Implications:

- Whether an artefact is Complete, Sufficient and Comprehensible is determined by the person who will use the artefact not by the person that produces the artefact.

Metrics:

- Raw: Number of artefacts labelled "satisfactory" by those that use them.
- Raw: Number of artefacts labelled "unsatisfactory" by those that use them.
- Derived: % of "satisfactory" artefacts.

Structured Modelling

We hold and manage information in structured rather than unstructured forms.

Rationale:

- If information is held in unstructured forms, there is a great risk that it cannot be reused, related to information it depends on or related to information that depends on it.
    - Reducing the ability to relate information and see a clear line of sight between it, greatly increases the risk of making bad decisions.
- If information is held in unstructured forms, there is a great risk that any problems it contains will not be seen and corrected until much later.
    - Seeing problems much later than when problems are introduced greatly increases the risk of wasting resources and the risk of not achieving what was planned.

Implications:

- Appropriate Tools and Processes will be required.
- It can take longer to create and work with information in structured forms.
- Increase time and resources will likely be required.

Metrics:

- Raw: Amount of information in use, stored in unstructured forms.
- Raw: Amount of information in use, stored in structured forms.
- Derived: % of unstructured vs structured information in use.

Relationships & Traceability

We ensure that Information (Structural & Transformational) used for transforming the Enterprise is related.

Rationale:

- Relationships are the key to understanding the impact of change which enables informed decisions.
- IT consists of a large number of different things (e.g. applications, databases, objectives, technologies, etc).
- In addition IT operates within a business context of different things (e.g. business processes, people, locations, requirements, objectives, etc).
- Whilst these things are important it is the relationships between them that allow the best decisions to be made and allow IT to make sure that what it does has concrete business value. (e.g. mapping Business Objectives to Requirements to Solutions, etc)
- The relationships allow impact analysis and the implications of decisions to be made clear.

Implications:

- A repository and various tools (EA Modelling, Requirements Analysis, Portfolio Management, etc) are required to enable these different things and their relationships to be modelled effectively.
- There will be a learning curve to be able to use these tools.
- There will be a population curve while the information is initially loaded.

Metrics:

- Raw: Is there an appropriate EA modelling tool in place?
- Raw: % of the Enterprise using the EA Model.
- Raw: % complete of the Strategy domain model.
- Raw: % complete of the Business domain model.
- Raw: % complete of the Technology domain model.

Have a Sound Business case

We ensure that all projects are supported by a sound business case which addresses the total cost of ownership, plus any wider impacts on the Business and IT.

Rationale:

- All too often projects are initiated without a clear definition of the costs, benefits and therefore the true value of a proposition.
- Whilst costs and benefits are defined these values can often be "invented" to make the Business case stick and can also often miss the wider strategic and ongoing costs.

Implications:

- There are no IT projects, there are only Business projects that have a mixture of IT Change and Business change.
- All business cases need to articulate business benefits in business terms

♦ In order for ball park costs to be reasonably representative, a high level view of the solution options and lifecycle costs must be produced at an architectural level.

♦ This view can be produced in a very short space of time, by engaging with architects and business analysts. If it is not possible to determine a broad brush set of options and representative costs, it means that the initial business case would be for an investigation/feasibility study of possible solutions and associated costs, rather than for the solution which would then be contained in a later business case.

Metrics:

♦ Raw: % of programmes, projects and initiatives that have a business case.

♦ Raw: % of programmes, projects and initiatives that include solution options

♦ Raw: % of programmes, projects and initiatives that include lifecycle costs.

Items (Technology) Principles

Cultural Principles

Disagreement <> Confrontation

We ensure that any disagreement is taken as a positive opportunity for learning.

Rationale:

- In general, people can see disagreements as confrontations.
- In general people really hate confrontations and tend to do anything and everything to avoid them.
- That does not mean that they do not tell anyone, it just means they tell the wrong people.
- Allowing disagreements, rather than seeing them as confrontations to be avoided, allows people to understand and learn from one another and get to the bottom of any disagreement, instead of burying them.
- If we bury disagreements, they will only rear their head later where more damage will have been done.

Implications:

- Hearing disagreement can be challenging and threatening to some people.
- Everyone, regardless of their pay grade will be impacted.
- Some people may not like this principle if they have in the past, are used to being able to ignore anyone who disagrees with them.

Metrics:

- Raw: The number of times "Because I said so" is used.

Explain Decisions

We ensure that "...because I said so" will never be used as the reason or rationale for any decision.

Rationale:

- Allowing "because I said so" as a reason for decisions is deeply damaging to the Enterprise as a whole and to individuals. Allowing it shows people that there is no point in asking "why".
- It promotes a good culture to make sure people understand why decisions are been taken.
- This does not mean that all people will be happy with all decisions.
- If people understand the reason for a decision, they will accept the decision more readily even if they do not agree with it.

Implications:

- It takes time and energy to explain reasons to people.
- Some people may not like this principle if they have in the past been used to saying "Because I said so".
- This does not imply that every decision will be explained to every person. What it means is that if someone has reason to ask why a decision is being made then that decision will be explained.

Metrics:

- Raw: The number of times "Because I said so" is used.

Record Decisions

We ensure that people understand why decisions are made and that the reasons for those decisions are recorded.

Rationale:

- "You can please some of the people all of the time, you can please all of the people some of the time, but you can't please all of the people all of the time." - John Lydgate.
- A lot of "non-acceptance" of decisions stems from people not understanding why a decision was made.
- If decisions are explained, a lot of peoples "problems" with those decisions are likely to vanish.
- Explaining why decisions are made helps people accept them, and make them work.
- Even if people still do not like a decision, if they can see the rationale behind a decision, they are much more likely to "run with it".

Implications:

- It is the responsibility of the person making a decision to explain that decision to those who are affected by it.
- Requires time and resources.
- People need an environment that allows then to feel comfortable and to have the mandate to ask for decisions to be explained.
- Management needs to create that environment.

Metrics:

- Raw: Number of decisions taken.
- Raw: Number of decisions documented.
- Derived: % of documented decisions.

Consider Context & Implications

We ensure that all decisions are based on understanding the context that causes them to be made and the implications that making them create.

Rationale:

- Decisions made without first seeing and then understanding the full context, greatly increases the risk of making bad decisions.
- Decisions made without first seeing and then understanding the full implications, greatly increases the risk of making bad decisions.

Implications:

- The Context for Decisions must be documented.
- The Implications for Decisions must be documented.
- Appropriate Tools and Processes will be required.

- ◆ Increased time and resources will likely be required.

Metrics:

- ◆ Raw: Number of decisions made that did not consider the full context and/or implications.

Work Smart not Hard

We concentrate on expending the 20% of the effort that provides 80% of the benefit.

Rationale:

- ◆ "The Pareto principle", "The law of the vital few" or "The principle of factor sparsity" state that, for many events, roughly 80% of the effects come from 20% of the effort.
- ◆ If we concentrate on addressing the 20% that provide us with 80% of the benefits we will be as effective as we can reasonably be, whilst still allowing for further improvement.

Implications:

- ◆ Requires time and resources.
- ◆ People need an environment that allows then to feel comfortable and to have the mandate to think-out-of-the-box.
- ◆ Management needs to create that environment.

Metrics:

- ◆ Raw: Number of instances where the 8020 rule is applied.

Consider Efficiency

We consider how things are done, rather than only what things are done.

Rationale:

- ◆ The Enterprise will always have finite resources.
- ◆ Those resources are precious, and the return on their use must be maximised.
- ◆ What the Enterprise does, is not so much of a differentiator as how it does, what it does.
- ◆ Efficiency is a key to strategic success.

Implications:

- ◆ Requires time and resources.
- ◆ People need an environment that allows then to feel comfortable and to have the mandate to consider efficiency.
- ◆ Management needs to create that environment.

Metrics:

- ◆ Raw: Amount of resources spent on efficiency.

Consider Important Non-Urgent Work

We break the negative feedback loop of always spending more time on Important Urgent Work (Firefighting) to the detriment of Important Non-Urgent Work.

Rationale:

♦ Increasing time spent on Important Non-Urgent work, tends to reduce the amount of time subsequently required to deal with Important Urgent work (Firefighting).

♦ Reducing the amount of time dealing with Important Urgent work (Firefighting), tends to increase the amount of time available for Important Non-Urgent Work.

♦ Prevention is better than cure.

Implications:

♦ Requires time and resources.

♦ People need an environment that allows then to feel comfortable and to have the mandate to consider Important Non-Urgent work.

♦ Management needs to create that environment.

Metrics:

♦ Raw: Amount of resources spent on efficiency.

Consider Things of Fundamental Importance

We spend more time thinking more deeply about fundamental things and getting those things correct.

Rationale:

♦ Concentrating on things of Fundamental Importance are likely to yield better decisions and better outcomes than ignoring them or not giving them enough consideration.

♦ If you do not get fundamentals right, it is likely to cause serious problems further down the line.

Implications:

♦ Can be subjective.

♦ Requires time and resources.

♦ People need an environment that allows then to feel comfortable and to have the mandate to Consider Things of Fundamental Importance.

♦ Management needs to create that environment.

Metrics:

♦ Raw: Amount of resources spent on Considering Things of Fundamental Importance.

Consider the True Value of Things

We look deeper into things to see where true value lies rather than only looking at things with obvious value.

Rationale:

♦ .

Implications:

- ◆ Requires time and resources.
- ◆ People need an environment that allows then to feel comfortable and to have the mandate to Consider the True Value of Things.
- ◆ Management needs to create that environment.

Metrics:

- ◆ Raw: Amount of resources spent on Considering the True Value of Things.

Prioritize Substance over Style

We value the content and substance of ideas and argument over and above the way those ideas or arguments are communicated.

Rationale:

- ◆ The way something is said or a message is delivered can unduly influence those listening to and affected by it.
- ◆ The Halo Effect can mean that a decision with dubious value could be accepted.
- ◆ The Horns Effect can mean that a decision with great value could be rejected.
- ◆ "If the honourable gentlemen would pay more attention to what I am saying, rather than how I am saying it, he might receive a valuable education in spite of himself" - Margaret Thatcher.

Implications:

- ◆ People need to feel comfortable expressing their opinions even though they may not be delivered in a "professional" manner.
- ◆ People need to focus on the content of opinions rather that their delivery.
- ◆ Management needs to create that environment.

Metrics:

- ◆ Raw: The number of times substance is wins out over style.

Consider Future Benefit

We consider things from the point of view of future benefit rather than only in terms of short term benefit.

Rationale:

- ◆ Short term benefits satisfy the craving for low hanging fruit and immediate gratification, however, not balancing immediate needs for more longer term needs will usually cause longer terms problems that can easily outweigh short term gains..

Implications:

- ◆ Requires time and resources.
- ◆ People need an environment that allows then to feel comfortable and to have the mandate to Consider Future Benefit.
- ◆ Management needs to create that environment.

Metrics:

♦ Raw: Amount of resources spent on Considering Future Benefit.

Expose Individual and Contrary Opinion

We seek out and hear people with opinions that are contrary to the opinions of people that have more "seniority" or contrary to the opinions of the majority.

Rationale:

♦ Being senior does not mean that someone is right.
♦ Being in the majority does not mean that someone is right.
♦ Innovation and progress can come from seeing things that others cannot.
♦ If we do not allow (demand) contrary opinion, the risks of making bad decisions are greatly increased.

Implications:

♦ People in power may feel very uncomfortable allowing contrary opinions to be heard.
♦ People understanding that being in the majority does not automatically mean they are right.
♦ People need to feel comfortable and able to express contrary opinions.
♦ Management needs to create that environment.

Metrics:

♦ Raw: The number of contrary opinions heard.

Change Actions and Beliefs over Perceptions

We don't allow cognitive dissonance to corrupt decisions.

Rationale:

♦ Cognitive dissonance theory is based on three fundamental assumptions:
  ♦ Humans are sensitive to inconsistencies between actions and beliefs.
  ♦ Recognition of this inconsistency will cause dissonance, and will motivate an individual to resolve the dissonance.
  ♦ Dissonance will be resolved in one of three basic ways:
    ▪ Changing ones **Belief**.
    ▪ Changing ones **Actions**.
    ▪ Changing ones **Perception**.
♦ It is inherently very hard for people to change their Beliefs - otherwise they would not be Beliefs.
♦ It can be very difficult for people to change their Actions (one type of action is a decision)
♦ It is very easy for people to change their Perceptions to justify a Belief or an Action regardless of how erroneous the Belief or Action may be.

Implications:

♦ People will feel very uncomfortable changing their Beliefs or Actions.
♦ People need to fee that changing their Beliefs or Actions is seen as a positive rather than a negative.

- ◆ An environment will be required that stop people feeling uncomfortable.
- ◆ Management needs to create that environment.

Metrics:

- ◆ Raw: The Number of Beliefs that have changed.
- ◆ Raw: The Number of Actions that have changed.

Don't Jump to Conclusions

We don't unnecessarily jump to conclusions.

Rationale:

- ◆ A general (insatiable) appetite for quick wins and doing things faster can cause people to make snap decisions.
- ◆ Decisions that are taken without the required information to make them are not decisions, but arbitrary guesses.

Implications:

- ◆ "Analysis Paralysis" is a phrase often used when people who want to jump to conclusions or to repress others who may be more wary.
- ◆ Requires time and resources.
- ◆ People need an environment that allows then to feel comfortable spending the time required to make well founded decisions.
- ◆ An environment will be required that stop people feeling uncomfortable.
- ◆ Management needs to create that environment.

Metrics:

- ◆ Raw: The number of decisions that were going to be made incorrectly, but were changed.

Think Strategically

We make decisions to provide maximum benefit to the Enterprise as a whole.

Rationale:

- ◆ Decisions that are made purely from a tactical perspective provide less long term value than those made for the benefit of the Enterprise as a whole.
- ◆ All parts of the Enterprise only exist to enable and fulfil the goals and objectives of the Enterprise.

Implications:

- ◆ Some short term goals may need to be sacrificed in preference to larger and more strategic goals.
- ◆ Some projects may need extra funding to achieve this.
- ◆ IT systems and services will be evaluated in terms of the benefits to the whole Enterprise rather than to satisfy the needs of a particular project or group.

Metrics:

- Raw: Number of decisions which produce a multi project, multi department benefit as opposed to a singular benefit.
- Raw: The number of Applications shared across boundaries.
- Raw: The number of Services shared across boundaries.
- Raw: The number of Components shared across boundaries.

No Bullying

We make decisions based on rational thinking not on power, control or position.

Rationale:

- Bullying can take many forms, not just physical.
- Bullying: Anyone who holds some kind of power, control or position over someone else, and who uses that power, control or position to force another person to do (or not to do) something.
- Bullying only serves to benefit the individual and damage the Enterprise.

Implications:

- People who are used to using bullying as a tool to get things done will feel very uncomfortable not being able to.
- People who are used to being bullied will feel very uncomfortable exposing it when it happens.
- An environment will be required that stop people feeling uncomfortable.
- Management needs to create that environment.

Metrics:

- Raw: Number of Incidences of Bullying.

Expose Problems

We expose, evaluate and deal with problems when they occur, rather than ignoring or burying them.

Rationale:

- Solving problems as early as possible greatly limits the damage and knock on problems those problems can cause later.
- Hiding "bad news" only serves to benefit the individual and damages the Enterprise.
- Sometimes information can come to light that requires a very large change in what is being done.
- The bigger the problem, the more likely it is for people want to gloss over it and ignore it.
    - Either because they feel they may be looked on as having done something wrong, or because the implications of accepting it will cause an increase or loss of a large amount of time, money, effort, etc.
- However inconvenient and painful the truth is, it is usually an order of magnitude less that the pain that will be suffered later if it is not dealt with.

Implications:

- People who are used to hiding problems will feel very uncomfortable not being able to.
- People who are used to seeing problems hidden will feel very uncomfortable exposing them.
- An environment will be required that stop people feeling uncomfortable.
- Management needs to create that environment.

Metrics:

- Raw: Number of problems exposed.
- Raw: Number of problems hidden.
- Derived: Ratio of problems exposed vs hidden.

Proactive Business Leadership

We ensure that business and IT leadership engage proactively on Transformation planning activities.

Rationale:

- The Business is the key stakeholder, or customer, in the application of technology to address a business need.
- The business needs to be an active participant in order to close the gap between IT and the Business and to allow the Business and IT to operate within a partnership rather than a purely customer/supplier relationship.
- In order to ensure IT is aligned with the Business, all areas of the Business must be involved in all aspects of the IT environment.

Implications:

- To operate as a team, every stakeholder, or customer, will need to accept responsibility and accountability for developing the information environment.
- Commitment of resources will be required to implement this principle.
- The business experts from across the Enterprise and the senior technical staff responsible for developing and sustaining the IT environment need to come together as a team to jointly define their goals and objectives.

Metrics:

- Raw: Does a model of IT and Business leaders involved in Business Planning exist?
- Raw: % of roles, responsibilities and accountabilities defined for each
- Raw: % of leaders that have agreed their roles, responsibilities and accountabilities.
- Raw: Last 4 Quarters: Did the quarterly Business Planning meeting take place?
- Raw: % Business leaders attendance at quarterly Business Planning meetings.
- Raw: % IT leaders attendance at quarterly Business Planning meetings.
- Derived: % attendance at quarterly Business Planning meetings.

Recognise Responsibilities

We recognise and respect the responsibilities of business departments and the IT department.

Rationale:

Guidance

- ◆ Business departments are best placed to define **WHY** something needs to change.
- ◆ Business & the IT Department are best placed, together, to define **WHAT** needs to change.
- ◆ The IT department is best placed to define **HOW IT change** should be implemented.
- ◆ Business departments are best placed to define **HOW Business change** should be implemented.

Implications:

- ◆ Business departments are responsible for explaining to the IT department why something needs to change. If the IT department does not understand, the onus is on the business department to explain.
- ◆ Business departments and the IT department need to work together to determine what needs to change to achieve the desired outcome of a change.
- ◆ Whilst the IT department is always open to any discussions and recommendations regarding how its change processes could be improved, it is the IT department that will decide what processes must be followed to effect IT change and that these processes may impact business timescales and/or costs.
- ◆ Whilst business departments are always open to any discussions and recommendations regarding how its change processes could be improved, it is the business departments that will decide what processes must be followed to effect business change and that these processes may impact IT timescales and/or costs.

Metrics:

- ◆ Raw: % of instances where the IT department is not allowed to follow its change processes.
- ◆ Raw: % of instances where business departments are not allowed to follow their change processes.

> ## KEYPOINT:
>
> When categorising Principles, think in terms of those that guide HOW we effect Transformation (Means).

> ## ADOPTION:
>
> EA Project Team: Create Principles that guide HOW we effect Transformation (Means).

Guidance

Questions to Ponder

- ◆ Has your Enterprise defined principles that guide HOW you effect Transformation (Means)?
- ◆ If not, what problems does that create and what can you do to alleviate them?

KEYPOINT:

The Environment section of PEAF defines 'WHAT' tools and frameworks are required, 'WHERE' and 'WHEN'.

ADOPTION:

C-Suite: Instigate a review of the Tools and Frameworks used for Enterprise Architecture, to determine if their maturity is appropriate.

Questions to Ponder

- ♦ With respect to your Enterprises EA capability, what Environment (Frameworks/Tools) is used?
- ♦ Are those Frameworks/Tools documented? Understood?
- ♦ Are they fit for purpose?
- ♦ Are they used? All the time? Only when it suits?
- ♦ Which of them are Good? Why? Bad? Why?

Items > Frameworks > PEAF

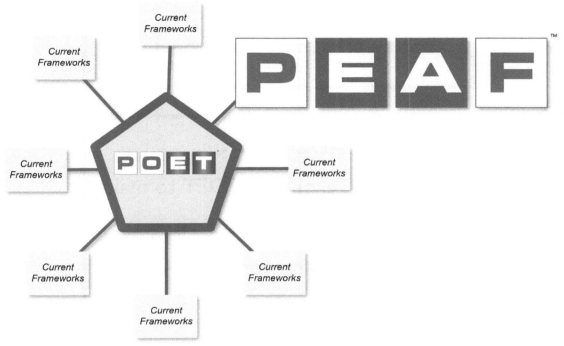

PEAF is obviously the framework in use here, however, we need to make sure that PEAF fits in with the other frameworks the Enterprise uses in the Enterprise Architecture domain (as defined by PEAF.

This section would therefore need expanding to include the frameworks you currently use and information on how they overlap and interact.

POET provides the basis for doing this which allows Executive Management to take a coherent and holistic view of the whole of the Transformation part of their Enterprise, by providing a coherent and holistic MAGIC framework which enables informed decision making about what to change and how.

Items

> ## KEYPOINT:
>
> Frameworks must work together.

> ## ADOPTION:
>
> EA Project Team: Use POET to make sure you know how PEAF integrates with other Frameworks you use or intend to use.

Questions to Ponder

- ◆ What Frameworks do you currently use?
- ◆ How do they relate to each other?
- ◆ Are there any overlaps or gaps?
- ◆ If so, does this present any issues or problems?
- ◆ What will you do to alleviate or solve them?

Items > Tools > Coverage

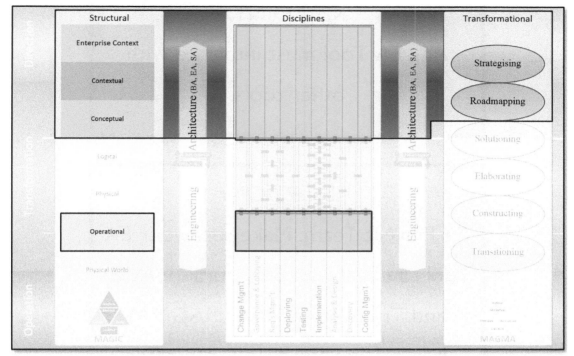

© Pragmatic 365 (2008-2021)

To carry out the work in the EA domain (Roadmapping) effectively and efficiency, tools are mandatory.

There are two fundamental domains (types) of information that any tool needs to be able to work with (Structural and Transformational) and this information is consumed and produced by various Disciplines.

In general (because of their history and initial focus) tools operating primarily on Structural information have tended to be called EA Modelling tools and tools operating primarily on Transformational information have tended to be called EA Planning Tools. This is not a hard and fast rule though as many tools describe themselves using various adjectives - it's not what they call themselves, it's what information they manipulate.

Although the output of "doing" EA is at the conceptual level, an EA Tool needs to also be able to model the Enterprise Context and Contextual levels, in order the EA work to be tied back to the information that drives it. In addition, it should also be able to contain (integrate with) information at the Operational Level (CMDB) in order for any EA work to be based on what actually physically exists within the Enterprise. This Operational information contains valuable information that can be abstracted and represented at these top three levels to allow us to understand how the current capability and operating models map to the physical world.

Items

KEYPOINT:

Any EA Tool must integrate with other tools.

ADOPTION:

EA Project Team: Make sure your EA Tool can deal with Structural (MACE) and Transformational (MAGMA) information and that it integrates with other related tools.

Questions to Ponder

- ◆ Which tools do you currently use for Enterprise Architecture?
- ◆ What domains (Structural/Transformational) do they cover?
- ◆ Are they adequate?
- ◆ If not, does this present any issues or problems?
- ◆ What will you do to alleviate or solve them?

Items > Tools > Vendors

  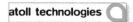 

 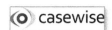  

Commercial   Open Source

Here we present all the EA Modelling tool vendors presently in the marketplace.

Detailed information about the companies, their tools and licensing can be found in the PEAF Toolkit.

Items

KEYPOINT:

Many of the EA Tool Vendors, are not EA Tool Vendors.

ADOPTION:

EA Project Team: Consider, all the EA Tool Vendors in the market.

Questions to Ponder

- ◆ Which Tool Vendors have you heard about?
- ◆ Which Tool Vendors tools have you used?
- ◆ What is your view of each of these Tool Vendors?

Importing	Exporting	Relationships	User Interface / Ease of use
Diagrams / Views	Impact Analysis	Meta-model	Target and Intermediate Models
Management	Supplementary	Expected Views	Expected Dashboards

Here we detail a set of **Pragmatic** requirements for EA Tool selection. These are the most important requirements that need to be met, not an exhaustive list and come under these general headings.

##END##

A. Importing

1	Can .CSV be used as a source?
2	Can .XML be used as a source?
3	Can .XLS be used as a source?
4	Can .MDB be used as a source?
5	Can relationships be imported as a list of the form <primary key1>,<primary key 2>,<attributes>?
6	Can relationships be imported as a grid where <primary key1> is listed across the top, <primary key2> is listed down the side, with an X in intersecting cells indicating the presence of a relationship?
7	Can .VSD be used as a source?
8	Can the objects be mapped to entities in the Meta-model and imported as such?
9	Can the connectors be mapped to relationships in the Meta-model and imported as such?
10	Is the diagram imported the same type as a diagram created within the tool?
11	Can the user import the data without the display properties of the graphics?

12	Can the user import the data with the display properties of the graphics?
13	Can the diagram produced be manipulated in the same way as a diagram that was drawn natively in the tool?
14	Is it possible to perform round-trip engineering via Visio?
15	Can Hierarchical Information be imported of the form <name>,<parent name> where <parent name>'s are previously defined <names>s?
16	Is this hierarchical information imported as entities linked by relationships?
17	Can other types of relationships supported be imported?
18	Can the tool handle conflicts?
19	Is it possible to configure rules to resolve conflicting information being imported from multiple sources?
20	Are there any tools/functionality to enable the synchronisation of entities and/or relationships stored outside the tool (e.g. CMDBs, portfolio management tools, change management tools)?

B. Exporting

1. Can .CSV be used as a target?

2. Can .XML be used as a target?

3. Can .XLS be used as a target?

4. Can .MDB be used as a target?

5. Can relationships be exported as a list of the form <primary key1>,<primary key 2>,<attributes>?

6. Can relationships be exported as a grid where <primary key1> is listed across the top, <primary key2> is listed down the side, with an X in intersecting cells indicating the presence of a relationship?

7. Can .VSD be used as a target?

8. Can Hierarchical Information be exported of the form <name>,<parent name> where <parent name>s are previously defined <names>s?

9. Can other types of relationships supported be exported?

C. Relationships

1. Are relationships a fundamental type?

2. Are there fundamental types such as Hierarchy, Composition etc that a relationship can be based on?

3. Are all relationships stored as relationship entities linked to the related entities rather than attributes on entities?

4. Can I view and manipulate relationships visually by creating, deleting and moving lines between entities?

5. Can I use a matrix to view, create, delete and modify all non-hierarchical relationships?

D. User Interface / Ease of use

1. Can I use a combination of the thumbwheel and the shift and ctrl keys (or equivalent) to easily pan and zoom diagrams (ala Visio)?

2. Can I drag/create graphics (representing entities) onto the diagram and then immediately be able to move things without having to change the drawing tool into a select tool?

3. Do open windows auto update when changes in other windows are made?

4. Is there a fully featured (Diagrams, entities, properties, fully hyperlinked) "viewer" interface for consumers of the model to use to navigate the model that allows viewing but not updating?

E. Diagrams / Views

1	Can I define the graphic used to display entities on diagrams?
2	Can I define the properties to be displayed on the graphic?
3	Can I define the appearance (font, colour, size, alignment) of the properties displayed on the graphic?
4	Can I fully define the location of each attribute on the graphic?
5	Can the displayed properties be conditionally set (e.g. make the text colour red if a property of the associated entity equals a value)?
6	Can I define the graphic used to display relationships on diagrams?
7	Can I define the properties to be displayed on the graphic?
8	Can I define the appearance (font, colour, size, alignment) of the properties displayed on the graphic?
9	Can I fully define the location of each attribute on the graphic?
10	Can the displayed properties be conditionally set (e.g. make the text colour red if a property of the associated entity equals a value)?
11	Can I define different properties to be displayed on the beginning and ends of the graphic?
12	Can I define different properties to be displayed on the middle of the graphic?
13	Are all predefined entities provided with associated graphics?
14	Are all predefined relationships provided with associated graphics?
15	Can I create fully configurable custom diagrams (e. g. Management Dashboard View)?
16	Can I model processes using BPMN (e.g. Activities, processes)?
17	Can I model Data using logical ER diagrams (e.g. to model business data models)?
18	Can I create a diagram, drop any number of entities of any number of types at any level of abstraction, and have the tool draw in the relationships?
19	Can I use that diagram to change the relationships and entities?
20	Can I automatically navigate the data at varying levels of detail where the relationships of those lower levels are summarised and displayed as relationships as there are expanded or collapsed?
21	Can I assign entities to a "group" and then have the tool draw a bounding polygon showing the entities in the group and those without? Can I do multiple groups?
22	Do I have access to various tools to help me layout diagrams (e.g. arrange as Hierarchy, horizontally, verticals, block, circle, star)?
23	Do diagrams automatically update when the underlying data changes (I.e. text changes, addition or removal of entities and relationships)?
24	Can I use "layers" on diagrams?
25	Are there built-in views/dashboards/reports/questions available for the Business?

	(see "Expected Views & Expected Dashboards" Sections)
26	Are there built-in views/dashboards/reports/questions available for the Finance dept? (see "Expected Views & Expected Dashboards" Sections)
27	Are there built-in views/dashboards/reports/questions available for the IT dept? (see "Expected Views & Expected Dashboards" Sections)
28	Are there built-in views/dashboards/reports/questions available for Suppliers? (see "Expected Views & Expected Dashboards" Sections)
29	Are there built-in views/dashboards/reports/questions available for B2B Customers? (see "Expected Views & Expected Dashboards" Sections)
30	Are there built-in views/dashboards/reports/questions available for Governance? (e.g. Compliance to principles, polices, etc)

F. Impact Analysis

1	Can I perform impact analysis by navigating a hierarchical textual representation of the model?
2	Can I perform impact analysis by navigating a hierarchical graphical representation of the model?
3	Is it possible to view the deltas between different versions of a model?

Items

G. Meta-model

1	Does your Meta-model cover Strategy (e.g. Vision:Goals:Objectives, Mission:Strategies:Tactics, Policies:Rules, etc)? List the entities provided.
2	Does your Meta-model cover Assessment Architecture (e.g. Trends, Influences, SWOT's, etc)? List the entities provided.
3	Does your Meta-model cover Business Architecture (e.g. Products, Sectors, Segments, Services, Customers, Enterprise, Locations, Activities, Processes, etc)? List the entities provided.
4	Does your Meta-model cover Information/Data Architecture (e.g. Business Data Model, Logical Data Model, etc)? List the entities provided.
5	Does your Meta-model cover Technology Architecture (e.g. Services, Applications, Datastores, Databases, Technologies, Devices, etc)? List the entities provided.
6	Does your Meta-model cover Governance (e.g. Principles, Policies, Waivers, etc)? List the entities provided.
7	Do you provide an easily navigable Meta-model documentation consisting of a high level view with the ability to drill down?
8	Can I change the Meta-model visually?
9	Can I add and remove new entities?
10	Can I add and remove new relationships?
11	Can I add and remove attributes to existing and user defined entities?
12	Can I add and remove attributes to existing and user defined relationships?
13	Is the Meta-model totally flexible or are there limitations? (If so what are they?)
14	Can attributes be simple (e.g. text, number, list, date, money)?
15	Can attributes have rules associated (e.g. limit number of chars, limit numbers/dates to a defined range)?
16	Can attributes be complex (e.g. an attribute consisting of a group of attributes)?
17	Can I automatically navigate the model using TOGAF as a navigation structure?
18	Can I automatically navigate the model using Zachman as a navigation structure?
19	Can I define new navigation structures?

H. Target and Intermediate Models

1	Does the model fundamentally understand and support the concepts of target and intermediate models and the special relationships between them?
2	Does the model offer specific functionality for the definition, management and analysis of target and intermediate models and the gaps between them?

I. Model Management

1	Are all changes to the model subject to version control and management?
2	Is it possible to "check out" whole models?
3	Is it possible to "check out" partial models?
4	Does it allow branching and merging of entities, relationships and diagrams?
5	Is there any workflow built in to allow the acceptance or rejection of changes to the model through a lifecycle (e.g. discussion, draft, authorised, published)?
6	Can I load inconsistent and/or missing attributes into the model and then use the tool to manage the consolidation and completion of the data?
7	Can I generate syntax, semantic and consistency, and completeness reports?

J. Supplementary Questions

1	Does the tool possess Application Portfolio Management capability or do you have another tool that does?
2	Do you have any out of the box integrations with 3rd part APM tools?
3	Does the tool possess Configuration Management Database (CMDB) capability or do you have another tool that does?
4	Do you have any out of the box integrations with 3rd party CMDB tools?
5	Does the tool possess Governance capability or do you have another tool that does?
6	Do you have any out of the box integrations with 3rd party Governance tools?
7	Does the tool possess Business Process Analysis and Simulation capability or do you have another tool that does?
8	Do you have any out of the box integrations with 3rd party BP Analysis and Simulation tools?
9	Does the tool possess Business Intelligence (BI) capability or do you have another tool that does?
10	Do you have any out of the box integrations with 3rd party BI tools?
11	List the EA Frameworks supported and describe how they are supported.
12	Describe/Illustrate the architecture of your tool including the use of any 3rd party software.
13	List the modelling notations supported and indicate any 3rd part products used to provide the functionality.
14	List any standard queries/reports (textual or diagrammatic - please indicate which for each).

K. Expected Views
(Does the tool provide answers to these questions)

1	What are the average costs for applications that support a particular business process?
2	What fundamental architectures are being used and numbers of each type?
3	What is the split between COTS and bespoke applications?
4	How many FTE's are requirement to support an application?
5	What applications support a business function?
6	What applications are not covered by a DR plan?
7	What applications or technologies are candidates for rationalisation
8	What applications are the most costly (value based)
9	What applications are the most important to the business
10	What are the transition plans for an application / process / etc
11	What are the recurring costs of an application
12	How critical is an application to a business process
13	How many users depend on an application
14	What is the usage profile/roadmap for an application
15	What skills are required to support an application
16	Which applications have the greatest impact on the business
17	Who are the business and technical owners for an application
18	Who are the owners of applications with no DR plans
19	Who is using an application

L. Expected Dashboards
(Does the tool provide these dashboards)

1	Executive Dashboard: Project Portfolio Impact Executive Summary
2	Executive Dashboard: Demands Executive Summary
3	Executive Dashboard: Portfolio Complexity Summary
4	Executive Dashboard: Goals and Strategy Executive Summary
5	Executive Dashboard: Spend Alignment Executive Summary
6	Executive Dashboard: Revenue Views of customers, segments, sectors, products, etc
7	Business And IT Executives: Business Demand
8	Business And IT Executives: Projects alignment to strategies
9	Business And IT Executives: Spend related to business need
10	Business And IT Executives: Programmes and projects roadmap
11	Programme and Financial planners: Applications related to Business Capability
12	Programme and Financial planners: Enterprise Application Roadmap
13	Programme and Financial planners: Spend related to Business value
14	Enterprise architects: Analysis of interrelationships
15	Enterprise architects: Model Enterprise
16	Enterprise architects: Ensure data is complete and accurate and up to date
17	Enterprise architects: Define Future State
18	Enterprise architects: Plan State transitions
19	Enterprise architects: Principles and policies related to goals and objectives
20	IT: Understand technology roadmap
21	IT: Analysis of interrelationships
22	IT: Impact Analysis
23	IT: Manage risks

Demonstrations

After short listing a set of Vendors/Tools by using the requirements defined in the previous section, it is important to receive demonstrations of each where a more qualitative assessment can be made.

The aim of demonstrations is not so much to find out if a tool does or does not provide a particular function but more to determine how well functions are provided.

There can be widely differing methods of particular functions provision. For example, one tool may be able to perform a function with one click of the mouse. Another tool performing the same function may require 10 button clicks.

The other point to consider is that because this assessment is qualitative it is also largely subjective. One person's view of what "sub-optimal" means may be very different to what someone else's view is.

The criteria below is to be used for this qualitative assessment and is a measure of how well the functionality/capability is provided (Qualitative)

- ◆ **Poor**   Provided for via a sub-optimal, indirect or unnecessarily convoluted way
- ◆ **Good**   Provided for but has some limitations or usability issues that makes its use sub-optimal
- ◆ **Excellent**   Provided for in a very good manner but wouldn't be called "Best in class". Some room for improvement
- ◆ **Outstanding**   Provided for in the best possible way. "Best in Class". If you were to write it from scratch this is how the functionality would be provided

The following items are deemed most pertinent for demonstration.

A. Importing

Show	Import a VSD + roundtrip if supported
Show	Conflicts and management/resolution
Describe	How Integration with CMDB works

B. Exporting

| Show | Relationship export as a grid |

C. Relationships

| Show | Creating/modifying/deleting relationships by editing a diagram |
| Show | Relationship matrix editor |

D. User Interface / Ease of use

| Show | Pan and zoom |
| Show | Viewer for freeform navigation of the model |

E. Diagrams / Views

Show   Graphic designer including relationships (lines)

Show   Custom views - e.g. dashboard

Show   Drop entities, let tool show relationships - save, change entities does diagram auto-update. Navigate/display at higher levels of abstraction

Show   Layout tools; hierarchy, star, block, align, etc.

Show   Built in Views/Dashboards

F. Impact Analysis

Show   Impact analysis

Show   Deltas between versions of a model

G. Meta-model

Show   Meta-model structure; Strategy, Guidance, Business, Information, Technology, Governance

Show   Meta-model navigation/discovery

Show   Making changes also Types of complex sets/groups of data

Show   Model mapping to Zachman, TOGAF, others

H. Target and Intermediate Models

Show   Current, Target, Intermediate and tools around them

I. Model Management

Show   Version control, management, check-in/out

Describe   Branching and Merging

Show   Workflow

Show   Management of inconsistent/missing/invalid imported data

Show   Syntax, semantic and consistency, and completeness reports

Items

X. Additional considerations.

XA - Tool Architecture

Show   XA1. Single Object Table

Show   XA2. 1st Order Relationships

Show   XA3. Heterogeneous Hierarchy

Show   XA4. Foreign Keys Relations

Show   XA5. Plain Text Encoding

Show   XA6. Time as a Fundamental

XC - Tool Configuration and Maintenance

Show   XC1. Bulk Upload

Show   XC2. Structured Upload

Show   XC3. Open ERD

Show   XC4. Graphical Meta-Model

Show   XC5. Hybrid Metamodels

Show   XC6. Flexible Notation

Show   XC7. Tool Integration

Show   XC8. Concerns & Viewpoints

XF - Tool Functionality

Show   XF1. Meta-Data Inheritance

Show   XF2. Dangling Relationships

Show   XF3. Explorer Drag And Drop

Show   XF4. Explicit Variants

Show   XF5. Analytic Charts

Show   XF6. Quantitative Analytics

Show   XF7. Catalogue Data Management

Show   XF8. Round Trip Engineering

> # KEYPOINT:
>
> When evaluating EA modelling tools,
>
> use a good set of requirements.

> # ADOPTION:
>
> EA Project Team: Use the Pragmatic
>
> EA Tool Requirements when
>
> reviewing EA Tools.

Questions to Ponder

- Do you agree with these high level requirement categories?
- If not, which ones would you add, change, remove?
- How would you rank them in terms of importance?

Out of the Box

The requirement **is met** (No Configuration or Customisation required)

Configuration

The requirement **is met** (Configuration is Required)

Customisation

The requirement **can be met** (Customisation is required)

No

The requirement **cannot be met**

Since the answer to most questions posed to a Tool Vendor are likely to be "Yes", it is not a question as to whether a Tool Vendor can satisfy a requirement, it is more in terms **How** they can satisfy a requirement. For this reason, each Tool Vendor was asked to rate their tool against each of the Requirements using a set of categories.

Out of the Box

This is the best way a Tool Vendor can satisfy a requirement. This means that the functionality is built in and can be utilised with no changes at all. Associated costs and risks are zero because no changes are being made. Subsequent releases of the tool can be adopted with no impact.

Configuration

This is the second best way a Tool Vendor can satisfy a requirement. This means that the functionality is built in but requires some configuration to be used, usually through a specific user interface or via configuration files. Associated costs and risks are low because only simple "changes" are being made. Subsequent releases of the tool can be adopted with very little or no impact.

Customisation

This is the worst way a Tool Vendor can satisfy a requirement. This means that the functionality has to be specifically added to the tool by the Tool Vendor. Associated costs and risks are high because changes need to be designed, coded, tested and maintained. This can produce severe problems in adopting subsequent releases of the tool.

> ## KEYPOINT:
>
> Tools that satisfy requirements by Customisation rather than by Configuration or Out-of-the-box, should be avoided.

> ## ADOPTION:
>
> EA Project Team: Ignore EA Tools that satisfy requirements by Customisation.

Questions to Ponder

- ◆ Do you agree with these high level evaluation categories?
- ◆ If not, which ones would you add, change, remove?
- ◆ How would you rank them in terms of importance?

Items

Items > Tools > Evaluation > Raw Scores

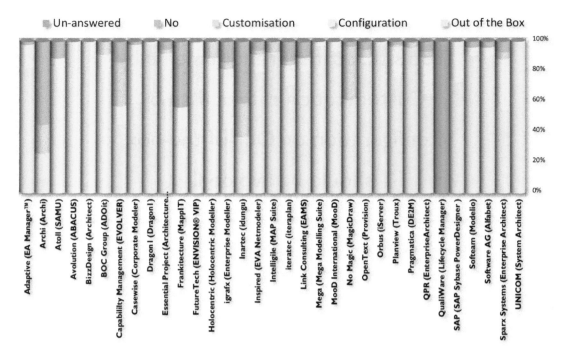

© Pragmatic 365 (2008-2021)

Here we see an overview of the vendor supplied scores against each of the requirements. The evaluation scores have been supplied by the vendors themselves. **Pragmatic** accepts no responsibility for the accuracy of the information presented. Accuracy and correctness of the information rests solely with the individual companies concerned.

This section only contains summary information. The detailed evaluation scores and comments can be found in the Tool Evaluation Excel spreadsheet.

Items

> # KEYPOINT:
> Be aware that many Tool vendors can be very economical with the truth.

> # ADOPTION:
> EA Project Team: Be very sceptical when talking to Tool Vendors.

Questions to Ponder

- If you already use an EA Modelling Tool, how does the tool you currently use fair?
- If you are not currently using and EA Modelling Tool, which Tool Vendors will you shortlist?

Items

Items > Tools > Evaluation > Weighted Scores

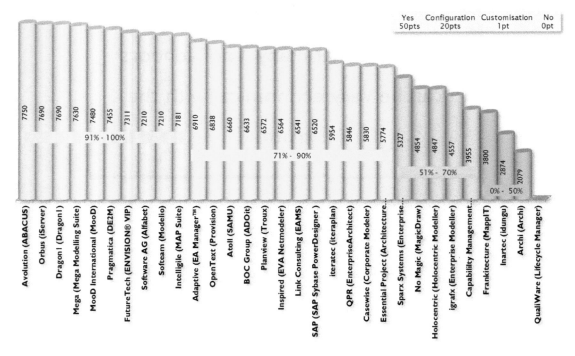

© Pragmatic 365 (2008-2021)

Here we have applied a **Pragmatic** weighting to the base scores.

Tools that can satisfy requirements out-of-the-box or just by configuration are much more favoured over those that require modification.

If you do not agree with these weightings, you can choose your own using the PEAF Tool Vendor Evaluation Toolkit spreadsheet

KEYPOINT:

Weighting vendors to downgrade "customisation" answers can be useful.

Questions to Ponder

- ◆ Do you think this weighting criteria is fair?
- ◆ If not, what weighting criteria will you use?

Items > Tools > Evaluation > X-Requirements

XA Architecture	XC Configuration	XF Functionality
• Single Object Table • 1st Order Relationships • Heterogeneous Hierarchy • Foreign Key Relations • Plain Text Encoding • Time as a Fundamental	• Bulk Upload • Structured Upload • Open ERD • Graphical Meta-Model • Hybrid Metamodels • Flexible Notation • Tool Integration • Concerns & Viewpoints	• Meta-Data Inheritance • Dangling Relationships • Explorer Drag And Drop • Explicit Variants • Analytic Charts • Quantitative Analytics • Catalogue Data Mgmt • Round Trip Engineering

© Pragmatic 365 (2008-2021)

The X-Requirements are fundamental core requirements, that Enterprises should consider applying to Tool Vendors, when evaluating EA Modelling Tools. These are the single most important features that, if not present, will seriously limit your use of a tool. The other detailed Tool Requirements documented elsewhere in PEAF are useful also, however, these much smaller set of X-Requirements can be used as critical gating criteria, to reduce a large number of Vendors down to a smaller set, for detailed evaluation.

They are split into three distinct sections:

♦ **XA - Tool Architecture**

How the tool is fundamentally architected and engineered. Why? Because if that's not done right, it will cause massive problems for all functionality and all users.

♦ **XC - Tool Configuration & Maintenance**

How the tool is Setup and administered by those people who are responsible for setting up all the reusable things such as meta-models, notations, standard viewpoints etc. that everyone else will use.

♦ **XF - Tool Functionality**

Key functionality that must be present if the tool is to be used for Enterprise Architecture.

#####

XA - Tool Architecture X-Requirements

XA1. Single Object Table

There should be a single table of all objects (e.g. Objects, Elements or Components) with their type indicated via a foreign key to a unique list of types, as opposed to an individual table in the database for each object type (i.e. separate Process, Application, Department tables).

Why?	Because without a single table for each object type, the underlying repository is completely rigid, and the inevitable configuring of existing objects for additional attributes or adding of new objects altogether is going to require some serious back-end customization. Not to mention the consequent business logic and presentation layer hacks that will be required. In some cases "spare" tables are provided or attribute "slots" but this is hardly configurable.

XA2. 1st Order Relationships

All relationships between the objects in the repository should be explicitly stored as a different collection of elements in their own right, as opposed to being only on the diagrams, or attributes on objects, or just some specific subset of objects).

Why?	Because without modelling relationships as 1st order entities, a tool fails as a real architecture tool (see IEEE 1471). These sorts of convoluted designs smack of being a kludged together. Most likely, relationships on the diagrams were an afterthought to be stored in the repository with some serious implications including the next few criteria.

XA3. Heterogeneous Hierarchy

The repository should use a heterogeneous hierarchy of objects (and relationships), as opposed to flat collections of objects with (for example) a 'decomposes' relationship between them or only homogenous hierarchies.

Why?	Because with a single flat collection of each object (or relationship) type, none of the principles of information hiding and role-based access are available. Slightly better are approaches that allow homogenous hierarchies where at least objects can be decomposed natively into objects of the same type (e.g. Processes into sub-Processes). These approaches are legacy of 'flatlanders' who simply compose Meta-models as 'boxes and lines' without any use of heterogeneous composition/aggregation or 'boxes within boxes'. Cars have four wheels, an engine, gearbox etc. ... not just sub-Cars.

XA4. Foreign Keys Relations

The relationships between the objects / entities in the repository should be defined and stored in the repository, rather than defined and stored in program or SQL code.

Why? Because if the relationships are stored in the program or SQL code, this creates serious limitations on what relationships can and cannot be defined and if you want to change them, you would have to change program or SQL code rather than just the data in the repository.

XA5. Plain Text Encoding

The objects / entities / tables and relationships in the repository should be coded as decipherable plain text data, as opposed to being binary objects from some other proprietary format.

Why? Because the practice of "wrapping" a proprietary data model as binary objects or other coded data in order to become "SQL Server" or "Oracle" compliant severely reduces the openness of the customer's data that is ultimately being stored there.

XA6. Time as a Fundamental

The repository should:

a) Allow any objects / entities and any relationships to exist in time., rather than just having a "time" attribute attached to them
b) Allow different versions of architectures / scenarios
c) Allow for relationships to exist between architectures / scenarios, rather than just storing different scenarios as separate repositories that cannot be related.

Why? Because EA Modelling tools are built to allow Enterprises to transform things over time. This mandates modelling the structure of the Enterprise at various points in time. It is therefore paramount to be able to model relationships between these different point-in-time models. If time has not been properly considered and designed in to the tool from the beginning (i.e. architected) you will face serious limitations when you come to create and maintain roadmaps and different scenarios - which, after all, is the whole point of an Enterprise Architecture.

####

XC - Tool Configuration and Maintenance X-Requirements

XC1. Bulk Upload

It should be possible for a user to bulk upload 1000's of rows and columns of structured data to the repository in a single step from MS Excel, MS Access and/or MS SQL Server with the base product, as opposed to one-by-one copy-pasting data into forms or requiring professional services support.

Why?	Because users may well assume this to be the case and then be surprised by a large cost required to either enter data by hand or to pay for professional services to do the work.

XC2. Structured Upload

It should be possible to bulk upload objects, relations and attributes all at the same time, as opposed to a single flat collection of an individual object type and their attributes at a time.

Why?	Because, as POET teaches us, "The value is in the lines, not in the boxes". If you can only upload lists of single entities at one time, there is very limited ability to easily build a connected repository.

XC3. Open ERD

Documentation of the complete Entity-Relationship-Diagram (ERD) / Object Model (OM) for the repository should be provided to clients on request, as opposed to being kept secret, and the relationships between the objects / entities / tables should be explicitly defined as relationships in the database technology being used, as opposed to being coded in application logic. It should be clear by looking at the datamodel utilised by the repository how all the tables are related.

Why?	Because if the datamodel (which may or may not include its relationships) is either non-existent or hidden, this profoundly inhibits users from running reports using other external tools of their own without requiring potentially costly professional services fees to achieve it.

XC4. Graphical Meta-Model

It should be possible to use a graphical and navigable representation of the Meta-model(s), as opposed to creating (and maintaining) a dummy set of entities based on that Meta-model or by editing cryptic configuration files.

Why?	Because understanding and maintaining the Meta-model(s) used, is crucial for the correct and streamlined management of an EA Modelling Tool. This can be highly complex, and attempting to do it purely by editing "configuration" text, is fraught with difficulty.

XC5. Hybrid Metamodels

It should be possible to concurrently utilise and relate multiple Meta-model implementations out-of-the-box.

Why?	Because the Meta-model(s) used by any Enterprise will generally be a mixture of Meta-models rather than just one. e.g. P3O + BPMN + Archimate + PEAF + BMM. Without this ability, you will find it extremely difficult to create "your" Meta-model(s) and even more difficult to utilise them effectively.

XC6. Flexible Notation

It should be possible to change the iconography of the Explorer / Object Browser and shapes used for the objects themselves on the diagrams, through simple drag-and-drop operations in the standard UI, as opposed to hacking code or some convoluted editing of a cryptic configuration file.

Why?	Because a lot of the frameworks don't have agreed notations so it is essential that the appropriately trained / skilled users can easily reconfigure the look-and-feel of the views for maximum business impact without needing vendor support or ever writing a line of code of customization.

Items

XC7. Tool Integration

The tool should provide the ability to seamlessly integrate with other tools, and be able to synchronise precisely with the data they contain, without any need for translation or transformation of their data, such that changes made in the EA Modelling tool are pushed out to other tools, and changes made in other tools are incorporated back into the EA Modelling tool, all in a controlled way and without any loss of data.

Why?   Because no tool exists in a void. The tools you choose must cooperate together into a coherent whole. If your EA Modelling Tool cannot integrate and synchronise faithfully and easily with data in other tools (without the need for any transformation of the data) all you will do is create another island of data, with all the risks and costs related to duplication of data, and those data becoming out of date and therefore useless.

XC8. Concerns & Viewpoints

In addition to the obvious requirement for a Metamodel (and the requirement for Hybrid Meta-models) an EA Modelling tool should also allow for the definition of:

    a)   Users - Who will use the tool to answer questions?
    b)   Concerns - What questions do those stakeholders require answers to?
    c)   Viewpoints - How those questions are answered?

Why?   Because as POET teaches us "There is no reason to model anything unless it will be used to answer a question." In order to do that in a reasonably coherent way, the tool also needs to define who wants the question answered, what are the questions that require an answer and how that question will be answered.

#####

XF - Tool Functionality X-Requirements

XF1. Meta-Data Inheritance

It should be possible to define meta-data on a general entity in the repository, that can be inherited and then extended by local object or relationship instances, as opposed to simply having a relationship type called Generalizes or Generalized By (or Specializes / Specialized By or Realizes / Realized By etc) between two existing objects.

Why?	Because a lot of tools provide a 'flat' repository with tables of objects (and possibly foreign-key relationships between them). This approach ignores the concepts of inheritance and meta-data. Invariably these tools are then kludged to provide a specific relationship type called 'Generalizes' or 'Realizes' between two existing objects. This approach does not exploit the benefits of inheritance including efficiency, meta-data re-use and specialization.

XF2. Dangling Relationships

It should be possible to detach the end of a relationship from an object on a diagram and leave it unattached (i.e. 'hanging in space') and then re-attach the same end of the relationship to a different object.

Why?	Because if a tool merely has a drawing SDK on top of a RDB it is probable that only some of the drawing features are 'linked' to the RDB. For example, to allow there to be a detached relationship at some point in time on a diagram (as a minimum) the relationships need to be explicitly contained in the repository (not just an 'attribute' of the objects) and there needs to be tight coupling between the diagrams and the repository.
	If a user cannot detach then re-attach relationships, when you inevitably want to change the attachments, the user will have to delete and recreate them, losing all the information associated with the relationship, and its occurrence in any other views.

XF3. Explorer Drag And Drop

It should be possible (using the "Explorer" or "Object Browser") to re-order items in any way using simple drag-and-drop, as opposed to, for example, just a forced sorting of alphabetical 'A-Z' or 'Z-A'.

Why?	Because there is often a logical ordering to the group of objects that isn't alphabetical, e.g. Business - Information - Application - Technology. If the sorting is forced, then you end up prefixing all the objects with a numerical index to control the sort order.

XF4. Explicit Variants

It should be possible to explicitly model variants / scenarios / what-ifs / options etc as separate collections of (the same baseline) objects relationships and views, as opposed to just 'tagging' the one set of objects / relationships with flags saying which variant they are in.

Why?   Because just 'tagging' objects seriously limits the amount of difference / gap analysis that is possible, and more or less negates the ability to do trade-off analysis at all.

XF5. Analytic Charts

It should be possible for the tool to produce standard charts like pies, lines, bars etc.

Why?   Because if the tool can't produce simple charts, it may struggle to produce other more complicated diagrams or analytics.

XF6. Quantitative Analytics

The tool should allow for quantitative ways of analysing the information in the repository, not only simple analytics such as "how many", but more detailed analysis for KPIs from the Financial (e.g. Total Cost of Ownership (TCO), ROI, NPV) to the Technical (e.g. Resource Utilization, Response Times, Availabilities) to the environmental (e.g. Carbon Footprint, Resource Re-use, Sustainability, Heat & Power Consumption).

Why?   Because the purpose of an EA Modelling tool is to model various Structural states of an Enterprise and to quantitatively analyse the differences between them, for the purposes of:

a) Roadmapping - Analysing differences between states at different points in time - for the purpose of creating a roadmap to move from one state to another, and
b) Options - Analysing differences between states at the same point in time - for the purpose of selecting which one is more appropriate.

XF7. Catalogue Data Management

It should be possible to manage a catalogue / list of elements (e.g. objects, entities, relationships) and their properties natively in the tool, as a tabular list of data through the standard UI, as opposed to hacking into or querying the back-end repository / database (assuming it's possible to understand).

Why? Because tabular data entry / management is fundamental to efficient portfolio management of data around objects / relations, and simply providing a single form / screen per object and relationship for data editing, is going to guarantee data obsolescence very quickly.

XF8. Round Trip Engineering

It should be possible to export information into Excel and Visio, allow someone to edit that data, and then reimport the changes they made back into the repository.

Why? Because Excel and Visio are widely used applications that most people are familiar with and most Enterprises already own. To be able to lever this existing investment and to give people information in a format they are familiar with allows many more people to be involved with the creation, maintenance and consumption of the information in the repository.

Items

> # KEYPOINT:
>
> X-Requirements are the key when assessing EA Modelling Tools.

> # ADOPTION:
>
> EA Project Team: Use the X-Requirements as the key gating criteria when assessing EA Modelling Tools.

Questions to Ponder

- Do you agree with these high level X Requirements?
- If not, which ones would you add, change, remove?
- How would you weight them in terms of importance?

> # KEYPOINT:
>
> The Culture section of PEAF defines the "The roles and the culture required.

> # ADOPTION:
>
> C-Suite: Instigate a review of the Culture used for Enterprise Architecture, to determine if its maturity is appropriate.

Questions to Ponder

- ♦ With respect to your Enterprises EA capability, what Culture exists?
- ♦ Is the Culture documented? Understood?
- ♦ Is it fit for purpose?
- ♦ Are they used? All the time? Only when it suits?
- ♦ What parts are Good? Why? Bad? Why?

Culture

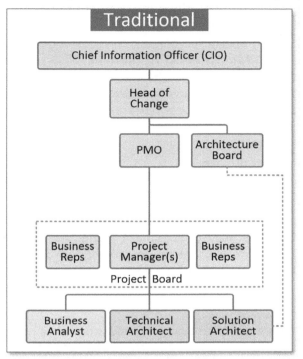 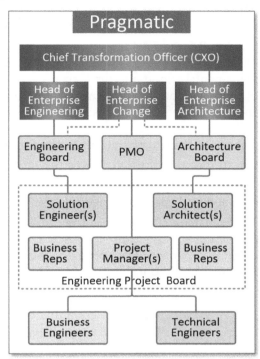

© Pragmatic 365 (2008-2021)

Although Enterprise Architecture has more to do with Roadmapping than Project Execution, EA still has a role on projects and that is one of Governance & Lobbying. Since much damage can be inflicted upon an Enterprise by how Projects execute, EA also has a remit to make sure the relationships in "projectland" work together cohesively.

Traditional Model

Any project today tends to be run with three key roles. The names may change from Enterprise to Enterprise or from country to country but broadly speaking these three roles exist:

- ◆ The **Business Analyst** is accountable for the Functional Fitness for purpose, takes Functional Requirements as input, and produces a Changed processes and provision of a functional capability as output.
- ◆ The **Technical Architect** is accountable for the Technical fitness for purpose, takes Non-Functional Requirements as input, and produces a Operating hardware and software as output.
- ◆ The **Solution Architect** is accountable for the whole logical design of the solution, taking the Conceptual Designs produce by Enterprise Architects as input and produces a Logical Solution Design as output.
- ◆ The **Project Manager** is accountable for the Project Budget and Deadlines, takes a Project Plan as input and produces a Completed Project as output.

Traditional

In the traditional model usually found in most Enterprises, the relationships are usually dysfunctional.

In spite of these dysfunctional relationships (which is at the expense of the Enterprise as a whole) things tend not to change because the people with the power required to change them are usually the ones that are incentivised to perpetuate them.

The SA, BA and TA "report" to the PM, with the PM being "in charge". The PM's voice is the loudest and tends to overrule the SA, BA and TA most (99%) of the time. This creates fundamental and important (negative) implications, but since the PM is not measured on any of them, he doesn't really care. And why should he, if that is how he is driven. This is normal and understandable, because everyone agrees that most projects these days run over time, budget etc, etc and therefore we need a "good" hard PM to keep everyone in check and make sure the project hits its budgets and timescales.

It is strange therefore that given this structure most projects fail.

The truth is that while this "power structure" is imposed to ensure projects complete on time and on budget, it is precisely this structure that causes them to fail. Doh!

The fundamental problem in the Traditional model, is that the work of the Solution Architect can discover significant problems or opportunities that could fundamentally change the project, other projects or even the Enterprise Architecture in operation. The Solution Architect must go to his boss (the PM) and try to convince him to either:

- Remove work from his project and put it in another existing project, then make his project dependent upon that project.
    - This never happens because PM's do not like being dependent on other things that could influence the success (time and budget) of their project.
- Remove work from another project and put it in his project, then make the other project dependent upon his project.
    - This never happens because PM's do not like having extra work added to their project that could influence the success (time and budget) of their project.
- Remove work from his project and put it in a new project, then make his project dependent upon that project.
    - This never happens because a) starting a new project requires a full cost/benefit analysis to be done and the project portfolio and budgets have already been agreed and cannot be changed and b) because PM's do not like being dependent on other things that could influence the success (time and budget) of their project.

And so, many serious problems, that could be fixed, are ignored and the project fails, while the PM and management still say it succeeded.

Alternatively, the unsolved problems cause so much knock-on effect that the project has to extend its deadlines and ask for more budget, while the PM and management still say it succeeded.

Alternatively, un-grasped opportunities do not make the savings or benefits they could have, while the PM and management still say it succeeded.

Alternatively, all of the above.

Pragmatic Model

In the **Pragmatic** model, the work of Solution Architecture (5-10% of most projects overall budget?) is taken out of projects. Projects therefore become Engineering projects and do not even start until the work of the Solution Architect is nearing completion.

In this way, all the problems identified in the Traditional Model (and witnessed by be on every single project I ever worked on as a Solution Architect over 20 years) are solved. All fundamental architectural concerns, problems and opportunities are ironed out without the hindrance of Project Managers.

In addition, we have renamed Business Analysts to Business Engineers because Business Analysts do not only Analyse, they also Design, largely at the physical level (composition/decomposition is used extensively, and composition/decomposition is not architecture). We have also renamed Technical Architects to be Technical Engineers because a) they are largely dealing with physical designs not logical designs and b) the Architecture title is given to many very experienced engineers, and c) to match the Business Engineer moniker.

KEYPOINT:

Solution Architecture is too

important to be owned by Projects.

ADOPTION:

Management: Move Solution

Architects work out of projects.

Questions to Ponder

- Does your Enterprise have SAs reporting to PMs?
- Does it create any problems?
- If so, what do you need to do to solve them?
- Do your Project Boards hear from the PM and SA or just the PM?
- If not does this cause any problems or issues?
- If so, what do you need to do to solve them?

Type 1	Type 2
Improving EA	**"Doing" EA**
Increases Enterprise Architecture Maturity	Strategic Transformation Planning and Governance

© Pragmatic 365 (2008-2021)

There are two types of Enterprise Architects:

- ◆ **Type 1** - This type of EA is responsible for increasing an Enterprises Maturity in its use of EA.
- ◆ **Type 2** - This type of EA is responsible for "doing" Enterprise Architecture.

Most (99.999%) Enterprises only ever recruit for a Type 2 Enterprise Architect - and therein lies the problem…

Whilst the job of the Type 2 EA is massively important and the things they produce are of massive benefit to the Enterprise, they are, in most cases, severely limited by the context of MAGIC that they are forced to work within.

But I hear you cry:

> "A good workman never blames his tools"

This is a common saying ("tools" = "context") and does have some validity.

However, it is also true to say that if you force a surgeon to:

- ◆ Save money – by not washing his hands before an operation (**Immature Methods**),
- ◆ Save money – by using untested blood and medicine (**Immature Artefacts**).
- ◆ Save money – by not following the guidance of the GMC (**Immature Guidance**).
- ◆ Save money – by using carving knife instead of a scalpel (**Immature Items**).
- ◆ Save money – by not living the Hippocratic Oath (**Immature Culture**).

You can hardly complain when patients keep dying.

Stopping patients dying is not achieved by replacing the Surgeon with another surgeon operating (no pun intended!) in the same context. Stopping patients dying is achieved by

Culture

improving the Methods, Artefacts, Guidance, Items and Culture that they are forced to work within.

It is not in the Surgeon's power to increase the maturity of the Methods, Artefacts, Guidance, Items and Culture that surgeons are forced to work within, that is the job of Management -either with the guidance of Surgeons (hopefully!!) or by Management giving the Surgeons a mandate and resources to do so themselves.

I say hopefully because the National Health Service (NHS) in the UK demonstrates time and time again Management's utter lack of involving and listening to people who actually do the work regarding how to increase its maturity. But this is only one sad example of a much bigger cultural problem which exists all over the world today. A culture which effectively says, that people who are more senior are the ones who somehow magically know how to improve things. This used to be the case many decades ago when the Manager did know everything because he did the job himself for 40 years before he became the Manger, but in the 21st century Managers do not get appointed on that basis. They get appointed for all manner of strange reasons, all of which do nothing to help them actually do their job properly.

As we have said before, every Enterprise is already "doing" EA (operating on patients), it's just a question of their maturity in **How** they do it.

And in the same way that a surgeon cannot improve his context without a mandate, the same is true of a Type 2 EA. If the Type 2 EA's job description does not give him a mandate to increase maturity, then he is doomed to work within the constraints of his predecessor and almost certainly produce the same results. This always seems to come as a complete shock to Management who then blame that EA and go recruiting for a "better" one. Doh!

What is happening is that Management (because of Cognitive Dissonance) is actually ignoring the fundamental problem - which is themselves!

> "We have seen the enemy, and the enemy is us!"
>
> *- W.E.Deming*

We could also say:

> "A good manager never blames"

KEYPOINT:

Recognise that there are two types of EA: 1. Those that improve how EA is done. 2. Those that "do" EA (Strategic Transformation Planning and Governance).

ADOPTION:

Management: Ensure everyone in the Enterprise understands that there are two types of Enterprise Architect.

Questions to Ponder

- Does your Enterprise recognize these two types of EA?
- How much time is spent on the duties of Type 1 vs Type 2?
- If you spent more time improving EA, would that reduce the amount of time spent "Doing" EA?

Culture

Purpose	Works With	Term
Helps an Enterprise to increase their EA maturity	Executive Management and the EA Team	Typically transitory / consultant

Focus	Qualitites	Behaviours
Communication, guiding and mentoring	Pragmatic, Enthusiastic, Agnostic, Articulate, Persistent, Strategic, Altruistic, Diplomatic, Open, Generalist.	Persuade, Learn, Investigate, Abstract, Expose, Facilitate, Lead.

EA Experience	Business Experience	IT EA Experience
Detailed	General	General

It is possible for one person to fulfil both roles (if given the mandate to do so), however, they are different in some fundamental respects.

The Type 1 Enterprise Architect's main role is not to "do" EA but to increase an Enterprises maturity in its use of EA - to ultimately allow those who "do" EA to be more effective and efficient.

This type of EA does not need any detailed business or IT knowledge, but they do need detailed knowledge about the EA profession, EA Frameworks and how to increase an Enterprise's EA maturity. That can come from their own innate knowledge and experience (a framework - even though it doesn't have a name and is not written down), from a published framework such as PEAF, or more likely a mixture of the two.

They can work in any type of Enterprise and can be equally as effective. It doesn't matter to a Type 1 EA whether the Enterprise is a bank, an oil company, a medical centre, the tax office, a university, an aircraft manufacturer, a hotel, an online retailer or a dog grooming company.

How transformation is effected and how its maturity can be increased is independent of the type of Enterprise. How Transformation is effected and the approach to the Transformation of Transformation is the same. What will ultimately be transformed (the Enterprise) can be very different but How transformation is effected is fundamentally the same irrespective of the type of Enterprise.

This type of EA therefore, is not an expert in your Enterprises Operations. They are (should be) an expert in the Enterprise called Transformation - that exists within all Enterprises. When interviewing for this type of person it is futile to ask questions such as "How much Banking Experience do you have".

KEYPOINT:

Type 1 Enterprise Architects help an Enterprise to increase their EA maturity.

ADOPTION:

Management: Ensure everyone in the Enterprise understands what a type 1 EA does.

Questions to Ponder

- ◆ Do you agree with these basic requirements for a Type 1 EA?
- ◆ If not, what would you change?

Strategising	Evangelise the benefits of EA. Expose the fundamental problem and opportunity and propose the fundamental solution.
Roadmapping	Evangelise the benefits of EA. Work with the EA project board to select an EA framework.
Solutioning	Evangelise the benefits of EA. Train the EA Team in the selected Framework. Work with the EA Team to a) articulate the EA vision and gain buy in from business and IT leaders across the organisation. b) define the EA Risks and mitigation strategies
Elaborating	Support the EA Team to a) Document the organisation's current EA maturity, b) define a target maturity level and the benefits of attaining that level, c) define a detailed implementation plan
Constructing	Support the EA Team to a) mitigate the risks, b) define the target Methods, Artefacts, Guidance, Items and Culture, c) define the transition plan
Transitioning	Support the EA Team to rollout the changes to the Methods, Artefacts, Culture and Items

© Pragmatic 365 (2008-2021)

The Type 1 EA is involved in Transformation. Not the Transformation of Operations (What the Type 2 does) but the Transformation of Transformation.

As such he also follows the standard Transformation phases of Strategising, Roadmapping, Solutioning, Elaborating, Construction and Transitioning, but these phases should not be confused with the phases in the context of the work a Type 2 EA does. For example, the Type 1 Roadmapping work is not concerned with creating the Roadmaps of the Enterprise, it is concerned with the roadmap to increase the Enterprise's Maturity in its use of EA.

Hence the phases we refer to here are the phases of the maturation of the EA capability.

> ### KEYPOINT:
>
> Type 1 Enterprise Architect's work, is primarily to; 1) Evangelise the benefits of EA. 2) Support the internal EA Team to mature how EA is performed.

> ### ADOPTION:
>
> Management: Ensure everyone in the Enterprise understands what a Type 1 Primary Tasks are.

Questions to Ponder

- Does anyone in your Enterprise perform these duties?
- If not, who will perform them?
- Are there people in your Enterprise already capable of performing these duties?
- If not, where will you get them from?

Purpose	Works With	Term
Strategic Transformation Planning and Governance	Strategic planning team & EA Steering Group	Typically permanent

Focus	Qualitites	Behaviours
Transformation Planning and Governance	Pragmatic, Enthusiastic, Agnostic, Articulate, Persistent, Strategic, Altruistic, Diplomatic, Open, Generalist.	Persuade, Learn, Investigate, Abstract, Expose, Facilitate, Lead.

EA Experience	Business Experience	IT EA Experience
General	Deatiles	Detailed

© Pragmatic 365 (2008-2021)

The Type 2 Enterprise Architect's main role is "do" EA for which he/she needs detailed (architecturally) Business and IT knowledge.

They need to really understand whatever the primary business role of the Enterprise is (be it a bank, an oil company, a medical centre, the tax office, a university, an aircraft manufacturer, a hotel, an online retailer or a dog grooming company) but also the Enterprise Context that that Enterprise Operates within.

They also need to really understand the place of IT within the Enterprise but also in the Enterprise Context in terms of vendors, products, services and technologies - both old, existing and upcoming - as part of their job is to highlight Technology Catalysts where a particular vendor, product, service or technology is exposed to the senior business executives that might provide competitive advantage.

```
KEYPOINT:

Type 2 Enterprise Architects do

Strategic Transformation planning.
```

```
ADOPTION:

Management: Ensure everyone in the

Enterprise understands what a type 2

EA does.
```

Questions to Ponder

♦ Do you agree with these basic requirements for a Type 2 EA?
♦ If not, what would you change?

Strategising	Evangelise the benefits of EA. Contributing to the Enterprise Strategy (Business & IT). Supporting the modelling, structured description, and the relationships between the parts of the Enterprise Strategy (Business, Motivation & Capability models)
Roadmapping	Evangelise the benefits of EA, Creating the Enterprise Transformation Strategy (Current, target and intermediate Capability and Roadmap models). Lobbying up to Strategising Phase, highlighting missed problems and/or opportunities.
Solutioning	Governance down to Project Execution, ensuring strategic guidance is followed. Accepting Lobbying up from Projects when missed problems and/or opportunities are discovered by Projects
Elaborating	Supporting
Constructing	Supporting
Transitioning	Supporting

© Pragmatic 365 (2008-2021)

The Type 2 EA is involved in Transformation. Not the Transformation of Transformation (What the Type 1 does) but the Transformation of Operations (or Support or Direction).

As such he also follows the standard Transformation phases but is only concerned with the Strategising, Roadmapping and Solutioning phases and the Governance and Lobbying between them. He may be required to participate in subsequent phases but only usually when there is a panic or specific strategic guidance is required.

KEYPOINT:

Type 2 Enterprise Architect's work,

is primarily to; 1) support

Strategising. 2) perform Roadmapping

3) Govern executing projects.

ADOPTION:

Management: Ensure everyone in the

Enterprise understands what a Type

2 Primary Tasks are.

Questions to Ponder

- Does anyone in your Enterprise perform these duties?
- If not, who will perform them?
- Are there people in your Enterprise already capable of performing these duties?
- If not, where will you get them from?

"In many organizations, despite any rhetoric to the contrary, **people are rewarded for dealing with crises and problems**. The MVP is the one who came in at 3 a.m. to fix a problem, or who reacts instantly to the customer's complaint. Such an organization overlooks the fact that these MVP's are putting out fires that **either they set themselves and/or they failed to do anything to prevent**. Then when we promote the MVP, **we wonder why nobody follows any processes** and everyone is always too overloaded to get anything right the first time. Why? **Because that is the behaviour that is rewarded."**

- Douglas Brown (*Chief PMO - US Department of Defense*)

© Pragmatic 365 (2008-2021)

Here we see a very insightful quote from the Chief PMO of the US DoD.

It's something insidious, that happens within almost every Enterprise. Insidious because on the surface, it appears to be a laudable thing. Something to be celebrated. Who could say that a White Knight who rides in on a White Charger and saves the day, is a bad person?

But it's not the White Knight that is the problems. It is the environment (culture), that rewards people who put out fires but vilifies people who want o stop fires being started in the first place. And the culture is set by the management.

> ## KEYPOINT:
>
> While "firefighters" are always necessary, more resources need to be brought to bear as "fire prevention officers".

> ## ADOPTION:
>
> C-Suite: Reward those who prevent fires, as much as those that put them out.

Questions to Ponder

- ◆ How does your Enterprise reward people for dealing with crises and problems?
- ◆ How does your Enterprise reward people that try to prevent crises and problems?
- ◆ What will you do to change your Enterprise's approach?

- # Personal Motivation

- # Career Outlook

- # Financial Motivation

Here we compare "The Management" and "The Workers" in various ways. Obviously the comparisons shown here will not apply to every Manager and every Worker in every Enterprise. For example, there will be managers who stay at one Enterprise the whole of their life, and there will be Workers that change jobs every two years. It is also accepted that there can be in many cases a blurring between "The Management" and "The Workers".

This section just highlights the general differences that can exist. Whether they do or not, and to what extent, will depend on each individual Enterprise.

You are invited to create your own depending upon the specifics of your Enterprise.

Personal Motivation

- ♦ Management
    - ♦ Short term.
    - ♦ Driven by challenge and money.
    - ♦ Know that they will probably not be around when any long term problems they create come to pass, and therefore concentrate solely on today's problems.
- ♦ The Workers
    - ♦ Long term.
    - ♦ Driven by stability and money.
    - ♦ Know that they will probably have to deal with any long term problems that are created and therefore try to "head them off at the pass" whenever they can by highlighting them to Management.

Career Outlook

- ♦ Management

- Generally look to move on to a different Enterprise every 2 or 3 years.
- They recognise that career development mostly comes from changing Enterprises and not from promotion within an Enterprise.
- A move to another Enterprise is seem as an exciting new challenge.
- The Workers
  - Generally look for stability and to stay at one Enterprise for long periods.
  - Things have to get pretty bad before they do anything about changing Enterprises.
  - A move to another Enterprise is seen as a worrying and disrupting event.

Financial Motivation

- Management
  - Short Term.
  - Bonuses based on this year's achievements and paid almost immediately.
- The Workers
  - Long Term.
  - Bonuses based on this year's achievements and usually paid over long periods to avoid the possibility that large numbers of employees will leave after they get their bonus.

> # KEYPOINT:
>
> You cannot change what you don't understand and you cannot understand what you cannot see.

> # ADOPTION:
>
> EA Project Team: Model the culture between the Management and Workers.

Questions to Ponder

- In which ways would you compare "The Management" vs "The Workers"?
- How does the personal motivation of "The Management" and "The Workers" in your Enterprise compare?
- How does the career outlook of "The Management" and "The Workers" in your Enterprise compare?
- How does the financial motivation of "The Management" and "The Workers" in your Enterprise compare?
- Does that create any tensions or problems or issues?
- What do you need to do to solve them?

Culture > IT vs "The Business" > Is IT Special? > What vs How

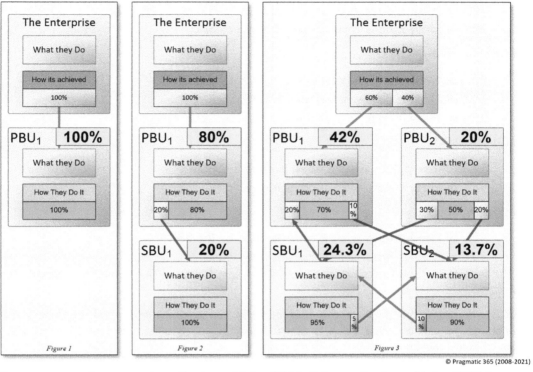

Figure 1   Figure 2   Figure 3

© Pragmatic 365 (2008-2021)

An Enterprise is split into various Business Units (BUs). Primary Business Units (PBUs) equate to those Business Units that perform the main role of the Enterprise such as Sales, Banking, Drilling oil wells, etc. Supporting Business Units (SBUs) are those which support the PBU's, usually supporting multiple PBU's

Each BU (be it Primary or Support) can be split into two fundamental notional parts.

♦ **What** they do - This relates to the business function they perform - be it selling things, drilling for oil, recruitment, training people, providing financial reports and auditing, etc.
♦ **How** they do it - This relates to how they perform their business function and with what.

Figure 1.

Here the Enterprise has one department - PBU₁.

100% of the **How** is work is carried out, is carried out by PBU₁.

Figure 2.

In a larger more complex Enterprise there may be another department - SBU₁.

While PBU₁ is still responsible for 100% of the **What**, it is now only performs 80% of the **How** - as the other 20% of the **How** is now carried out by SBU₁.

Figure 3.

An even more complex Enterprise may be structured as follows:

♦ PBU₁ is responsible for 60% of **How** the Enterprise achieves what they do.
♦ PBU₂ is responsible for 40% of **How** the Enterprise achieves what they do.

Considering PBU₁

♦ 20% of **How** it does what it does, is done by SBU₁
♦ 70% of **How** it does what it does, it does itself.
♦ 10% of **How** it does what it does, is done by SBU₂

Considering PBU₂

♦ 30% of **How** it does what it does, is done by the SBU₁
♦ 50% of **How** it does what it does, it does itself.
♦ 20% of **How** it does what it does, is done by SBU₂

Considering SBU₁

♦ 5% of **How** it does what it does, is done by SBU2
♦ 95% of **How** it does what it does, it does itself.

Considering SBU₂

♦ 10% of **How** it does what it does, is done by the SBU₁
♦ 90% of **How** it does what it does, it does itself.

On the face of it, PBU₁ looks like the most important BU and PBU₂ looks the second most important. However…

If we work out **How** each of the BUs contributes to doing the work necessary for the Enterprise, we can see that SBU₂ is actually the second most important BU, not PBU₂, in terms of **How** the Enterprise does what they do.

♦ PBU₁ is responsible for 42% of the **How**.
♦ PBU₂ is responsible for 20% of the **How**.
♦ SBU₁ is responsible for 24.3% of the **How**.
♦ SBU₂ is responsible for 13.7% of the **How**.

> ## KEYPOINT:
>
> HOW each part of your Enterprise does what they do, shows the real contribution toward achieving the Enterprises Mission.

> ## ADOPTION:
>
> C-Suite: Instigate an initiative to calculate how much each part of the Enterprise contributes to it's Mission.

Questions to Ponder

- ◆ Does your Enterprise consider what percentage each department contributes to what they do?
- ◆ How many PBUs and SBUs does your Enterprise have?
- ◆ What are their names and what are their relationships?

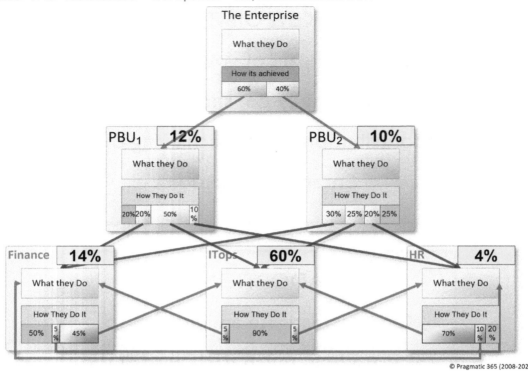

© Pragmatic 365 (2008-2021)

With a third SBU, we are beginning to approximate the complexity of many Enterprises today. We have also replaced the SBU monikers with representative names of Finance, IT and HR.

Essentially we are showing that a large proportion of How the PBUs do what they do, is done by IT. We are also showing that a large proportion of How Finance and HR do what they do, is also done by IT.

Given these percentages we can work out **How** each of the BUs contributes to doing the work necessary for the Enterprise.

(These figures are not entirely accurate because of the circular/recursive nature of them, however, they do illustrate the point, and it's not the accurate numbers that are important but the overall story the numbers are telling us.)

- PBU₁ is responsible for 12% of the **How**.
- PBU₂ is responsible for 10% of the **How**.
- Finance is responsible for 14% of the **How**.
- ITops is responsible for 60% of the **How**.
- HR is responsible for 4% of the **How**.

These percentages are not a reflection of the "importance" of each BU, nor do they reflect how much each BU contributes financially to the bottom line, however it is an important way to look at which areas do the most work. If ITops is doing 60% of the How, why would an Enterprises deem it to be a Cost centre rather than a Profit centre?

In a world before IT, no BU grew so much to completely dwarf other BUs because if it did, it is likely that it would have been divided up into more manageable PBUs or SBUs. When IT first began to be used by Enterprises, the IT BU was only responsible for a very low percentage of the overall **How**.

As time has gone by, the use of IT has grown and grown. More and more of the **How** was taken out of the BU where that work is done and wrapped up in IT systems. In many Enterprises this has now grown to such a point that in the example shown above where ITops is responsible for 60% of the **How**.

So, IT is a special case, but not because it's IT. IT is a special case because it is responsible for the majority of the **How** of an Enterprise.

> ### KEYPOINT:
>
> IT is special not because it is IT, but
> because IT tends to be responsible
> for a large part of HOW an
> Enterprise does what it does.

> ### ADOPTION:
>
> Management: Ensure everyone in the
> Enterprise understands that IT is
> special, but not because its IT.

Questions to Ponder

- Does the Leadership of your Enterprise understand how much IT contributes to the bottom line?
- Does your Enterprise treat IT Operations as a cost centre or a revenue stream?
- What percentages would apply to your Enterprise?
- Which PBU or SBU is responsible for most of the "How they do it" of your Enterprise?

© Frankie Goes to Hollywood

© Pragmatic 365 (2008-2021)

In many Enterprises it may not necessarily be that IT and "The Business" are at war but in most they are most definitely two tribes. This does not necessarily mean there is a problem. It's OK to have two (or many) tribes. It only becomes a problem when one tribe seeks to control the other.

Even if you do not believe or accept that IT and the Business is at war, perhaps it's because it's more of a cold war.

Whatever the status within your Enterprise, the relationship between IT and "The Business" is one of monumental importance and therefore understanding that relationship and improving it should be a strategic aim of the Business.

A Marriage of Convenience

The relationship between IT and the rest of the Enterprise is usually one of uneasy bedfellows. In fact the relationship could be thought of like a marriage than anything else.

It starts out with huge amounts of love and positivity. The two cannot bear to be separated for more than 10 seconds at a time. But as time goes on, they can begin to start to see the cracks and the little annoyances.

Some marriages work well, some do not.

In marriage, one party can get so fed up they find another partner they do like and commit adultery. In Enterprises adultery is represented by parts of the Enterprise sourcing systems and IT for itself or using small consultancies under the wire, working directly for the rest of the Enterprise instead of through IT.

In marriage, when the relationship breaks down irrevocably there is divorce. In Enterprises divorce could be synonymous with outsourcing….which may lead to another marriage…

The thing to remember is that it all comes down to relationships (which basically is all about communication) and if people/groups are flawed in the way they approach relationships (e.g.

Culture

flawed in communication) it doesn't matter how many flings or divorces they have, they will always have relationships that fail. It's not a matter of if, but a matter of when.

> "Men are from Mars, Women are from Venus"
>
> "IT is from Mars, The Business is from Venus"

Mind the gap!

For a marriage to be successful both parties need to work on the relationship on a daily basis. Whether the marriage is between two people, two Enterprises or two groups within an Enterprise. That is why communication is the most important aspect of EA's tenet to "Bridge the gap between the rest of the Enterprise and IT".

In fact that oft used phrase is actually fundamentally flawed. Bridging the gap intimates that the two parts continue to be separate and that there is a gap which needs to be bridged.

EA will not, and does not bridge the gap.

EA helps to reduce and ultimately remove the gap.

There is only a slight change of words but the implications are profound.

Continuing the marriage analogy, you can think of Enterprise Architects (the people), Enterprise Architecture (the process) and Enterprise Architecture (the product) as a kind of marriage counsellor or mediator, helping both parties to find a way to get back in touch with each other. EA, like counselling, doesn't bring answers, it allow the parties to communicate in positive ways so they arrive at their own decisions about how they want to change.

> ## KEYPOINT:
>
> Recognise and deal with the fact that
>
> IT and The Business do constitute
>
> "Two Tribes".

> ## ADOPTION:
>
> C-Suite: Instigate an initiative to bring
>
> the two tribes (Business and IT)
>
> together.

Questions to Ponder

- ♦ Is your IT department at war with "The Business"?
- ♦ Do they work together in a coherent and holistic partnership?
- ♦ Are they somewhere in between?
- ♦ Does that create any tensions or problems or issues?
- ♦ What do you need to do to solve them?

340 - Culture

Culture > IT vs "The Business" > Should IT Ever Say No to "The Business"?

Should IT ever say NO to "the business"?

IT should never say no.

EA does not make decisions.
EA is a facilitator.

IT should always say yes, but...
Pros, Cons, Costs, Risks, Implications.

© Pragmatic 365 (2008-2021)

Should IT ever say "No" to the Business?

In a word. NO! Or, to put it another way **NO. Never. Ever. NO!**

I know what you are thinking...

> "There will be sometimes when we (IT) just have to say no because what
> they want us to do is just plain wrong, illogical, stupid, crazy, etc, etc, etc.
> Like if they asked us to give all their customers a Tablet and expect us to
> maintain them, or if they asked us to remove all the backup storage, or if
> they told us to use COBOL instead of JAVA….."

The point is - who is to decide what is wrong, illogical, stupid, crazy, etc, etc, etc.

"The Business" will have access to much more information than IT and therefore IT will never be in a position to say what they are being asked to do is wrong, illogical, stupid, crazy, etc, etc, etc. From an IT persons perspective things may well look wrong, illogical, stupid or crazy but from the Business perspective things may look so obviously right that they find it hard to understand why IT is saying no and appearing to be trying to block things.

This does not, of course mean that IT will not have an opinion and may offer recommendations, but that is very different.

When IT starts to make decisions and therefore effectively refuses to do what the Business asks of it, it immediately puts IT in the role of a blocker, a problem, a difficult child, a loose cannon, a "difficult person". IT being seen in this light is a major major problem - for IT itself but more importantly for the entire Enterprise.

IT needs to understand its place (and especially the role of EA) is to make "The Business" aware of the implications of what they are asking IT to do. By doing so, IT forces "The

Business" to take accountability for those decisions. If not, the IT department will continue to be its own worst enemy.

The business is in control of an Enterprise but many have lost control of the IT department. EA puts the business back in control of Enterprise Transformation, including the IT department, and at the same time allows the people in the IT department to sleep at night.

The caveat is, of course, if "The Business" bestows on IT the power to make certain decisions within specified limits. If this happens, it is still not IT making the decision. It is still the Business making the decision. IT is merely the messenger, and if problems accepting that decision come about, then it is ultimately the business whose responsibility it is to defend or change it.

> # KEYPOINT:
>
> IT should never say "No" to the Business. It should say "Yes, but…".

> # ADOPTION:
>
> Enterprise Architect: Don't ever say No to the Business.
>
> The Business: Own the implications of your requirements

Questions to Ponder

- Do people in your IT department ever say no to the business?
- Does that create any tensions or problems or issues?
- What do you need to do to solve them?

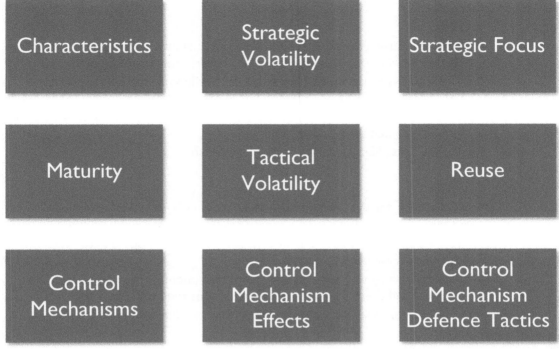

© Pragmatic 365 (2008-2021)

It is useful to analyse the differences between IT and the Business. These are, of course, generalities and need to be reviewed in light of each individual Enterprise.

Characteristics

- ◆ The Business
    - ◆ Analog.
    - ◆ Very grey - no rights or wrongs .
    - ◆ The Business don't want things to be black and white.
    - ◆ Grey is where opportunities lie.
    - ◆ Women - Venus - right brain - intuitive, thoughtful, subjective.
- ◆ IT
    - ◆ Digital
    - ◆ Very black and white - things work or they don't.
    - ◆ IT's ambition is to reduce the grey and increase the black and white.
    - ◆ Grey is where problems lie.
    - ◆ Men - Mars - left brain - logical, analytical, objective.

It in no way asserts that women cannot be logical, analytical or objective.

It in no way asserts that men cannot be intuitive, thoughtful or subjective.

Men and women are equal, but different. In the same way that an apple and an orange are equal but different.

The Business and IT are equal, but different. Instead of pretending they are the same, both sides need to understand the other to be able to work together in harmony. Like a marriage.

Culture

Strategic Volatility

- ◆ The Business
  - ◆ High.
  - ◆ Major strategic change/direction could occur at any time, e.g. legislative change, market opportunity, hostile takeover, acquisition opportunity.
  - ◆ The world is a fast moving environment. Businesses that don't react and react quickly tend to suffer at the hands of those that do.
  - ◆ Therefore The Business wants to be agile and definitely does not want to be tied into a fixed plan/strategy.
  - ◆ The Business likes things to be fluid and flexible.
- ◆ IT
  - ◆ Low.
  - ◆ IT Strategy doesn't really change much from year to year. Technology changes very fast but the IT Strategy tends to be reasonably stable.
  - ◆ The focus tends to be the same and tends to be focussed on cost reduction and service availability.
  - ◆ Strategic change can have a massive and detrimental effect on IT and The Business and there any large strategic changes tend to be avoided.
  - ◆ IT likes things well defined and locked down and prescriptive.

Strategic Focus

- ◆ The Business
  - ◆ Business Verticals - Banking, Manufacturing...
  - ◆ Increase Revenue- Sell more, acquisitions...
  - ◆ Decrease Costs - Use less, outsource, common services
- ◆ IT
  - ◆ IT Service Management - Availability, DR...
  - ◆ IT Project Management - On Time, to Budget...
  - ◆ IT Cost Reduction - Rationalisation, Outsourcing...
  - ◆ IT Planning - Architecture, Roadmaps, Governance...

Maturity

- ◆ The Business
  - ◆ Generally speaking other SBUs and the functions they perform have existed for hundreds of years and have generally not changed much.
  - ◆ The services they provide to PBUs and the SBU's are generally identical.
- ◆ IT
  - ◆ IT is a new kid on the block and as such is not as mature and standardised as the other SBUs.
  - ◆ The services IT provides to other SBUs have not changed much in function but have changed radically in how they are provided and implemented.
  - ◆ The services IT provides to PBUs have changed radically over generally short timeframes and have also changed in how they are provided and implemented.

Tactical Volatility

- The Business
    - Low or High - Small number of changes with potentially massive impact.
    - The Business may make tactical decisions at any time - these tactical decisions at The Business level (although 'simple') could have (or more likely are constrained by) massive changes required to effect the changes required, especially in IT.
- IT
    - High
    - Large number of changes to respond to every little change in the Enterprise.
    - Emphasis on reducing this - key to stopping this is to decouple.

Reuse

- The Business
    - Very low.
    - At a high level
    - The only common/ reused services are Locations, HR, Finance, Procurement and IT, etc, etc.
- IT
    - Very High.
    - At a low level.
    - Servers, databases, applications, data, components, racks, networks, workstations, builds, etc, etc.

Control Mechanisms

- The Business
    - The Business tries to control IT by limiting time, money, resources, the scope of projects or any combination thereof.
- IT
    - IT tries to control The Business by forcing it to be more and more prescriptive with the documentation of its strategies and project requirements.
    - IT also tries to control The Business by forcing projects to comply with a set of prescriptive IT principles, IT policies and IT standards.

Control Mechanism Effects

- The Business
    - The Business views IT as very inflexible and thinks IT is more interested in technology that The Business it is meant to support.
- IT
    - IT views The Business as meddling in their affairs and forcing them to do sub-standard work which The Business then blames IT for.
    - Projects over run timescales and budgets and do not provide the services The Business requires.

Control Mechanism Defence Tactics

- The Business

- ◆ The Business knows that IT will always want more money and time and therefore restricts time and money as a defence tactic.
- ◆ IT
  - ◆ IT knows that The Business will always restrict time and money and therefore inflates project estimates to "counter the cuts".

> # KEYPOINT:
>
> You cannot change what you don't understand and you cannot understand what you cannot see.

> # ADOPTION:
>
> Enterprise Architect: Model the culture between IT and "The Business".

Questions to Ponder

- ◆ How does The Business and IT compare in your Enterprise?
- ◆ Does that create any tensions or problems or issues?
- ◆ What do you need to do to solve them?

Culture

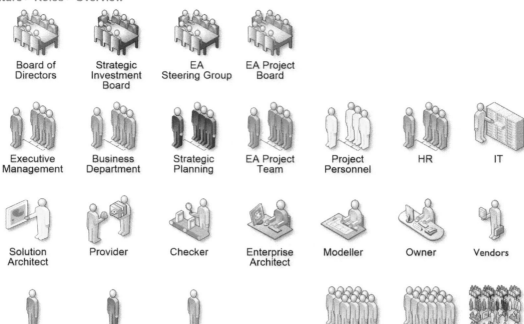

© Pragmatic 365 (2008-2021)

The following table details the graphics used to represent people or groups shown on the PEAF process diagrams.

Boards

Board of Directors (BOD)
The Statutory company board of directors for limited companies or for government bodies/agencies, the group of individuals responsible for setting policy and direction.

Strategic Investment Board (SIB)
A group, with budget, that can decide, or not, to provided extra time, money, people, scope to projects if it would create strategic benefit or competitive advantage.

EA Steering Group (EASG)
A group with powers devolved from the SIB and the BOD which ensures that solutions conform, where appropriate, to strategic principles and roadmaps and ensures that Transformation Debt™ is uncovered and documented.

EA Project Board (EAPB)
The project board of the EA Implementation project.

Groups

Executive Management
The Enterprise wide group of people responsible for turning the Enterprise strategy into reality and managing all work undertaken.

Business Department
Any department in the Enterprise playing a primary business role.
(i.e. Any department not playing a supporting business role)

Strategic Planning
The group of people responsible for annual business planning and the formulation of Business and IT Strategy to support the Enterprise Strategy.

EA Project Team
The group of people tasked with increase the Enterprise maturity in its use of Enterprise Architecture.

Project Personnel
Anyone working on a project. e.g. Project Mangers, Business Analysts, Architects, Developers, etc.

Human Resources (HR)

Information Technology (IT)

Employees

Users

Individuals

Culture

Enterprise Architect - Type 1 (Increasing EA maturity)
Enterprise Architect - Type 2 ("doing" EA)

Solution Architect

Vendor

Provider (Modelling)

This role is Responsible for finding and extracting the information from wherever it currently resides and providing a consolidated set of information to the Checker and tends to be the people who currently use this information.

This role will almost certainly be fulfilled by people already working for Enterprise.

Checker (Modelling)

This role is Responsible for analysing the information and making sure that all the information collected is consistent and correct.

This role will almost certainly be fulfilled by team leaders and managers already working for the Enterprise.

Modeller (Modelling)

This role is Responsible for taking the Quality Controlled information provided by the SME and entering it into the modelling tool.

This role could be fulfilled by individuals already working for the Enterprise (having received appropriate training) or equally could be fulfilled by the tool vendor's professional services team.

Owner (Modelling)

This role is Accountable for keeping the information in the model up to date, consistent and correct.

> # KEYPOINT:
>
> PEAF refers to various roles, most of which will already exist in an Enterprise.

> # ADOPTION:
>
> EA Project Team: Map Pragmatic Roles to your Enterprise's roles.

Questions to Ponder

- Do these roles exist within your Enterprise?
- Are they called the same names?
- Which ones are missing?

Purpose
Release more resources (people, time, money, increased scope, etc) where it is in the best interests of the whole enterprise to do so

SIB

Budget Holding	Escalation Route
Strategic Investment Budget	None

Permanent Members	Transient Members
• Business Directors • CTO/CIO/IT Director • Enterprise Architect	• Project Managers • Solution Architects • Business Analysts

© Pragmatic 365 (2008-2021)

Culture

KEYPOINT:

An SIB with allocated budget and power is mandatory for Governance & Lobbying to operate effectively.

ADOPTION:

EA Project Team: Create a Strategic Transformation Investment Board (SIB) with allocated budget and power.

Questions to Ponder

- ◆ Does your Enterprise have an SIB?
- ◆ If not, does it create any problems?
- ◆ If so, what do you need to do to solve them?

Culture > Roles > EASG (Enterprise Architecture Steering Group)

Purpose
Ensure that solutions conform where possible to strategic principles and roadmaps. Ensure that cross projects synergies are exploited where possible. Ensure that all Transformation Debt™ is exposed. Request more resources (people, time, money increased scope) where it is in the best interests of the enterprise to do so

EASG

Budget Holding	Escalation Route
Delegated from the Strategic Investment Board	Strategic Investment Board

Permanent Members	Transient Members
• Enterprise Architect • Head of Business Change • Business SMEs • Head of IT Development • Head of IT Operations	• Project Managers • Solution Architects • Business Analysts

© Pragmatic 365 (2008-2021)

The Enterprise Architecture Steering Group {{James McGovern}} exists to guide the execution of Transformation as it progresses, and to ensure that any deviations from roadmaps, principles or policies are recognised, understood and evaluated.

> # KEYPOINT:
>
> An EASG with delegated budget and power is mandatory for Governance & Lobbying to operate effectively.

> # ADOPTION:
>
> EA Project Team: Create an Enterprise Architecture Steering Group.

Questions to Ponder

- Does your Enterprise have an EASG?
- Does it hold delegated budgetary responsibility from the SIB?
- Does it have an escalation route to the SIB?
- If not, does it create any problems?
- If so, what do you need to do to solve them?

APPENDIX

KEYPOINT:

The Appendix section contains

information on the background of

PF2, POET, PEAF and the author.

WHY?	• We Care About Enterprises • We Care About the People who Direct, Operate, Transform and Support Enterprises

WHEN?	• PEAF 2008 • POET 2014 • PTMC 2018

WHERE?	• Born from Observing Failure

HOW?	• 150,000 Hours of Thinking • 20,000 Hours of Creating

USING WHAT?	• Architecture, Engineering, Altruism • Honesty, Integrity, Persistence, Passion • Common Sense, Logic

© Pragmatic 365 (2008-2021)

Why Were They Created?

Because I care. Because I care about Enterprises. Because I care about the people who Direct, Operate, Transform and Support Enterprises. Because I am angry about how much time is wasted. Because I am angry about how much money is wasted. From the Afghani to the Zloty, I guarantee you are wasting it. Big time!

This work was inspired by all those who seek to make the world a better place rather than those that seek to own it.

When Were They Created?

PEAF was initially launched in November 2008 and POET in 2014.

Where Did They Come From?

All Pragmatic Ontologies and Frameworks were created from observing failure. That is:

- ◆ Seeing why people fail
- ◆ What problems they encounter
- ◆ Providing things to reduce the risk of others failing in the same way
- ◆ Providing things to alleviate the problems people have.

Around 2002 I began to be interested in something called "Enterprise Architecture". The term started to appear more in publications and people started to talk about it more - although from listening to them there never seemed to be a concrete definition of what it actually was that everyone agreed with (some say that's still the case today!). Using logic and common sense I could surmise that it was not Project level Architecture (because that already had a name - Solution Architecture) and therefore it must be something at a "higher level" - not just bigger. Something related to:

♦ What goes on before projects execute and before Solution Architects start working on those projects.

♦ Enterprise Centric, or more specifically Enterprise Transformation Centric, rather than Project Centric and/or IT Centric.

At that time it all seemed to be a bit of a black art (some say it still is!) and so, being an Architect and not wanting to reinvent the wheel (others call it being lazy!), I surmised that there must be something out there (a bit like Prince or ITIL or MSP for example) - a framework - that might help people to "do" EA by:

♦ Helping people understand what EA was.

♦ Helping people increase the maturity in how an Enterprise "does" EA.

So, I consulted the mighty Google (sorry Oracle!). Google told me about something called Zachman and something called TOGAF. And so I went off to investigate further.

From what I could tell, Zachman's message seemed to resonate well with me in terms of general thinking I had built up over the preceding 20 years, namely:

♦ You can't change what you can't see - hence the need to model things - in a structured way.

♦ There must be Phases involved in Transformation to get from Strategic intent at the top down to real physically deployed things at the bottom.

These basic messages haven't changed and are as valid today as they always were - although the important distinction between Enterprise Architecture and Enterprise Engineering that **Pragmatic** makes today was not (and still is not) recognised in Zachman (despite my attempts to do so). But, whilst these fundamental things (modelling and phases/levels) were a good start, they were much too high level to provide any practical help in using them (which is what a framework is supposed to do) and so I invested more time looking into the much more detailed TOGAF.

As I looked into TOGAF, the first thing that struck me was "Where the hell do I start?". The material was immense, complex, confusing, very dry, hard to consume and offered no guidance about how to adopt it. So, assuming it was my ignorance that was the problem I booked myself on a TOGAF course. Within the first 2 hours of the first day it became clear that it was centred around Project level IT centric Architecture.

Nothing wrong with Project level IT centric Architecture, but not Enterprise Architecture.

Fantastic for those Enterprises that had still not figured out that the complexity of the IT landscape had grown to such a level that using Architecture as a discipline on IT Projects (Solution Architecture) was almost mandatory (unless you wanted to waste a shed load of money and deliver a shed load of bad IT to customers), but not Enterprise Architecture.

Great for those Enterprise that wanted to formalise their Solution Architecture discipline, but not Enterprise Architecture.

Great for those Enterprises that wanted to continue to treat "The Business" as a second class citizen to "IT", but not Enterprise Architecture.

At least not the Enterprise Architecture that logic and common sense dictated to me.

Anyway, I got through the course, passed the exams and became TOGAF Certified. Over the next few years I worked at various organisations and my TOGAF certification served me well in terms of getting me job interviews and most of the subsequent contracts. Having got a contract (because I was TOGAF certified) I then endeavoured to first discover how much and what parts of TOGAF were being used. The conversation (over many days, sometimes weeks) usually went something like this:

> K: "Hi Allen, I'm new here. I've been told that you use TOGAF, can you tell me what parts you are using and which you aren't?"
>
> A: "Hi Kevin, Errrmm, Yeah sure - you need to talk to Steve, he's the one that did the training."

<time passes….>

> K: "Hi Steve, I'm new here. I've been told that you use TOGAF, can you tell me what parts you are using and which you aren't?"
>
> S: "Hi Kevin, Errrmm, why are you asking me?"
>
> K: "Allen told me you did the training and you would know."
>
> S: "Err yeah, but I was only one of the twenty people who did it, I wasn't the main person. Listen - I'm a bit busy on this CRM project at the moment, can you go and ask James about it - I think he was the main guy."

<time passes….>

> K: "Hi James, I'm new here. I've been told that you use TOGAF, can you tell me what parts you are using and which you aren't?"
>
> J: "Hi Kevin, Errrmm, why are you asking me?"
>
> K: "Steve told me you did the training and you were the main guy so you would know."
>
> J: "Err yeah, but I was moved off that onto this ESB project. Listen - I'm a bit busy at the moment, Dave took over that TOGAF thing - go talk to Dave."

<time passes….>

> K: "Hi Dave, I'm new here. I've been told that you use TOGAF, can you tell me what parts you are using and which you aren't?"
>
> D: "Hi Kevin, Errrmm - why are you asking me?"
>
> K: "James told me you did the training and you're now the guy in charge of TOGAF adoption."
>
> D: "Err No! That's Chris, you need to talk to Chris"

<time passes….>

> K: "Hi Chris, I'm new here. I've been told that you use TOGAF, can you tell me what parts you are using and which you aren't?"
>
> C: "Hi Kevin, Errrmm, why are you asking me?"
>
> K: "James told me Dave did the training and he was the guy in charge of TOGAF adoption, but that Dave says it wasn't him, it was you"

> C: "Err Yeah - well I went on the course, but to be honest we never did
> anything about if after that, you should go talk to Allen, he knows what's
> going on"

In every case, after being passed from pillar to post, it always transpired that no one was actually using TOGAF at all.

So, I began to build up my own intellectual capital (documents, checklists, presentations, spreadsheets, ideas, concepts, processes, products, etc) so that I could bring them to bear as a set of quick start artefacts for subsequent contracts.

During 2008 it suddenly dawned on me that all this intellectual capital that I had built up, actually constituted what I thought an EA framework should contain. So, in addition to cleaning up and structuring the material so others could adopt and use it easily, I had to choose a name. So, I thought, what one word would sum up my approach? A core of fundamental things - the 20% that would give 80% of the benefit - that would reduce or remove 20% of the risks that cause 80% of the failures. Cutting through all the smoke and mirrors and Cutting EA to the Bone. And so the name **Pragmatic** chose me.

How Were They Created?

POET and PEAF have taken more than 10,000 hours to produce in terms of physical work, born from approximately 150,000 hours of thinking. The graphics were not just drawn - like most good things they evolved - and while many of them look quite simple, it took an awful lot of work and pain to get to those simple graphics. To an outside observer, those diagrams could appear as if someone just sat down and drew them but each one has had many versions as it has evolved, coalesced, fragmented, reconstituted, gone down the wrong track, fragmented, coalesced again and then finally thrown away, only to be resurrected when a light bulb went on somewhere in the deepest darkest recesses of my feeble brain.

Elegance and simplicity takes a lot of hard work to achieve but, anything **Pragmatic** must be so.

> "Je n'ai fait celle-ci plus longue que parce que je n'ai pas eu le loisir de la
> faire plus courte."
>
> *- Blaise Pascal ("Lettres Provinciales", 1657)*

Which loosely translates to

> "If I Had More Time, I Would Have Written a Shorter Letter"

In fact, the amount of things and work I have thrown away greatly outweighs what now exists.

I believe that POET and PEAF have achieved elegance and simplicity to some degree but, of course, "we don't live in a perfect world" (as so many Managers I have worked for in the past have reminded me on so many occasions) and there is always more work to do. POET and PEAF will evolve, as everything must do, but for now, it is good enough.

With the benefit of time to think of a suitable response to those Managers, my response now would be:

> "We don't live in a perfect world?
> I know - Believe me I know!
> If we did, we wouldn't be having this conversation ;-)"

What Was Used to Create Them?

Basically, common sense. It has always amazed me, how many things in business (and in life) do not seem to adhere to any common sense at all, which probably explains why a lot of things that are created to help people improve or mature something, contain a lot of common sense. In addition I have a brain split into two parts (Architecture and Engineering) that work together but also conflict a lot of the time. But it is from this conflict that progress lies.

Methods

♦ Architecture, Engineering, Logic.

Artefacts

♦ Input - Air, Water, Nespresso, Earl Grey, Toast, Ham Eggs & Chips, Bombay Sapphire (Tonic), Johnny Walker Black Label (Coke Zero), Whiskers, Paper, Ink, Blood, Sweat, Tears.

♦ Output - PF2 Book, POET Book, PEAF Book, **Pragmatic365**.org Website

Guidance

♦ Common Sense, W.E. Deming, J. Zachman, T. Graves.

Items

♦ Biological Technology - Kevin - Generally all of him, but mostly his brain, eyes and hands. (His stomach, colon and bladder put in an appearance occasionally, with his posterior providing a supporting role :-), Murphy the cat.

♦ Mechanical Technology - 25 Buttermere, Braintree, Essex, CM77 7UY, UK, Desk, Chair, Whiteboard (Pens and Eraser).

♦ Electrical - Challenge Fan Heater, Creative GigaWorks T40 Series II 2.0 PC Speakers

♦ Information Technology

♦ Hardware - Dell Latitude E6520 (Intel i7-2760QM @ 2.4GHz, 8GB RAM), 2 * 32in 2560x1600 LED Monitors, 2 * 24in 1920x1200 LED Monitors, HP Officejet Pro X576, Samsung Galaxy Note 8.

♦ Software - MS Windows 10, MS Visio, MS Word, MS Excel, MS PowerPoint, Paint.NET, Integromat, CognitoForms

♦ Languages – VBA, VBscript, Javascript, SQL, ASP, HTML, CSS

♦ Data – (mp3) David Bowie, Pet Shop Boys, Dean Martin, Chris Rea.

Culture

♦ God, Honesty, Integrity, Pragmatism, Altruism, Persistence, Passion, Psychology

> # KEYPOINT:
>
> Use POET and PEAF to make sure
> you don't make the mistakes that
> cause 90% of all EA initiatives to fail.

Questions to Ponder

- Do you think that observing failure is a good way to figure out how to improve things?
- What failures have you witnessed in the past?
- What does that tell you about how to improve it?

- ## Kevin Lee Smith

- ## 40 Years in all phases of Enterprise Transformation

- ## MBTI: (INTJ) Mastermind, (INTP) Architect

- ## DISC: (7414) Result-Oriented

© Pragmatic 365 (2008-2021)

- ## Belbin: Plant, Shaper

Who Created The Pragmatic Family of Frameworks (PF2)?

A simple man.

My career began at the age of 16 in 1978 as an Electrical and Electronic Apprentice with Marconi Radar Systems (Blackbird Road, Leicester, UK) At that time I was really into electronics and had been playing with little circuits for a few years. It was really exciting. I spent my time between college and "The Factory" where I got the chance to work in many different departments. It was really exciting. Around 1980 I ended up in a Department (New Parks, Leicester UK) called TEPIGEN (TElevision PIcture GENerator) who had built the visual system for a ship simulator. Six million Pounds of custom built hardware (that had less processing power than the CPU in the phone that's in your pocket) consisting mainly of four racks of "Picture Processors" (Motorola 68000s) driven by a PDP11. It was really exciting. The output was on three channels each delivering 40 degrees field of view which drove three large Barco projectors. Interestingly at one point there were black speckles that kept appearing on the displays, moving about in random patterns and appearing and disappearing in the same apparently random fashion. After months of software and hardware investigation the problem was identified. It was a test Radar across the apron from where our Portacabins where located that was spraying us periodically with microwaves! It was really exciting.

I began my time there hand entering the data which described the terrain and buildings and which fed the picture processors, and wrote my first program in DEC BASIC. Over the next four years or so my programming skills grew, and I moved from BASIC to FORTRAN and then to PASCAL. It was really exciting. The ship simulator turned into a flight simulator which meant it was the biggest video game in the world. It was really exciting. So much so that I would work late into the night (sometimes 48 hours at a stretch) and go into work on Saturdays or Sundays. Right from the beginning it wasn't so much the code I wrote that I got excited about it was more HOW I wrote the code that interested me. I would often spend hours writing a program and finally get it working, only to tear it to pieces and rewrite it in a

Appendix

new and elegant way, often with more features, less code and more opportunity to reuse things later. It was really exciting. Even at that time I spent more time throwing things away than I spent creating things. I believe this is where progress comes from. Sounds totally counter-intuitive I know, but most things of value are counter-intuitive!

Around 1986 the plug was pulled on TEPIGEN and I moved to another department (Fleet, Hampshire, UK) who produced a system called TELEVIEW (an improvement on Teletext and a forerunner of "The Web") for Singapore's Telecom Company (SingTel). I had moved on to C as a programming language. The most elegant and powerful language I have ever used. It took me a while to understand it but after reading the perfect "The C Programming Language" (Kernighan and Ritchie) the penny dropped. It was really exciting.

A brief spell at SD Scicon (1989-1991) was followed by three years working for Deutsche Bank (Singapore) where I found the best food in the world and where my architectural tendencies came to the fore. It was really exciting. While there I created and sold a numerical analysis package for lottery numbers called Mega4D. Returning in 1994 I spent six years working for Eurobase Systems (Chelmsford, UK) doing Application Architecture and creating Architectural and programming frameworks.

From 2000 to 2011 I spent my time working for various Enterprises as a contractor. While interesting, it wasn't very exciting, but all the time, whatever domain I worked in I was always interested in improving it. Each time this met a limit and the limit was always as a consequence of things being done less than effectively and less than efficiently in the preceding step. Hence my roles moved from Application Architecture, Data Architecture and Technology Architecture into Technical Architecture (a bit of a misnomer!) then Solution Architecture then Enterprise Architecture and finally the entire Transformation domain.

Since 2011 I have devoted my time to **Pragmatic**. It is really exciting.

Whilst I have never been an academic person, and never went to university (I have always preferred to "go out and do stuff") I have recognised over the last year that Psychology plays such a vital role in Enterprise Transformation (for good or bad) and so in February 2014 I began a BSc (Honours) Psychology degree with The Open University. It is really exciting.

MBTI

My MBTI is a split between **INTJ** and **INTP.**

INTJ - Sometimes referred to as the "Architect," or the "Strategist," people with INTJ personalities are highly analytical, creative and logical.

Strengths: Enjoys theoretical and abstract concepts. High expectations. Good at listening. Takes criticism well. Self-confident and hard-working.

Weaknesses: Can be overly analytical and judgmental. Very perfectionistic. Dislikes talking about emotions. Sometimes seems callous or insensitive.

INTP - People who score as INTP are often described as quiet and analytical. They enjoy spending time alone, thinking about how things work and coming up with solutions to problems. INTPs have a rich inner world and would rather focus their attention on their internal thoughts rather than the external world. They typically do not have a wide social circle, but they do tend to be close to a select group of people.

Strengths: Logical and objective. Abstract thinker. Independent. Loyal and affectionate with loved ones.

Weaknesses: Difficult to get to know. Can be insensitive. Prone to self-doubt. Struggles to follow rules. Has trouble expressing feelings.

DISC

My DISC Profile is 7414 and categorised as **Result-Oriented.**

Result-Oriented people display self-confidence, which some may interpret as arrogance. They actively seek opportunities that test and develop their abilities to accomplish results. Result-Oriented persons like difficult tasks, competitive situations, unique assignments, and "important" positions. They undertake responsibilities with an air of self-importance and display self-satisfaction once they have finished.

Result-Oriented people tend to avoid constraining factors such as direct controls, time-consuming details, and routine work. Because they are forceful and direct, they may have difficulties with others. Result-Oriented people prize their independence and may become restless where involved with group activities or committee work. Although Result-Oriented people generally prefer to work alone, they may persuade others to support their efforts especially when completing routine activities.

Result-Oriented people are quick-thinkers, and they are impatient and fault-finding with those who are not They evaluate others on their ability to get results. Result Oriented people are determined and persistent even in the face of antagonism. They take command of the situation when necessary, whether or not they are in charge. In their uncompromising drive for results, they may appear blunt and uncaring.

Belbin

Belbin categorises me as a **Plant** (Creative and inventive individuals, Plants are the ones in the team most likely to come up with new ideas and suggestions. The name comes from Dr Belbin's original research. It was discovered that there was no initial spark of an idea in a team unless a creative person was "planted" in each team) and a **Shaper** (Shapers are people who challenge the team to improve. They are dynamic and usually extroverted people who enjoy stimulating others, questioning norms, and finding the best approaches for solving problems.).

Putting MBTI, DISC and Belbin together just about sums me up to a tee.

Different people have different profiles, and different profiles fit into different roles in different ways. We all kind of know this but do we ever take it into account?

> # KEYPOINT:
>
> Use people for the type of person they are, not the type of person you want them to be. If we were all the same, nothing would ever get done.

Questions to Ponder

- ♦ What are the MBTI, DISC and Belbin profiles of the people in your Enterprise?
- ♦ Do they all suit their roles?
- ♦ Have you ever found someone to be a "difficult person" or a "loose cannon"?
- ♦ If so, did their MBTI/DISC/Belbin profile taken into account?

PEAF enables you to mature your EA capability. Pragmatically.

The Adoption section of PEAF defines 'HOW' it should be adopted and used.

Designing Changes allows you to decide what to change from PEAF to your own XOET.

Use PEAF to design your own XEAF.

There are many risks related to increasing your EA maturity. 99% of these are misconceptions. If you do not address them, YOU WILL FAIL.

Many people will hate EA because: 1. It exposes problems and mistakes, 2. It breaks down silos and fiefdoms, 3. It's about long term benefits to the Enterprise, rather than short term benefits to individuals.

If you do not continually communicate, your initiative will fail.

Developing Changes allows you to create your own XOET.

Use P3 to develop your own XEAF.

Without proper governance, EA will most likely not deliver much value.

Without the fundamental processes, EA will most likely not deliver much value.

Without an EA metamodel, we won't be able to do any sensible modelling.

Without continuous education, EA will not be sustainable.

If you don't change the culture, you will FAIL.

Without a proper EA modelling tool, we won't be able to do any sensible modelling.

Rollout Changes allows you to rollout your own XOET for people to use.

Use P3 to train your staff in your own XEAF

Without the fundamental processes, EA will most likely not deliver much value.

Without an EA metamodel, we won't be able to do any sensible modelling.

Without continuous education, EA will not be sustainable.

If you don't change the culture, you will FAIL.

Without a proper EA modelling tool, we won't be able to do any sensible modelling.

The Guidance section of the Adoption section of PEAF defines what is used to guide people in their decision making.

EA is about bridging the gap between Strategy and Execution

X Architecture, is the fundamentally important structure of X, set in the context of things outside of X, that affect it, or are affected by it.

EA and SA are not the same thing. EA is not just big SA.

If you want to know the purpose of EA, ask 300+ people.

300+ people use a lot of different words when describing the purpose of EA.

If you ask 100 people what is the purpose of EA you will get 100 different responses that only together are likely to give you the full picture.

Removing synonyms, 300+ people use a small number of different words when describing the purpose of EA.

Arranging the words of 300+ we get a description of the Why (purpose), How (by) and What (using) of EA.

When asking 300+ people the question "What is EA?", the answer is surprising simple when you remove all the noise.

Using a PM framework will not guaranteed success. Not using a PM framework will not guaranteed failure.

Using an EA framework will not guaranteed success. Not using an EA framework will not guaranteed failure.

The "scope" of EA (at a point in time) is determined by the Enterprise Strategy (at a point in time) not on a Department or Business Unit level.

If you cannot invest in an increase in EA Maturity as part of an EA Catalyst, you probably never will.

The Objectives that EA provides, comes from the Enterprise Strategy.

EA Goals must be born from the Enterprise Strategy.

EA Strategies must be born from the Enterprise Strategy.

EA Tactics must be born from the Enterprise Strategy.

The Objective of using an EA Framework must be born from the Enterprise Strategy.

Be aware of the pros, cons and implications of using a Visio/Excel or a Visio/DB or a Custom Tool.

As the complexity and volume of information grows, the ability to use the information can quickly become impossible unless a custom EA modelling tool is used.

As the complexity and volume of information grows, the effort to maintain it can quickly become impossible unless a custom EA modelling tool is used.

Modelling tools should be architected and built on 4 fundamentals: 1) Entities. 2) Relationships. 3 Properties. 4) Views.

You cannot use your CMDB as you EA modelling tool because their purpose and content are totally different.

CMDBs Only contain a subset of information you need to work with in an EA modelling tool.

CMDBs Only contain a subset of Current Technical information you need to work with in an EA modelling tool.

CMDBs Only contain a subset of Current Technical Attributes you need to work with in an EA modelling tool.

The Methods section of PEAF defines 'WHAT' should be done, 'HOW' and 'WHEN'.

Roadmapping is phase that is part of the EA domain.

EA supports the Strategising phase.

If Enterprise Strategy is not captured in a structured way, we can't use it.

Many Enterprises only create Capabilitiy Models for Operate and miss the strategically important Direct, Transform and Support domains.

Many Enterprises only consider the capabilities from the point of view of Method Capabilites.

Roadmapping is "doing" EA.

Accumulated Transformation Debt™ is reviewed during Roadmapping.

EA is not a destination. EA is not a journey. EA is a way of travelling.

Intermediate models satisfy Business and Technical Objectives from the Enterprise Strategy.

The Project Portfolio effects transformation between the intermediate models.

The Enterprise Transformation Strategy is composed of interlocking Business and IT Transformation Strategies.

Solutioning is "doing" Solution Architecture.

If Solution Architecture is not carried out properly, any EA will be seriously compromised.

EA performs Governance down to projects, and accepts Lobbying up from Projects.

Reviewing Options and Solutions is the heart of Governance.

EA Governance is the highest level of Transformation Governance.

EA work has to integrate with your project processes (SDLC).

Don't confuse the Tactical/Strategic reasons for doing projects, with the Tactical/Strategic methods of executing them.

Transformation Debt™ Agreements expose Transformation Debt™ Value.

Over time, increase the ratio of Strategic to Tactical work.

Modelling anything must follow a pragmatic process, if it is to be of value.

Populating a model is a Data Migration exercise.

Without continuous EA Education,
EA will die.

The Artefacts section of PEAF defines
'WHAT' information is consumed
and produced and 'WHEN'.

Enterprise Context, Contextual and
Conceptual information levels are
part of the EA domain.

Enterprise Strategy is the Business Motivation and Capability models, set in the context of the Business Model. Transformation Strategy is the Roadmap and Operating models, set in the context of the Capability and Business Motivation models.

Make sure you have the correct input information for the model you are building.

The Business Strategy and IT Strategy are inherently linked and cannot be thought of separately.

> Specific Entities are required to define the Business Motivation and Roadmap models

> The purpose of a Transformation Debt™ Agreement is to expose Transformation Debt™.

> The purpose of a Transformation Debt™ Agreement is to expose Transformation Debt™.

> Specific Entities are required to define the Enterprise Context, Enterprise Capability and Operating models.

The Guidance section of PEAF defines what information is used to guide people in their decision making.

Principles come from Best Practice and your Enterprise's Strategy.

Don't think in terms of Business and IT principles. Use MAGIC to categorise them.

When categorising Principles, think in terms of those that guide WHAT we want to achieve (Ends).

When categorising Principles, think in terms of those that guide HOW we effect Transformation (Means).

The Environment section of PEAF defines 'WHAT' tools and frameworks are required, 'WHERE' and 'WHEN'.

Frameworks must work together.

Any EA Tool must integrate with other tools.

Many of the EA Tool Vendors, are not EA Tool Vendors.

When evaluating EA modelling tools, use a good set of requirements.

Tools that satisfy requirements by Customisation rather than by Configuration or Out-of-the-box, should be avoided.

Be aware that many Tool vendors can be very economical with the truth.

Weighting vendors to downgrade "customisation" answers can be useful.

X-Requirements are the key when assessing EA Modelling Tools.

The Culture section of PEAF defines the "The roles and the culture required.

Solution Architecture is too important to be owned by Projects.

Recognise that there are two types of EA: 1. Those that improve how EA is done. 2. Those that "do" EA (Strategic Transformation Planning and Governance).

Type 1 Enterprise Architects help an Enterprise to increase their EA maturity.

Type 1 Enterprise Architect's work, is primarily to; 1) Evangelise the benefits of EA. 2) Support the internal EA Team to mature how EA is performed.

Type 2 Enterprise Architects do Strategic Transformation planning.

Type 2 Enterprise Architect's work, is primarily to; 1) support Strategising. 2) perform Roadmapping 3) Govern executing projects.

While "firefighters" are always necessary, more resources need to be brought to bear as "fire prevention officers".

You cannot change what you don't understand and you cannot understand what you cannot see.

HOW each part of your Enterprise does what they do, shows the real contribution toward achieving the Enterprises Mission.

IT is special not because it is IT, but because IT tends to be responsible for a large part of HOW an Enterprise does what it does.

Recognise and deal with the fact that IT and The Business do constitute "Two Tribes".

IT should never say "No" to the Business. It should say "Yes, but…".

You cannot change what you don't understand and you cannot understand what you cannot see.

PEAF refers to various roles, most of which will already exist in an Enterprise.

An SIB with allocated budget and power is mandatory for Governance & Lobbying to operate effectively.

An EASG with delegated budget and power is mandatory for Governance & Lobbying to operate effectively.

The Appendix section contains information on the background of PF2, POET, PEAF and the author.

Use POET and PEAF to make sure you don't make the mistakes that cause 90% of all EA initiatives to fail.

Use people for the type of person they are, not the type of person you want them to be. If we were all the same, nothing would ever get done.

All Pragmatic books contain a Keypoint section.

www.Pragmatic365.org is the official source for all PF2/POET/PEAF related materials, and is constantly evolving.

Pragmatic EA is a non-profit research company, dedicated to developing Best Practice in relation to the structure and transformation of Enterprises.

Sources

- Book cover: Tropical Storm Lee - NASA/NOAA GOES Project Science Team.
- Stereogram used on "Hitting the Wall" produced by Easy Stereogram Builder - www.easystereogrambuilder.com
- "Brain Function with gears and cogs" used on the "Slaves to Psychology" graphic from BigStock - www.bigstockphoto.com/search/digitalista
- Technical Debt - www.wikipedia.org/wiki/Technical_debt
- Zachman Framework - www.wikipedia.org/wiki/Zachman_Framework
- TOGAF (The Open Group Architecture Framework) - www.opengroup.org/togaf/
- Business Motivation Model - www.omg.org/spec/BMM/
- Enhanced Business Motivation Model - www.MotivationModel.com
- ITIL (IT Infrastructure Library) - www.itil-officialsite.com
- COBIT (Control Objectives for Information and Related Technology) - www.wikipedia.org/wiki/Cobit

Resources

- www.Pragmatic365.org is the official source for all **Pragmatic** related materials.

Here is listed various sources and references to things referred to in the **Pragmatic** Frameworks.

You can always access the most up to date material online at www.Pragmatic365.org.

KEYPOINT:

www.Pragmatic365.org is the official source for all PF2/POET/PEAF related materials, and is constantly evolving.

Pragmatic 365

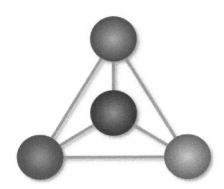

CONNECTING THE DOTS

> # KEYPOINT:
>
> Pragmatic EA is a non-profit research company, dedicated to developing Best Practice in relation to the structure and transformation of Enterprises.

Lightning Source UK Ltd.
Milton Keynes UK
UKHW052223180521
383943UK00001B/2